The Legacy of Tamar

Raye Springfield

The Legacy of Tamar

Courage, Faith, and the Common Road of Hope in a West Tennessee Community

The University of Tennessee Press / Knoxville

Copyright © 2016 by Raye Springfield.
All Rights Reserved.
First Edition, 2000.
Second Edition, 2016.

Frontispiece: The grandsons of Tonnie and Opal Springfield. Courtesy of Bridgette Mercer Carter.

Library of Congress Cataloging-in-Publication Data

Springfield, Raye.
The legacy of Tamar : courage and faith in an African American family / Raye Springfield.—1st ed.
  p. cm.
Includes bibliographical references and index.
ISBN 978-1-62190-226-3
1. Afro-Americans—Tennessee—Haywood County—Biography. 2. Afro-American families—Tennessee—Haywood County. 3. Afro-Americans—Civil rights—Tennessee—Haywood County—History. 4. Afro-Americans—Tennessee—Haywood County—Social life and customs. 5. Haywood County (Tenn.)—Race relations. 6. Haywood County (Tenn.)—Social life and customs. 7. Haywood County (Tenn.)—Biography. 8. Taylor family. 9. Springfield family. I. Title.
F443.H4 S68 2000
976.8'22300496073'00922—dc21   99-050585

for Sonia Karin Carter
Samuel Keenan Carter
. . . and all who come after

In loving memory of
Opal Taylor Springfield,
November 9, 1909–
October 26, 1999

In a nation torn by war and divided against itself, he was able to look us in the eye and tell us that . . . no matter how persistent the poverty or the racism, no matter how far adrift America strayed, hope would come again.

—**Barak Obama,** speaking about Robert F. Kennedy in 2005

Contents

Preface to the Second Edition   xiii
Preface to the First Edition   xxi
Acknowledgments   xxv

1. Old Crossroads Place   1
2. Kinfolks   15
3. On Springfield Road   34
4. Sweet Gum Trees   50
5. Fighting Odds   70
6. Winfield Lane   95
7. Forced Dancing   116
8. The Mourning Bench   136
9. We Are Not Afraid   154
10. Hulls Dinner   179
11. Hope for Reunion   197
12. The Storm   209

Epilogue: Offering to the Ancestors   226

Notes   239
Bibliographical Essay   251
Index   255

Illustrations

Following Page   xxvi

The Elbert Williams Memorial Service, June 20, 2015
Mayor William Rawls Jr, Dr. Cornell Brooks, and Edward Stanton III
Dr. Cornell Brooks, Raye Springfield, and Edward Stanton III
Elbert Williams Historical Marker
Elbert Williams in 1939
The Springfield Family at Old Country Store, July 2012

Following Page   94

The Western District of Tennessee
Taylor's Chapel Church
Cornerstone of Taylor's Chapel Church
Willow Grove Baptist Church
Campgrounds of Tabernacle Methodist Church
Dempsy Taylor
Jim Springfield
Ada Springfield
Jim Springfield
Tonnie Springfield
Opal Springfield
Arizona Johnson
Cloria and Reverend Baskerville
Brown and Crettie Mae Springfield

Following Page   *208*

Aaron Springfield
Salathiel Springfield
Lois Springfield
Springfield Family Reunion
Tonnie Springfield
A. D. and Catherine Springfield
Avery Springfield
Dan Springfield

Preface to the Second Edition

The Legacy of Tamar was first published in April 2000, telling the story of five generations of the Taylor and Springfield family and at the same time incorporating the history of Brownsville, Haywood County, Tennessee. It's a fascinating history, made even more so because for over a century the black population in the county has outnumbered the white population by about two to one. The story documents the family's experiences through two world wars, the Great Depression, and the turbulent civil rights period. It follows the families through significant change and social upheaval brought about in part by geography and demographics, and it shows their enduring courage, faith, and strength as passed on to future generations.

Beginning in 1913 Polk Taylor dreams the death of five family members, and Tamar, born a slave, is thrust into the role of family matriarch. The Taylor and Springfield families join when Tonnie Springfield marries Tamar's granddaughter, Opal. We follow this now united family, one of the few black land-owning families in the county, their efforts to maintain family and farm, and the changing way of life they face in later years in large part due to out-migrating family members and a diminished interest in farming. As the country shifted from rural to urban living, and from farm subsistence to industrial labor, the Taylor Springfield family restructured accordingly. The social shifts that occurred in Haywood County mirrored the changes at a national level as well.

Additionally, *The Legacy of Tamar* introduces us to the people of Haywood County told against the background of a system of segregation and the racial climate of the 1930s and 1940s. A voter registration campaign lead to an organized reign of terror that resulted in the lynching of Elbert

"Dick" Williams, one of the local leaders of the National Association for the Advancement of Colored People, and an investigation by the U.S. Department of Justice. It also brought Thurgood Marshall, who would later become Supreme Court Justice, to Haywood County. The 1950s and 1960s renewed a local civil rights movement in the county along with resulting local conflicts. In the midst of all this and the family's own evolution, we see how Tonnie and Opal held on to their demonstrable faith and the realization that education would create a better life for their children and future generations of Haywood County.

But, as Virginia Woolf argued in *A Room of One's Own*, "books continue each other." Woolf was speaking to the continuity of centuries old literature; however, the same basic premise is no less applicable here. In the early part of 2015, I realized that *The Legacy of Tamar* had reached its fifteenth anniversary. During the intervening years since the first edition, many things had changed in Brownsville and in the country as a whole. Therefore, for the second edition, it was suggested that I write a new preface to bring the book into the twenty-first century. In this second edition, the stories of the people of Haywood County, and the story of our nation, represent a continuation of past events.

When I initially wrote this book, I thought I wanted to tell the story of my family and my hometown so my children would know their history and from where they came. Over the past years, I have come to accept the fact that the book is much larger than that notion. Since Haywood County is one of only two of the 95 counties in the state of Tennessee with a higher black population than white, it has an interesting history that for the most part had remained untold. *The Legacy of Tamar* documents those experiences of blacks in the county that until now had been ignored or simply left out of history texts. Many who have had the opportunity to read the first edition have indicated they related to the Taylor-Springfield history. The story of my mother's childhood friend, Dick Williams, and the early civil rights struggle in Brownsville, receives more attention today than it ever did historically.

I've known from the inception of this book that, in addition to family, I had to write the Dick Williams story. I grew up in Brownsville at a time when a family's oral history was often past down while simply passing the time with storytelling. I heard my mother retell the story many times of, "what they did to Dick Williams." The story always resonated with me, though to this day I can't explain exactly why. Perhaps it was because even after decades had passed the emotion was still raw and the pain she described was quite palpable. While it took extensive research, numerous oral interviews with some people alive at the time, pouring through texts, microfilm, and reading through massive NAACP files in the Library of Congress and National Archives, it was important for me to tell the true story of what happened.

According to author Patricia Sullivan in *Lift Every Voice: The NAACP and the Making of the Civil Rights Movement*, "Elbert Williams was the first known NAACP official killed for his civil rights activities." In March 1939, prominent citizens in town, including businessmen and educators, held meetings to charter a Brownsville branch of the NAACP. The group of fifty-two charter members organized to secure the right to vote in the 1940 presidential election. What followed was a campaign of terror unleashed against local blacks that included intimidation, threats, beatings, and killings. On June 20, 1940, Williams, secretary of the branch, was taken from his home and lynched.

Chapter five of this book describes the civil rights struggle in Haywood County, the ensuing mob activities, and the subsequent investigation by NAACP leaders, including Thurgood Marshall. Although early indication was that blacks were being targeted because they were seeking to vote in the 1940 Presidential election, it later became clear the reason was much more systematic. Many blacks in Haywood County had started their own businesses, and a group of whites who desired to purge them from the county. Once blacks like Williams were killed, and others were threatened and forced to leave town, their property, both real and personal, was taken without any compensation. This system of injustice spanned decades. In Dick Williams' case, while there was an investigation by the U.S. Justice Department, it was less than thorough and unfortunately brought no relief.

As fate would have it, the fifteenth anniversary of the *The Legacy of Tamar* is the same year as the seventy-fifth anniversary of the lynching of Dick Williams. Until now, the bravery and courage, which Williams and other NAACP Brownsville branch members exemplified, received little attention. Today, there is considerable discussion about the civil rights movement in this country. Contributing to this discussion is the fact that the year 2015 also focuses attention on another anniversary—the fiftieth anniversary of the marches in Selma, Alabama, which was also the subject to the major motion picture, *Selma*. The movie brought new attention on the civil rights struggle of the 1950s and 60s and reminded us of the sacrifice of everyday citizens who simply wanted the right to vote. What people fought for, then, is justice in a country that claims to be the definition of democracy. And Williams made the ultimate sacrifice against a system of racial injustice years before those with more well-known names. He is an example of the struggle that continues today, with recent racially charged shootings of unarmed black men by police officers.

In Haywood County, and throughout the United States as the nation faces mounting mistrust of its justice system, we still have a segment of the black population disregarded in areas of economic, political, and social progress. A directly related area of contention is voter disenfranchisement created by new voter ID laws. (The state of Tennessee has one of the most restrictive voter ID laws in the country.) This especially has a negative impact on African Americans when it's estimated that 1 in 10 do not have photo identification. In a recent study commissioned by the city of Brownsville, sixty-five percent of the city's population identify as African American, thirty percent as white, and four percent as Latino. Although the distinctive racial and cultural mix can be seen as an asset, the city lags behind the surrounding counties in income and educational attainment. But even though the past decades have brought problems resulting in significant hardship and uncertainty in black communities, it would be disingenuous to suggest that Haywood County and the country have made no progress during this period.

One indication of progress was the November 2008 presidential election, when the nation elected its first African-American President, Barak Obama, over Republican challenger John McCain, who carried Tennessee by a landslide. (Haywood County was one of only five Tennessee counties to vote Democrat.) If for only a brief period, most of this country overflowed with the idea of new possibilities and was swept up in the euphoria of hope. President Obama was re-elected in the 2012 race against Republican opponent Mitt Romney. Two years later, in this small rural west Tennessee town, more progress was made. On June 16, 2014, the city of Brownsville took steps at moving beyond its dark, sordid past by electing its first African American Mayor. William "Bill" Rawls Jr. is a profound symbol of how much things have changed in the seventy-four years since the lynching of Dick Williams. In a historic election, Mayor Rawls beat his opponent, the city's first female mayor, by 65 percent to 35 percent of the vote. Rawls, a Morehouse College graduate, is passionate about his city and the challenges ahead. "As Mayor I can see something and get it done," he stated, adding that, "I have been entrusted with the opportunity to restore hope to our community."

On June 20, 2015, seventy-five years to the day Dick Williams was taken from his home in the middle of the night and lynched, the people of Brownsville, and many from other places, joined together to commemorate him. More than 500 people packed the Haywood County High School gymnasium for a memorial service to honor the man for his sacrifice. Perhaps it was only fitting that the service began with the singing of *Glory*, the original collaboration by Common and John Legend for the movie *Selma*. The Elbert Williams Memorial Singers, a group assembled for the event, lifted their voices singing, "One day when the glory comes, it will be ours...."

June 20, 2015, was proclaimed Elbert Williams Day by both Brownsville Mayor Rawls and Haywood County Mayor Franklin Smith. The State House of Representatives issued a Resolution noting that Elbert Williams was the first NAACP official in the nation killed for his civil rights activities. It was further noted that Roy Wilkins praised Williams when speaking on the death of Medgar Evers, a NAACP official killed June 12, 1963, for his civil rights activities. A video presentation of United States Congressman John Lewis was played with him saying we have an obligation to leave this land more peaceful and more just for generations to come.

Dr. Cornell William Brooks, National President of the NAACP, was the featured speaker for the occasion. Despite having been in Charleston, South Carolina, the previous day, giving repeated interviews about the killing of nine blacks by a white man, in a historically black church in that city, he was in Brownsville for the early morning program because of a "call of history." Dr. Brooks called Williams a martyr of the civil rights movement whose life was taken because of his beliefs and conviction. This was the story of an ordinary man at the crossroads of history who joined the NAACP when membership was a danger, he said. The record of the 1939 Brownsville branch shows Williams signed his name and paid the $1.00 fee as a charter member.

The second phase of the honor was dedication of a historical marker at the corner of East Main Street and Jackson Avenue in downtown

Brownsville. The location was chosen because it is near the site of the old Sunshine Laundry where Williams was employed at the time he was killed. A large group from the high school gathered for the unveiling of the historical marker. It briefly detailed what had happened to Williams and the Department of Justice's failure to prosecute. The faces of those in positions of historical authority and who refused to take action to deliver justice for Williams have changed. Today the chief United States prosecutor is a black woman, Attorney General Loretta Lynch, and the current U.S. Attorney for the Western District, Edward Stanton III, is a young black man. The diversity in those positions and the office of mayor signals progress at multiple levels of government, a fact not lost on the congregation attending the dedication ceremony.

The third and final event was a pilgrimage to Taylor Chapel Cemetery where Williams was buried on June 23, 1940, immediately after his body was removed from the Hatchie River. Although Williams was laid in an unmarked grave, we gathered at the place that the family believed to be the burial site. Williams was denied a service in 1940 but would receive one with the large crowd of people. Though there to honor Williams, I was overcome with feelings for my own family, those five who died beginning the winter of 1914, each one buried in these same grounds. With the short service over, the throng of blacks and whites marched down the dirt road together singing, "Pray on a Little While Longer."

Williams and his wife Anne did not have children, but there were family members present who were descendants of his sister, Julie. She had married Tamar's grandson, James "Meedie" Taylor. They fled to Michigan in the early 1940s and had ten children. It was their great granddaughter who spoke for the family at the memorial service, and it's interesting to note that, since Julie married Tamar's grandson, all Elbert Williams' remaining family from his sister are a direct bloodline of Tamar and the Taylors of Taylor's Chapel.

The NAACP Brownsville branch, re-organized in 1961, was also represented at the services for Williams, all wearing bright yellow tee shirts. As in previous years, the NAACP remains at the forefront of the civil rights fight. They are still battling for equal rights in America. It's what they wanted in the movements of 1940s, the 1960s, and the reason the struggle continues.

Finally, on an April morning this year, I received a telephone call that perhaps put in proper perspective not only the far-reaching effect of *The Legacy of Tamar* but also how much times have changed. A young woman phoned to tell me how much she enjoyed reading my book. She explained that she was the great-granddaughter of Harbert Thornton Sr., which meant she was a descendent of owners of the Taylor plantation. Both are mentioned several times in this book. She talked about how the history of the black people and white people in the county paralleled, making them seem related. That statement reminded me of the words of Richard Wright about the differences between black folk and white folk not being blood or color, and "the ties that bind us are deeper than those that separate us." She helped confirm the conclusion reached in the first edition that despite all our diversity, a common thread runs through our collective past. Before hanging up, the young woman made this comment about the book: "You know how you said that you wanted to teach your children their history, well you are teaching me my history too." Then she added, "I know you never thought about that, did you?" And to that I say, "There is always hope."

Raye Springfield
Nashville, Tennessee

Preface to the First Edition

This previously untold story traces the lives of one family in a small, rural west Tennessee town and reveals a history of the rural south. The place is Brownsville, county seat of Haywood County. The people are primarily the Taylors and Springfields, but the story would not be complete without including the many others who have touched their lives. The story begins in the year 1913, because the events of that year, and the Taylors' response to them, illustrate the enduring courage, faith, and strength that have been passed down to subsequent generations.

The Legacy of Tamar chronicles five generations of the Taylors and Springfields, farm families in Haywood County, Tennessee. The story begins with Polk Taylor's disturbing dream that foretells the death of five family members. His widow, Tamar, the daughter of the first generation of slaves in the county, valiantly accepts her new role as matriarch of the family. The Taylor and Springfield families are joined in 1926 when Tonnie Springfield marries the young Opal Taylor. For the next four decades, Tonnie's father, Jim Springfield, served as the leader and moral compass for the family. Their story traverses two world wars, the Great Depression, the civil rights movement, and beyond.

The book spans the period from when many black farmers in the rural south, like the Taylors and Springfields, owned a significant share of the land to the virtual demise of the Negro-owned farm. We follow their efforts to maintain family and farm as a changing way of life was produced, in part, by the migration of family members that dwindled the workforce. The diminished interest in the farm gradually restructured the family and put a new face on the community. The changes in this family remarkably mirror the national change that took place as the country shifted from rural to urban and from farming to industry.

The story is told against the background of a system of segregation and the racial climate of the 1930s and 1940s, when a voter registration campaign lead to a reign of terror that resulted in the lynching of one local leader of the National Association for the Advancement of Colored People and an investigation by the U.S. Department of Justice. It also brought a man who would later become Supreme Court justice to Haywood County to investigate. The 1950s and 1960s renewed the civil rights movement and local conflict. At the same time, the family coped with its continued evolution while realizing that education would provide better days for the next generation. During the later years, we witness Tonnie and Opal Springfield's exceptional demonstrable faith, which was their sustaining power through the years. Their story is one of struggle, resilience, and triumph of the human spirit.

The Legacy of Tamar introduces us to the people of Haywood County, one of only two counties in the state of Tennessee where, for the last century, the black population has outnumbered the white. The U.S. census for 1910 recorded a Negro population in Haywood County of 17,710 and a white population of 8,199.[1] At the time that this story begins, and for many years thereafter, the ratio of blacks to whites in the county was around 68 percent to 31 percent.[2] Of the 17,000 blacks, less than four hundred were landowners. This circumstance made for a unique history, one that for the most part has remained untold. *The Legacy of Tamar* tells who some of these people were; how they lived; the role of gender, religion and tradition; and how geography shaped their lives.

In 1939, the editor for the *States-Graphic*, Brownsville's weekly newspaper, supplied information about the history of the city for the Federal Writers Project. In response to a question concerning its churches and educational institutions, the number provided did not include the black institutions in the county.[3] Black history was simply not included as part of the Brownsville, Haywood County, Tennessee, history. This is one reason that I have written *The Legacy of Tamar*. Through this story, I have attempted to document the experiences of blacks in Haywood County that until now have been ignored, overlooked, or left out of history texts. The reference to colored people and Negroes is to keep the usage consistent with particular periods.

Preface to the First Edition

Tennessee has a diverse social, cultural, and racial history. *The Legacy of Tamar* records a different story about people of the state who have made significant contributions, both as slaves and as free men and women. This book focuses on their experiences in Brownsville, but as the story unfolds it reveals that this small town is but a microcosm. The story of this family is living proof that despite all our diversity, a common thread runs through our collective past. As Richard Wright said, "The differences between black folk and white folk are not blood or color, and the ties that bind us are deeper than those that separate us. The common road of hope which we all have traveled has brought us into a stronger kinship than any words, laws, or legal claims."[4] *The Legacy of Tamar* shows our commonality is greater than our differences. And that, ultimately, it is our humanity that must prevail.

Acknowledgments

This book would not have been possible without the people who granted me interviews and provided valuable information. In additional to the people I mentioned in the bibliography, I am especially grateful to Aunt Louise Cook and all the relatives in Decatur, Illinois, and to Cousin Ada Averyheart and Clarence Taylor, who opened their homes to me and shared their stories of the past.

I am grateful to Dr. Bobby L. Lovett for his comments, direction, and historical perspective. Much appreciation to Dr. Sonya G. Smith for her support, and encouragement, and to Martha Staley, who encouraged me in the beginning, when I had doubt about attempting such a project. Thanks to Mary Slater for her assistance in the development stage of this book. I owe a tremendous debt of gratitude to Loretta Green, the one person who read my drafts and edited the manuscript before anyone else. Without her insight, support, encouragement, and friendship this book may not have been completed.

I am grateful to Jennifer Siler, Scot Danforth, and all the people at the University of Tennessee Press for their assistance and patience, and for believing there was a book in my manuscript. I express thanks to the people at the Tennessee Library and Archives for their assistance on my many visits.

My deepest gratitude to my mother, Opal Springfield, for without her sharing her memories of the family and of the past with me, it would have been impossible to write this book. My love to Karin and Keenan for their unwavering belief in me.

The Elbert Williams memorial service, June 20, 2015. From left, Mayor William Rawls Jr, NAACP State Conference President Gloria Sweet-Love, NAACP National President Dr. Cornell Brooks, U.S. Attorney for Western District Edward Stanton III; and David Johnson.

Mayor William Rawls Jr, Dr. Cornell Brooks, and Edward Stanton III.

NAACP National President Dr. Cornell Brooks, Raye Springfield, and Edward Stanton III.

Elbert Williams historical marker dedicated in his honor on June 20, 2015.

Elbert Williams, charter member of the Brownsville branch of the NAACP, in 1939.

The Springfield family at Old Country Store, July 2012.

1.

Old Crossroads Place

On March 4, 1913, when Woodrow Wilson took office as the twenty-eighth president of the United States, the country had not lost its innocence. The beginning of the first World War was still a year off; a majority of Americans lived on farms or in rural areas; the Negro had not begun his migration from the South to the North; people held largely to unchanging moral values; and in Haywood County, Tennessee, the Negro population was helping shape the history of the state.

Because the state of Tennessee settled from east to west, most of its residents originally came from North Carolina and Virginia. Many of the settlers in the western part of the state previously lived for a period of time in Middle Tennessee, around the Nashville–Davidson County area. Early settlers traveling to Haywood County, located in rural West Tennessee, experienced the gradual change in the landscape, ranging from the mountains in the eastern part of the state to the flat lands in the west. Going west from middle Tennessee, these settlers encountered the rugged terrain of the Highland Rim, which runs for several miles just outside Davidson County. As they continued west, they saw miles and miles of rolling hills, with their peaks completely covered with indigenous trees. About seventy-five miles out of Nashville the settlers came to the Tennessee River, on its second run through the state, flowing from its source high in the mountains of east Tennessee. Upon crossing the river, travelers officially arrived in the west Tennessee region. As settlers traveled the next seventy-five miles to Haywood County, they beheld a countryside in stark contrast to the mountainous eastern part of the state.

After 1820, early settlers finally entered Haywood County, with most passing through Madison County, which borders on the east. Few travelers to the area crossed through the other counties that border Haywood County: Crockett County on the north, Tipton and Lauderdale Counties on the west, and Hardeman and Fayette Counties on the south. The settlers were struck by the beauty of the vast wide open space, with hills that roll ever so gently, breaking the monotony of flatness all around. Later, Haywood County had large farms with acres and acres of green fields, with sheep, horses, and cattle grazing in nearby pastures. Much smaller farms had only a few animals, some with only a single cow in a small fenced-in area near the house.

Those who settled here found the land ideal for farming, and in open fields grew enormous crops of corn, tobacco, oats, hay, wheat, sorghum, and cotton. By 1913, cotton had become king in Haywood and some of the other surrounding counties. The need for cheap farm labor accounted for the large Negro population in Haywood County and made it one of only two of the ninety-five counties in the state where Negroes out numbered whites, a fact that would play a significant role in the lives of the people for years to come.

This story begins early in the fall of 1913, on a dirt road off Highway 54 in the northwest corner on Haywood County, the night Polk Taylor had a dream. Everything about Polk's dream was perfectly clear. He was a preacher man, so he was not usually one to worry needlessly, but he could not shake his concern. Except for the slight chill in the air, that day had started no differently than many others for Polk and Tamar. Their daughter Ora; her husband, Howell; and the children made their usual visit. The four girls, Tamar, Cloria Vean, Arizona, and Opal spent time with their Grandma Tamar while Walter helped his daddy in the fields. Polk felt good knowing that as long as the children were at his home, Ora got her much needed rest. She was expecting another baby at the end of the year or the beginning of the next year. Howell, especially, wanted a boy, and Polk had to admit that another grandson would be nice. Later, when supper was over and everyone had returned home, Polk and Tamar retired early like they always did. Now, lying there under the covers close to Tamar, with the events of the day replaying in his head, it disturbed Polk to think that this dream may hold a special meaning for his family.

Howell Taylor, a tall, slim, handsome man, had married Ora Taylor in 1899. He was nineteen and she was fourteen. Ora was part of the large Taylor family that lived in the Taylor Chapel community in Haywood County. Howell had grown up in the little town of Whiteville, located near Stanton and Somerville. He was born in 1880 to Howell and Fannie Taylor, who were part of a smaller family of Taylors that lived in the Whiteville area. Howell did not talk very much about his family. He had several sisters, of which one was named Nora, and a younger brother, Milton. Milton lived with Howell and Ora for few years and worked with Howell on the farm until Walter was old enough to help.

By 1913, Howell spent most of his time working with his only son, Walter. Growing straight and tall, Walter looked more like his mother. His complexion was somewhere between Ora's light skin and Howell's rich brown color. Walter spent a lot of time with his father, and he was beginning to take on the mannerism of Howell. The young boy loved working with his father. After sometimes working to exhaustion, Howell would strike out singing one of his favorite songs. He had a deep, powerful bass voice that he raised to sing in the church choir on Sunday morning. Howell would start humming and slowly raise his voice until the woods around them echoed with song. There were many days when Howell could be heard singing, "Don't you want to go to that happy land? Don't you want to go to the land so fair?"

At nine, Walter was at the age where the two of them could handle the farm together. Sure they needed help at harvest time, but Howell and Walter did the day-to-day work that was required to run the farm. Walter threw seeds as Howell plowed the cotton fields. When the time was right, Walter helped chop cotton, which actually meant cutting the grass from around the cotton. In late summer and fall, Howell and Walter picked the cotton. Since his in-laws lived a short distance across the field, Howell relied on Polk and Tamar, and also lots of Taylor cousins to help at cotton-picking time. But, Howell and his son tended the animals and did most of the everyday labor on their farm.

Howell rented the farm from a white woman named Miss Bessie Sorrelle. Miss Bessie was a member of the Bradford family, who owned hundreds of acres of land in Haywood County, and a descendant of the white Taylors in the county. Although married to Dr. Alfred Sorrelle, as custom dictated, everyone called her "Miss" Bessie. Dr. Sorrelle gained respect as a physician since moving to Haywood County, where he met and married Miss Bessie. Howell considered the Sorrelles fair when they settled with him for the use of their land. Thus, unlike many black people who rented land from whites, Howell was able to save enough money from his crops to start a savings account at the local bank. He was not content to stay on the white folks land. Howell wanted a better life for his family.

Howell was a devoted family man who took pride in his wife and children, so he worked hard to provide for his young family. As his family continued to grow, Howell made plans for the future. He wanted very much to buy his own farm. Putting aside a little at a time, he saved enough money to make a down payment on the land he wanted. Although a lot of colored people had difficulty purchasing land even when they had the money, because they could not find a white landowner to sell to them, Howell did not think this was would be a problem for him. He knew Ora had uncles and other relatives who owned lots of land. Howell was confident that someone would sell to him. He had already bought farm equipment, chickens, and livestock. His dream of becoming a landowner was finally about to come true.

Then came January 1914. Young Walter had taken ill, and he stayed sick for what seemed like weeks. The doctor thought he had contracted pneumonia. Everyone said he caught it from some children before school was out in December. Howell sat by the boy's bed for hours. Walter's lungs were filled with fluids and he labored to breath. At times, his small body would convulse with coughing. Howell continued his vigil by the boy's bedside for days, watching him fight a futile struggle. After all the work and all of his plans and hopes for the future, Howell could not afford to lose his son. He felt his future and the future of his family were tied to Walter.

On January 22, Howell summoned the doctor. The old white doctor treated Walter for two days, but the boy still showed no sign of real improvement. Walter did not respond to either the medicine left by the doctor nor to the home remedy prescribed by his grandmama. The family did all they could just to keep the child warm. This being the middle of winter, when the weather was the coldest, the menfolk constantly hauled logs to put on the fire. They piled quilts on the sick child and sat with him around the clock. But on January 24, 1914, at about one o'clock in the morning, the young schoolboy gave up the struggle to live. Walter Howell Taylor, born September 16, 1904, at nine years and four months, was the first to die.

Howell's grieving was so severe that shortly after burying Walter, he took to his bed. None of the others in the family had ever before seen him so despondent. At first the family thought it was just a father grieving the death of his son. By January 29, when Howell still did not get out of bed, they began to get worried. Ora figured it was more than depression and said as much. She had her father call the doctor for the second time. He gave Howell some large white tablets to take. Two days later he returned to check on Howell and made the last visit to his patient. The doctor listed the cause of death as pneumonia. Everyone else knew that Howell had died more from a broken heart over losing his beloved son than from the sickness in his body. Howell Taylor died on January 31, 1914, exactly one week after the death of his son.

The ringing of the bell at Taylor's Chapel C.M.E. Church signaled the arrival of the funeral procession. The large bell was encased in a wood structure that extended from the roof. The dome-shaped structure hung just above the small porch at the front of the little shotgun church. One of the churchmen usually pulled the long, thick rope swinging from the iron mass to ring the bell. At other times, young children playing nearby ran and tugged on the rope as soon as they saw the hearse approaching. The family in their horse-driven buggies and wagons followed closely behind. As the old bell swayed from side to side, its sound traveled through the woods for miles. The tolling of the bell announced to the community that another funeral was about to begin.

Howell was buried in the Taylor burial ground, about a mile down the road from the church. To reach the cemetery, the procession turned on the narrow road running alongside Tabernacle Church, the place of worship for the white folks. They followed the narrow, bumpy road a short distance before reaching the entrance to the cemetery, and the two horses pulled the hearse as close as possible to the gravesite. The buggies and wagons carrying the family and other people in the community pulled to the side of the road behind the hearse. Owners tied their horses to nearby hitching posts and small trees. Howell's brother, Milton, and Ora' brothers, Tom, Clifton, and Bishop, served as pallbearers, and slid the coffin from the back of the hearse. After balancing the wood box, they walked slowly to the open grave and laid the coffin east to west. In keeping with the Negro custom, the head was laid to the west in preparation for the Resurrection.

On that cold first day of February, Polk, Tamar, and the rest of the family gathered around, along with the few other people from the community. They stood near the mound of fresh dirt where just a few days earlier they had come together to bury young Walter. The choir Howell had so much enjoyed being a part of braved the cold weather as they stood shoulder to shoulder and raised their voices in song. Howell's brother-in-law, Dempsy Taylor, also sang in the choir.

In tribute to their former member, the choir chose Howell's favorite song. They had to sing a cappella, but since they did not have a piano at the church they were accustomed to singing without instruments. Not that long ago, Howell had led the choir at the Sunday services, and after church everyone complemented him on his "good voice." They sang: "Don't you want to go to that happy land? Land so fair. Where the weary shall rest. Will you meet me there? Will you answer yes, I want to go?" Only the bass singer was missing.

Funerals in the community usually served as social events. Traditionally, all the women in the church prepared food for the family of the deceased. The morning before the funeral, the church ladies sent the food they had prepared to the home of Polk and Tamar. After the solemn graveside service, the family and their guests, who were mainly people from the community, gathered at the house, where dinner was served and everyone sat around and talked. Traditionally, men would slip out back to take a few sips of corn whiskey, but Polk never wanted anything to do with drinking and did not allow it in his home. Though these gatherings were sometimes known to take on an atmosphere of celebration, as people almost forgot that a family member had recently died, this time no one could forget what the last few weeks had been for the Taylor family.

Three weeks earlier, on January 11, 1914, in the midst of her son's illness, Ora gave birth to another child. As usual, when her labor began Howell went to get the midwife. The children were sent to stay with their Grandma Tamar until after the baby was born. Grandma Tamar always helped with the children until Ora was on her feet, then the children went back home, where they found a new brother or sister waiting for them. Howell got his wish, and Ora delivered a baby boy. She was glad the child was a boy because she knew how badly Howell wanted another son. Ora had given birth to three other sons before the new baby, but one boy was stillborn and Livingston had lived for just a few months, so Walter had been the only boy to survive. Walter's illness was the one thing that tempered the excitement of the family as they welcomed their newest male member. Ora chose the name one of her neighbors had suggested: Benjamin Franklin. Ora had seen the first name in the Bible, and she liked its sound.

On Tuesday morning, February 3, Ora appointed her brother Tom to help her handle the business involving Howell's estate. Taking care of matters related to the estate meant a trip to the courthouse in town. Brownsville, located almost in the center of Haywood County, is one of the best laid out towns in Tennessee, since there are no winding streets.[1] Roads lead out of the city in the direction of the neighboring towns of Ripley, Covington, Alamo, Bells, Somerville, Jackson, and southwest to Memphis, the state's largest city. North of the city, the Forked Deer River forms the northern border of the county, and south of town the Hatchie River runs across the county, flowing for a little more than twenty miles to the Mississippi River.²

The courthouse sat in the middle of a nearly three-acre public square. Four brick buildings at the corners of the courthouse yard served as law offices for local attorneys. On the east side of the square was the Brownsville Bank, and down the street south of the square was the First State Bank. On the north side of the square, Mr. Joseph Sternberger operated a general store. On the east side of the square was another general store, M. Rothschild and Son, which was operated by German immigrants, and Tamm's Department Store, owned by Mr. Emil Tamm. Felsenthal's Department Store, on the north side of the square, was known for its quality merchandise. However, a large granite stone next to the east wall of the store was reputedly used to auction slaves. West of the square stood the town's new public library, built with a $7,500 donation from Andrew Carnegie. The town's first automobile dealership, representing the Ford Motor Company, opened on East Main.³ Travelers coming into town from the north, as Ora and Tom did, had a clear view of the tall Confederate monument standing on the east lawn of the courthouse. The statute drew resentment from blacks as well as a surprisingly large number of white residents whose ancestors had served in the Union army and remained loyal to the United States.

Ora and Tom sat in the back of the courtroom as the clerk called the other cases. Finally, their turn came when they were the only two people remaining who had not been called. The clerk peered around the courtroom then read: "In the matter of appointment of Thomas Lewis Taylor as Administrator of the estate of Howell Y. Taylor, deceased, who departed this life January 31, 1914 at his home in number 5 Haywood County. The applicant Thomas Lewis Taylor, and the widow, Ora Taylor request the act."⁴ The judge informed Tom that a bond of fifteen hundred dollars was required to serve as administrator of the estate and told him to come back on Saturday since he was not prepared to post the bond.⁵

Saturday morning, February 7, Tom went back to court with his uncle Fox Taylor, who had agreed to sign on the bond. Fox, who was Tamar's brother, owned a large amount of land, so he had no problem helping Tom post the bond. The clerk read: "In the matter of a year's support for Ora Taylor, widow of Howell Y. Taylor, a year's support out of the property and effects of Howell Y. Taylor, deceased, is to be set apart in the amount of Three Hundred

Dollars of the money on hand and in the bank. Thomas Taylor having entered into proper bond with J. N. Gill and Fox Taylor as his surties, in the sum of fifteen hundred dollars and having been sworn to faithfully perform the duties of Administrator of said estate, it was therefore ordered by the court that he be clothed with all the power and charged with all of the duties of administrator of the estate of Howell Y. Taylor."[6]

As administrator, one of Tom's duties included filing an inventory of the estate. He made a detailed list of Howell's property: one black mare about ten years old; one bay mare, five years old; one bay filly about two years old; one bay filly colt, one year old; one bay horse colt, one year old; another bay filly colt, one year old; one jersey bull, two years old; one black heifer calf, one year old; one stock hog, one year old.[7] Howell had one hundred dollars cash in the First National Bank of Brownsville, and four weeks before he died he placed seven hundred in a certificate of deposit at the Brownsville Bank.[8] At thirty-four, this was all the property Howell owned, except for a few personal things and one other item. Ora paid five dollars to her husband's estate for his old buggy and harness.[9]

Ora Taylor was born in April 1885. She was Polk and Tamar's youngest daughter. She had a sister, Beulah, and five brothers, Bishop, Clifton, Alonzo, Tom, and Dempsy. Most people described Ora as very nice looking. She had inherited her skin color from Polk, who looked almost white. And her long, thick black hair hung down below her shoulders. When she married Howell, she was quite young and full of life. But after all the children came, she had almost lost her youthful appearance. Although still considered a young woman, Ora began to feel as though she was growing old much too soon.

Since Howell died, Ora and the children moved in with Polk and Tamar. Their home was large enough to accommodate their daughter and the children, and Ora needed her family's help. Grandma Tamar pretty much took over taking care of baby Benjamin. Tamar and Cloria Vean were old enough to help with their younger sisters, Arizona and Opal. Others in the family pitched in to help. Still, Ora became weak from all the strain in recent weeks.

On February 5, Polk once again saddled his horse and rode for several miles to the doctor's home. The white doctor, with his horse and buggy and black leather bag, followed Polk away from town, out into the country, to visit another family member. The doctor thought Ora, like Walter and Howell, might have also caught pneumonia. He prescribed the same medicine and bed rest. Ora did not appear to respond to the treatment. So, that next Friday the family called the doctor again. Even though Ora was nursing baby Benjamin, she did not return to her old self. Seeing how weak Ora looked, her mother continued to do the housework.

Tamar had taken over the care of her granddaughters. She cooked the meals, washed clothes, and fed the children. As she looked after her grandchildren, Tamar's concern for Ora continued. She wanted very much for Ora to get well. She had a very strong attachment to her youngest daughter, and she knew her grandchildren, who had just lost their father, needed their mother now more than ever.

Sunday morning, February 15, 1914, like other Sabbaths at the Taylor home, represented a day of rest and worship. The family did little work. They always went to church on Sunday. Ora got up early to feed baby Benjamin and help her mother with the other children. After the children dressed and had breakfast, Ora decided to comb the girls' hair. First she combed Arizona's hair and then she did Opal's hair. While combing Opal's hair, Ora felt herself getting tired. By the time she finished with Opal, she was feeling very weak. So Ora told her mother, "I'm feeling kind of tired, I'm gonna lay down." Just before lying down, she turned to Tamar and said, "I want you to stay home and take care of my children." Ora then lay down across the bed beside baby Benjamin. Tamar assured her daughter that she need not worry, but she did not get a response. Tamar's loud cries brought everyone running to see what was the matter. Polk tried in vain to comfort her, but Tamar kept on screaming. She was inconsolable.

The doctor said Ora probably died from an embolism or heart failure. This was due in part to the fact that she died so suddenly. He also thought pneumonia may have been a contributing factor. Since the county performed no autopsy, they had no way to be sure. In a period of less than three weeks, Ora gave birth to a new baby and lost her husband and oldest son. In her short life she had brought eight children into the world. Tamar thought Ora had grown tired, too tired to go on. The loss she had experienced in the period of less than a month was just too much for her to take, so she simply gave up. At about eleven o'clock that morning, she joined Howell and Walter. Ora Taylor was twenty-eight.

The next day, the bell at Taylor's Chapel Church tolled again. For the third time in less than a month the small community came together to support Polk Taylor and his family. Together they again made the cold ride to the cemetery. Tamar was almost overcome with grief when she first saw the open grave. She moved her mouth but did not utter a sound, leading some of those watching her to wonder if she was talking out of her head. But Tamar prayed to herself, over and over and over again, until she willed herself to be strong. That is how she held herself together and made it through the services. Ora Taylor was also buried in the Taylor's burial ground, with her head laid to the west.

On the morning of Saturday, February 21, 1914, Grandpa Polk and Grandma Tamar traveled to the county courthouse. They had to take care of some business. The matter before the court involved their grandchildren. Upon "order of the court," the clerk read, "Mann Wills was duly and regularly appointed Guardian of Tamo Taylor, Alonza Taylor, Chlave, Opal Taylor and Ben Franklin Taylor, minor heirs of Howell Y. Taylor."[10] The clerk continued to read, "Mann Wills, came into open court and was duly qualified as Guardian. He entered into and acknowledged his bond in the sum of Two Thousand Dollars. W. R. Wills was approved as security on the bond," and the court ordered the clerk to "administer the oath as prescribed by law" to Mann Wills.[11] Polk and Tamar sat watching as the local white attorney repeated the oath. Tamar thought they made a mess of her grandchildren's names, but she had been the one who said that she could not handle money matters for the children. Tamar had decided to see lawyer Wills, and Polk could not talk her out of it once she made up her mind. Now the court had granted the lawyer power to make decisions about what her grandchildren needed.

The Taylor family welcomed the arrival of spring 1914. The new season brought along with it the hope that the remainder of the year would be better. Polk and Tamar now had five of their grandchildren living with them full time. Last August, their youngest son, Dempsy, had married a young woman named Betty Taylor and they both moved into Dempsy's room at home.

The family's white house sat on a small hill, and the well that supplied the family with spring water was located in front of the house, near the road. Polk built a little white fence around the well, with a door on one side to allow entry. He always fastened the hook latch on the door to keep the children out. The house was surrounded on three sides by fields and green pasture with cattle and horses, and there was an old red barn and hog pen behind the house. Tamar was glad that the home, as she described it, was "pretty good size." Fortunately, she had enough bedrooms to accommodate the family that had more than doubled in size.

By May, Polk and Tamar had settled into their new role as parents to the grandchildren. Because the children were used to being around Polk and Tamar, they adjusted remarkably well. Polk worked hard to take care of Tamar and all the children. He was glad that he had Dempsy to help. Polk and Dempsy had been working in the fields for the past month, planting cotton, corn, and sorghum, but they still had a great deal more work left to do. Lately, Polk had not been feeling too well. He was reluctant to seek help and only agreed to Tamar sending for the doctor when, after several days, the pain in his right side did not go away.

May 13, 1914. The white men wearing white coats were making repeated trips in and out of the house. They brought in medical supplies and utensils from the buggy in the front yard, and two men carried a long folding table into the house. Dr. Alfred Sorrelle, carrying his black leather bag, followed close behind them. They worked quietly, setting up the table and putting everything in place. The men covered the table with white sheets. When the room was prepared, Dr. Sorrelle proceeded to operate on Polk. Opal, who was four, and Arizona, six, watched from outside their grandpa's house until one of the men came and closed the front door.

Dr. Sorrelle visited the house the day before to examine Polk. He said Polk's only chance of getting better was to remove his appendix. Tamar thought the little doctor had a friendly face and that he was nice enough. But he looked so young, and she hoped he knew what he was doing. At thirty-three, Dr. Sorrelle had been practicing medicine in Haywood County for seven years. After graduating from Memphis Hospital Medical College, he interned at Bellevue Hospital in New York and in Cook County Hospital in Chicago before he returned to the area.[12] Dr. Sorrelle now delivered babies and operated on people in their homes. Haywood County did not have a hospital.

The men stayed in the room with Polk for what seemed like hours. After the doctor completed the surgery, the men gathered everything they brought into the house and carried it back out. Dr. Sorrelle had successfully removed Polk's appendix. Tamar knew the doctor did all he could, but Polk did not look good. She had never seen him in such a condition. To Tamar, he looked like an old white man, with his pale skin and thin curly hair matted around the sides of his head. While she was not too comfortable demonstrating her affection, over the next two days, she took loving care of Polk. Tamar gave him his medicine, tried to get him to drink liquids, and talked to him. She tried to make him comfortable as best she could. Dr. Sorrelle came to check on Polk, but he was not getting any better. Tamar knew in her heart that Polk was not going to make it. He never got up out of the bed after his surgery. On May 15, 1914, at the age of sixty-eight, Polk Taylor died.

People in the community came to the house to dress the body for burial. First they removed the two coins from his eyelids, since his eyes were now tightly shut, then they readied the body for washing. Polk's body in death was cold and heavy, and they washed it from head to toe. They put on his undergarments, then his shirt and pants, and, finally, they pulled his socks on his feet, but no shoes. Then they stretched Polk's body out on the cooling board and covered it with a white sheet.

The next day, two horses pulled the hearse up to the front door. This time two black men arrived in Polk's yard. They carefully slid the coffin from the back of the hearse and brought it into the house. One man raised a corner of the sheet for a last look at the man he had known most of his life. Wrapping the sheet around Polk's body, they placed it inside the wood coffin. The horses slowly pulled the hearse down the road, with a procession of wagons carrying the family and their neighbors close behind. They traveled a short distance to the road that led to Taylor's Chapel Road. As they turned off highway 54, heading for the Taylor's Chapel Cemetery, Polk Taylor left the Old Crossroad Place for the last time. And the big church bell tolled again.

Most of the faces at the cemetery were the same as attended funeral services for the other family members. The preacher said Polk had been a faithful servant; and in this case, the words were true. The choir sang Polk's favorite hymn, "We Will Understand It Better By and By," and he was laid to rest beside mounds of earth now covered with spring grass. The fact that each mound represented the death of a family member since the new year did not escape the mourners. Later, family, friends, and neighbors dropped by the house, brought food, and talked. They expressed pity for the little children who had lost both parents and now their grandpa. Only those who did not know her well marveled at how Tamar was able to hold herself together.

After the funeral, Tamar thought about the dream Polk had told her of last fall—the one he had awakened from in the early morning, leaving him unable to sleep. She was sitting at the kitchen table when Polk told her about it. Tamar had recalled it many times since the beginning of the year. Polk said he dreamed that he saw five white horses. This would not have been unusual, but they were inside the house. He described them as the whitest horses he had ever seen, with long flowing white manes. He said it was odd that not one of the horses had a rider. "What does it mean?" Tamar had asked. "It means," Polk said, "that five people in my family will die." Then he added, "But, they will all be saved." Right now, this was Tamar's only consolation.

One Saturday morning, about two weeks after Polk died, Tamar got up earlier than usual. She and two of her sons, Tom and Dempsy, gathered up everything on the farm and brought it to the house. Polk owned several cows, horses, hogs, and chickens. Since he always raised large crops, he also had many farm tools. So they gathered his different plows and other tools from around the barn. They went back and forth, making trips between the barn and the house. Then they herded up the animals. It was still early in the morning when they finally finished moving the last things closer to the house. By this time, white men and their wagons spread across the yard. The men came to see what kind of bargains they could find. They had heard about the sale out at the Old Crossroads Place.

Tamar knew that with Howell and Polk now gone, she could not run the farm with just Dempsy and four little girls and a baby. She sold the cows and horses and the hogs. She sold all of the farm tools. The wagons kept coming all morning. Everyone walked around and inspected the animals and tried to decide which cow or horse they wanted. When the men questioned how much an item cost, Tom and Dempsy helped their mother deal with the white men.

At the end of the day, nearly everything that belonged to Polk and Howell had been hauled away. Tamar even sold Howell and Ora's favorite "buggy horses." Howell called his horse Old Lucy and Ora's horse was Old Annie. Tamar kept one cow, a horse, and some chickens. When the last wagon drove off, she sat down with her granddaughters to count her money. She said it was a pretty good sale, but come Monday morning, she had to take all the money to town.

Tamar sat in the little waiting room designated for colored people, tightly holding on to her pocketbook. She understood why she had to turn over to the lawyer the money she had collected, though some of her children vehemently objected when they learned of the arrangement. They said that Howell had worked hard for everything he owned. She could put the money she raised from selling his things with his money in the bank and save it for the kids. These children were their own flesh and blood, and they felt someone in the family would know what was best for Ora and Howell's children. The sons grumbled that the family had been getting by all these years without giving their money to a lawyer. To them, something about this just was not right. They thought that the white folks Tamar sometimes worked for had put her up to this. Still, all the talking did not change Tamar's mind. When lawyer Wills emerged from his office, Tamar took the almost six hundred dollars she made from her sale and gave the money to the middle-aged white man.

Later that year, Tamar buried yet another family member. Ora and Howell's baby boy, Benjamin Franklin Taylor, died on September 14, 1914. Again, the family sent for Dr. Sorrelle to treat the baby, but it was too late to do any good. The child died that same day. Dr. Sorrelle said the baby died of cholera.[13] He was seven months and three weeks old. As Tamar and the rest of the family grieved the loss of her grandchild, she allowed herself to think about everything that had happened since the beginning of the year. She could not help but wonder if things would have been different if Polk had gone to the hospital in Jackson or Memphis for his operation, like some people in Brownsville did. She would never know. It was now left up to Tamar to look after her four grandchildren. Being part of the large Taylor family in the Taylor's Chapel Community gave Tamar great comfort. She could count on her family to help if she needed assistance. She also had her deep faith.

Tamar stayed on at the Old Crossroads Place for a few years after Polk died. Then she decided the farm was more than what she needed for herself and the children. One morning soon after reaching her decision, Tamar and other family members loaded everything she owned onto the wagons. Tamar moved to a little house on Taylor's Chapel Road, where she had lots of family throughout the community. Tamar left behind the home where she and Polk spent most of their years together raising their family.

The place got its name because it was located where the road crossed, connecting Highway 54 and Taylor's Chapel Road, which was now Tamar's destination. The horses pulled the wagons along the same route that Polk and the others traveled for the last time. At the crossroad, they turned left down the little road, taking Tamar and her four grandchildren to their new home. As Tamar looked back at the old home place, she could not help but think about Polk and the song that he was always singing or humming: "By and by when the morning come. All the saints of God will gather home. We will tell the story how we've overcome. And we'll understand it better by and by."

2.

Kinfolks

By 1919, Tamar had settled into the little white house about eight miles outside of Brownsville, off Bells Highway. The house was located between the two churches in the neighborhood, Tabernacle and Taylor's Chapel. The official name of the road was actually Tabernacle, but the blacks chose to call it Taylor's Chapel, the name of their church. Tamar rented her place from William Taylor, a member of the large family of white Taylors in the county.

The Taylors were one of the first families to settle in Haywood County. In 1826, the same year that the town of Brownsville was incorporated, Rev. Howell Taylor and his five sons, Richard, Edmund, Allen, John, and Howell Jr., came to Haywood County. Richard Taylor, the youngest son, was the first in the family to arrive. The Taylors lived in Mecklenburg County, Virginia, before moving to Tennessee. In 1817, Richard Taylor traveled to Montgomery County, Tennessee, where he settled with his family. Nine years later, he packed up again and moved his family, cattle, turkeys, geese, and other belongings to Haywood County. The rest of the Taylors joined him later that year. Rev. Howell Taylor and his sons Allen, John and Howell Jr. settled with Richard northeast of town in the Tabernacle area. Edmund Taylor settled in Fayette County.[1] The Taylors were a well-respected family and quite prominent in the community.

Rev. Howell Taylor, the patriarch of the family, was a Methodist minister. He was proud of the fact that he could trace his lineage all the way back to Charlemagne and King Alfred the Great. He could also show descent from fourteen of the signers of the Magna Charta.[2] The family owned land in Virginia, where they had built a church some years earlier. According to the family, when Bishop Asbury crossed Roanoke River at the close of the

Revolutionary War, he was directed to the home of the Taylors. The bishop asked John, the "colored ferryman," if he knew anybody in the neighborhood that prayed. "Yes sir," John said. "My master lives in that large house on the hill. He prays." The bishop visited the home of Edmund Taylor, who, along with his wife, was a member of the Church of England. While there, the bishop prayed with Edmund Taylor, his wife, and their guests, and as a result of his visit, the family converted, which was the beginning of Methodism in the Taylor family.[3] Edmund Taylor was the father of Rev. Howell Taylor. When Howell's son Richard came to Haywood County in 1826, he built the first church, which also served as the first schoolhouse in the county. Richard Taylor also brought the first slaves to Haywood County. Thus, soon after building the church, he added a place for his slaves to worship.[4]

Sam and Isabel were two of the slaves that belonged to Richard Taylor. Whether they traveled with him to Haywood County or were the first generation of slaves born in the county, they grew up on the Richard Taylor plantation. Later, when the two decided to marry, Richard Taylor gave his approval. He had no reason to oppose this union, since Isabel had found someone on his plantation.[5] Isabel was happy because the master's approval meant their marriage would be sanctioned by the church, and not just some ceremony with them "jumping over a broomstick." Lots of slaves in other quarters lived together and raised a family outside of marriage. After a while, they thought of themselves as husband and wife. This was not what Isabel wanted for her and Sam.

Richard Taylor and most other masters in Tennessee did not deny their slaves the right to marry.[6] This practice however had nothing to do with the owner's benevolence to his slaves. Rather, owners had come to recognize the social and economic utility of stable unions among their slaves and saw the wedding ceremonies as important to celebrate the seriousness of the occasion.[7] Thus, slave marriages accompanied by ceremony were not uncommon. While many owners preformed the ceremony themselves, reading a passage from the Bible, Richard Taylor had a white minister to marry Sam and Isabel. Since Isabel carried the status of a favored house servant, her ceremony was planned as a festive occasion with dancing and lots of food for a big supper.

On the evening of September 22, 1848, with all the plantation slaves and the white Taylors in attendance to witness the occasion, Sam and Isabel were married. The only problem for Isabel was that they were not permitted to say "'Till death do us part."[8] Theirs was a Christian marriage that carried with it no rights under the law.[9] Regardless of this restriction,

Isabel and Sam knew that, in the eyes of God, they were committed for life, and together they had eight children. Their five sons were Nick, Nealy, Henderson, Pack, and Fox, and their three daughters were Nora, Nancy, and Tamar.

Plantation life for the Taylor slaves revolved around hard work. Isabel considered herself fortunate that at least she did not work in the fields. Since she worked in what was called the "big house," she did not want her children working in the fields either. Isabel knew that housework was more desirable because it meant better clothes, better food, and a better chance of being exposed to some education.[10] She was also glad that Sam was the handyman and foreman and did not work as hard as the field hands. Still, the slaves worked all the time. In January, Sam and the other men began the year cutting rails, putting up rail, and rolling logs to the mill. In the spring, the other men planted the crops. They planted corn and tobacco and hundreds of acres of cotton, and they planted all the vegetables that were later cooked for everyone on the plantation. They started chopping cotton in late spring and continued the labor for several weeks. On occasion, when someone gave the master different kinds of trees, Sam and the other men put out the peach trees, apple trees, cherry trees, and damson trees. In between the farming, the men helped to raise cabins for the new slaves the master bought. By the time September came around, all the slaves, except the house servants, went to the fields to pick cotton. They worked from sun up to sun down. When slaves finished with one field, they moved on to the next, picking cotton until almost the end of December. By then the weather was so cold that sometimes a layer of ice covered the ground. At other times, they worked while high winds blew blinding snow in their faces. Even when the cold weather killed large numbers of livestock, the men and women on the plantations kept working. They received a brief reprieve on Christmas Eve, when the master distributed a small amount of money to each family to take into town and do their Christmas shopping.

Fall was hog-killing time, and the master usually had many hogs to kill, along with beef cows. Cleaning, stripping down, and cutting up the pork and beef always required much work. The slaves applied this same process to the deer that whites brought back from hunting trips. They also cleaned the hunters' rabbits, coons, birds, and squirrels. They did all this while continuing to work in the cotton fields. All year long they worked, closing out one year's tasks and starting all over again. Most slaves lived their entire lives without ever leaving the plantation.

Tamar lived with her family on the plantation owned by John A. Taylor, son of Richard Taylor. Like slaves on other plantations and farms, Tamar's ventures outside Haywood County were infrequent. On a few occasions, she was instructed to accompany the master's wife, Nan, to Belle Eagle. Tamar remembered her mama talking about the places Master John and his brothers visited. Isabel always listened to them talk while she was working in the house. Later she would recount all the details of the trips. Isabel knew where they traveled, who they saw, and what they did. Isabel talked a lot about the trip that Edmund and Bob took to Arkansas in the summer of 1858.

The night before he left, Master Edmund said "all the Negroes are coming up to take their adieus." Before dark, all the slaves came up to the big house to see them off, because they expected this trip to be a long one. Early the next morning, Bob and Edmund drove into town and left their horses and buggy at the livery stable. They then took a short train ride to Memphis. That evening at dusk, they left on the steamer *R. W. Powell* for Helena, Arkansas. They rode the *Kate Frisbee,* the steamer *Arkansas,* and the *Virginia Belle* as they traveled down the Mississippi River and up the Arkansas River. The men examined crops along the Mississippi before going on to Little Rock. From Little Rock they took a stage to Pine Bluff to procure horses, but they were unsuccessful in their primary mission.[11]

On June 12, after having been gone for about two weeks, time came for the brothers to start the journey home. Bob and Edmund had a choice of two boats for the trip up the Mississippi. They chose the *Kate Frisbee* because she was a few minutes earlier than the *Pennsylvania.* At about six in the evening they were on their way up the Mississippi to Memphis. The next morning, they learned of a horrible accident on the other boat. It seems that during the night all the boilers on the *Pennsylvania* had exploded. When they arrived on the scene of the disaster, they saw such "intolerable suffering and agony" as they had never seen before. The boat was covered with dying people. Master Bob said, "Hundreds of poor souls were ushered into eternity" before the *Kate Frisbee* took on the wounded and dying. Another four or five people died before they reached Memphis.[12] Realizing what a narrow escape it had been, Bob and Edmund were feeling "unduly happy to get home safe and sound." That same evening, as they sat they sat around the table at supper, the two men described in detail everything they had encountered on their trip.

On March 4, 1861, when the news came that Abraham Lincoln was inaugurated as president of the United States, Tamar was one month shy of ten.

She was old enough to understand that the news created much concern on the plantation. Each night the grownups gave a report of everything they heard during the day. Since Isabel now cooked for Master John, she was able to get the latest news. This was especially true since Master John and his father and brothers frequently gathered at the house, where they invariably discussed what was going on locally as well as in the nation. The men shared the news they heard from talking to other businessmen in town, and Master John usually reported on what he read in the newspapers, including some northern papers. He constantly talked about the political affairs of "this great country being in such deplorable conditions." He and the others agreed that the election had led to much discontent in the South. Isabel prided herself with having excellent hearing and now, more than ever, when within earshot of the white folks talking, she made a point to use it well. While Sam, who worked as a handyman and foreman on the plantation, had more mobility than most slaves. The other slaves counted on both Sam and Isabel to provide them with reliable information.

In April 1861, news came from Charleston of the Civil War. The reports said cannons were firing in several directions. Everyone spent much of the time talking of the war and speculating about what it meant. Talks of the dreadful horrors of war and the nation being torn apart caused great anxiety for both blacks and whites. The town's people expressed concern for the future of the country, especially the South. Master John said he did not know why the North didn't just leave them alone, saying that, "The South has right on her side and her actions are in accord with the purpose and designs of God Himself." He believed the South would eventually prevail, so he kept praying, "Lord in heaven have mercy."

In June 1861, all the whites in the community attended a meeting to discuss the war, and many of them voted for Tennessee to secede from the U.S. government.[13] A few days later, Tennessee joined the Confederate States of America. Master John and many of the whites thought the South had done everything possible to avoid war, but now it was best for them to make their own rules. Although there were some whites, like almost all the blacks, who remained loyal to the Union, they were not among the whites who called on the Taylor plantation. Slaves compared notes on what they each heard about Tennessee leaving the Union, and they tried to figure out how that was possible. They heard that all the fighting was because the South wanted to keep them slaves. After initially sharing the master's sentiments on the war, most of the slaves started to think that maybe this war was not really that bad after all. One thing was certain, the war had everybody worried.

By the summer of 1861, whites had started holding regular meetings at the church at night to discuss the war. President Jefferson Davis announced that one day in June would be set aside for fasting and prayer for the Southern army. They all went to the church in the middle of the week to pray for the Confederate cause. In August, they met at the church almost every day and night, and sometimes the meetings went on all day and most of the night. A few months later, concerns heightened when they learned that Gov. Isham G. Harris had called out the militia of the state.[14] They talked about nothing but war. Yet all the meetings brought little encouragement. Convinced they needed to do more, men and boys showed up in town and volunteered to serve in the Tennessee army. The government asked each white man to provide one Negro to help the soldiers in their district. Whenever Sam returned from his trip into town, where he was sent to take supplies and to help sick soldiers, he reported on all the excitement among the people as the soldiers were getting ready to fight the war.

On some nights when the white folks were meeting, the slaves held their own secret church meetings under the stars. There were so many rumors being spread about the war that even Master did not know what was reliable and what was not, so Isabel and the other slaves no longer knew what to believe. They thought the reports were true about the war raging in different parts of the country and that a large number of lives were being lost. Master John said it had not been a good year on the plantation, with the war, all the rain, and the complaining Negroes. He kept on praying, "God in mercy defend the right."[15] And he often talked about how the South was going to rise up. He was almost fanatical in his belief that the "South was God's restored Israel." Despite the gloomy picture painted of the war, two young slaves, Pony and George, stood apart from the others and quietly hatched a plan to escape, join up with the Northern army, and be free. At the close of their meeting, to make sure they were not overheard, the men turned three big black kettles up side down to catch the sound as they prayed for the South's defeat.

Less than two weeks into the new year of 1862, the weather turned colder, the temperature dropped some forty degrees in a matter of hours, and the war continued to escalate. With so much fighting going on, most people had difficulty keeping track of all the incoming news. Master John and the other men met at the house more often to discuss not just the many rumors they heard and what they read in the papers, but also the very latest news that they received by telegraph. For a while, it seemed the tide was constantly shifting. First came reports of the North losing a number of battles, then in early February everything changed when they learned that Lincoln's gunboats had taken possession of Fort Henry and the railroad bridge over the Tennessee River. About a week later, they received news that there had been terrible fighting and the Confederate army of Tennessee had lost Fort Donelson. Then, on February 23, Nashville was occupied by the Union army. Isabel could not remember all the battles being fought, but she overheard the warnings when the Yankees began firing cannons on Memphis.

In April, Sam got an opportunity to see Northern soldiers firsthand when he and two other men were sent to work on Fort Pillow and discovered President Lincoln's soldiers already at the fort. Cannons fired all around them as they heard talk that the bridges across the Hatchie and Forked Deer Rivers were burned to prevent the Union soldiers from advancing. The plan failed. After the Confederates lost the Battle of Shiloh, all west Tennessee was open to full Union army occupation. Except for the excitement over cannons firing and seeing all the soldiers, life did not change much for the men and women on the Taylor plantation. The workers were still required to plow the fields; plant large crops of corn, cotton, and wheat; then cut and stack the grain and hoe the cotton, along with their other work. The heavy June rains caused concern about crops, then they got word that orders had been given for them to burn all the cotton. There was great uncertainty among the slaves. Still, they were perhaps more anxious about reports predicting the arrival of Northern soldiers in the city of Brownsville any day.

In August 1862, Union Gen. Ulysses S. Grant ordered the establishments of contraband camps at Grand Junction and other west Tennessee locations, including Brownsville, to hold the thousands of slaves who escaped area farms and plantations.[16] Sam and Isabel did not know anyone that was held in the camps. Almost every time one of the young slaves managed to escape from the plantation, he was captured and in a short time returned to Master John. They had never seriously entertained the idea of trying to escape themselves, not with all their children and other family members. Therefore they did not give much thought to the camps.

By fall, soldiers from the Northern army were encamped all around them. Several thousand soldiers had converged on nearby towns, and they became a common sight in the neighborhood, though their presence still created a source of much agitation. The soldiers made many trips to the plantation for supplies, and Sam and the other men had to bring some of their best horses and, reluctantly, turn them over. On several occasions when Union soldiers stopped by in the evening, Isabel cooked and fed them supper. At times, as many as twenty soldiers showed up to spend the night. But what really infuriated Master John, more than anything else, was having to ride into town and take the oath of allegiance to the U.S. government. That was one thing he swore he would never do.

In January 1863, word spread that President Lincoln had freed the slaves. The mood on the plantation was mixed. Tamar remembered her mama being very happy when she first told the family the news. Isabel could not believe her ears when she overheard Master John talking that day. Many of the others also expressed disbelief, but were later overcome with joy when Northern soldiers confirmed the reports. For days Tamar heard all the talk about being free. Master John and the other white folks were more than a little concerned by the news. They already claimed they had grass overtaking some of the crops because the Negroes had either left the plantation or were not doing their usual jobs. Master expressed much concern over harvesting the year's cotton crop. In previous years, the slaves had picked as much as five hundred bales of cotton in one fall. They now figured that no one could force them to repeat such efforts. But the joy among the slaves gradually faded when months passed and the news of freedom had not changed their situation. Tamar saw the disappointment in her mama and papa's face. Contrary to what they initially thought, things did not get better.

By the end of 1863, Federal soldiers made almost daily trips on the Taylor plantation to take property. They took hogs, mules, horses, and food. Isabel had to feed fifty men in one night, and she was afraid that soon there would be no food left for any of them. Thinking the same thing, some slaves started stealing food. Soldiers burned stores in Brownsville and committed other acts of destruction all around. Stories spread of Federal soldiers robbing others in the neighborhood and ransacking their homes. Tamar was eleven when the Federal soldiers came on the plantation and robbed Master John. She had been sent to help Miss Nan and the two were in the bedroom when several young soldiers barged in on them. The men proceeded to rummage through all the drawers, scattering articles of clothing and throwing items on the floor as they searched. A lady's white handkerchief landed almost under the bed near where Tamar stood. Miss Nan was too frightened to move. Tamar had seen her mistress with the handkerchief before, so she reached down by her foot, picked it up, and held it behind her back. The men ignored the child as they took the loot: a watch, ladies' pin, and a few other small items. After the soldiers left, Tamar handed Miss Nan the handkerchief, which had gold coins tied in one corner.

A year later, in April of 1864, word reached the plantation that Confederate troops had massacred a large number of Negro soldiers who had surrendered to Gen. Nathan B. Forrest at Fort Pillow, just a short distance from Brownsville.[17] All the slaves were disheartened by the latest news. They were beginning to think that this horrible war would never end. A few days later, their spirits were dampened even further when they watched a group of white men bring back Pony and George, who had finally gotten up enough nerve to attempt their escape.

In December 1864, word came of major victory for the North. A Union army of 43,000 black and white men had administered a decisive whipping to the Confederate army of Tennessee in the Battle of Nashville.[18] The Confederates would never lay claim to Tennessee again. Then in January 1865, the Tennessee General Assembly amended the state constitution to abolish slavery.[19] Finally, in April of that year, the Southern armies surrendered in Virginia. Sam and Isabel and the other Negroes on the Taylor plantation heard the news. Although their jubilation was tempered a few days later when President Lincoln was assassinated, the war was over. Isabel said God in heaven must have answered their prayers and Master's prayers too, because they were free. She recalled all those times when Master prayed and asked that the "Good Lord will cause the side of right and justice to triumph."

The newly freed blacks decided they were no longer willing to work as slaves, so they went on strike. Like blacks in other neighborhoods, Sam and Isabel were packing their few possessions, "settling up" with their former owners, and leaving the plantation. Although free, they and the other former slaves did not move very far. As important as their emancipation was, they stayed in the same area primarily for two reasons: they had developed a significant kin network with their relatives and other slaves on the plantation, and the Taylor plantation was the one place where they knew they could find work to support their families.[20]

The plantation where Tamar grew up with her parents was relatively stable. Most families were not disrupted by sales like those on other farms or plantations. John A. Taylor was considered by most to be a very religious man. He was small and somewhat frail, a real intellectual who was always writing books, articles, or daily journal entries. As a young boy, John gave his life to Christ after witnessing his mother's death, and some years later he was affected by the sudden violent death of his wife, caused when her horse ran away with her buggy. He probably treated his slaves better than most owners; however, he was still the master of the plantation and sometimes sold slaves, especially older ones, and continued to purchase new slaves.[21] He started out with ten slaves, and before the end of the war he owned about one hundred.[22]

Tamar remembered, around the time of the war, when Master sold Uncle Archer. The next year, he said the idea of buying Negroes from Virginia who belonged to his wife disturbed him. But that did not stop him from paying a man fifteen hundred dollars to go to the old country to buy them for him. Tamar also remembered one cold winter day when Master sent his cousin's young baby to the house for Tamar's mother, Isabel, to suckle. Isabel gave this child her milk when her own baby had died that morning. Tamar was saddened that her papa, who worked as a slave all his life, did not live long enough to enjoy his freedom. Sam Taylor died before the end of 1865.

Still, as a result of growing up in a well-settled community, Tamar was socialized to believe in the importance of family, morals, religion, and respect for one's elders. The community was composed primarily of blood relatives. All of Tamar's immediate family lived right in the same small community.[23] Those in the community who were not related often received kin titles. Out of respect, others within the community referred to all the older people as "uncle" or "aunt."[24] From this large kin network, Tamar's values were shaped. She was able to absorb the skills, tradition, morals, knowledge, and religion of her parents and other relatives. Tamar resolved to pass these values on to her grandchildren.[25]

A few years had passed since Polk died and Tamar returned to the Taylor's Chapel community. The community was similar to most of the others in Haywood County that acquired their name from the neighborhood church. Taylor's Chapel Church was built in 1895 on land given to the Negroes by John A. Taylor. The community surrounding the little church was made up of people who lived on the Taylor plantation and their relatives. Tamar now spent all her time working and taking care of her grandchildren. They worked in the field together, around the house, doing everything they could to keep the run of the place. With the help of Tamar's sons and her brothers, she continued to farm. When Tamar was not working on the farm, she cooked for the white folks. The first part of every year, Tamar and the girls received a check from lawyer Wills, the guardian of Howell Young Taylor's estate. That enabled them to make ends meet and to live comfortably.

Tamar Taylor had a tall, stout build and a dark brown complexion. As a young lady, she had long black hair, but having a rather soft texture it had grown thin over the years. Tamar was born April 24, 1851, on the Taylor plantation. She was fourteen before finally being able to live as a free person. She remembered the lessons she learned in the slave community. These were the things on which she relied for help in life. An intelligent woman with good business sense, Tamar believed in "fixing her clothes up nice," in being "real clean," and in "straight living." She also believed in working hard for everything that she received. Tamar was a strong Christian woman whose strength came from the church and God. And she imposed her moral code upon all those who came around her.

Tamar kept a close eye on everything her granddaughters did. She especially watched the young men that came around. She would not let just anybody come to see the girls. If the boy's family was not respected, he could not come to her house. Tamar defined "respected" as having good morals, being in the church, and being looked upon favorably in the community. Cloria Vean, Arizona, and Opal thought their grandmama was mean. Tamar was not so much mean as she was strict. It was important that the girls live right and grow up to be proper young ladies. Despite all her rules, Tamar's namesake found herself a young man to marry and left home.

Ora named her oldest daughter, Tamar, after Ora's mother. It was custom among Negroes, dating back to the early years of slavery, to name children for their grandparents and other extended relatives.[26] This was especially true for the firstborn child. The Taylor family was filled with children carrying the name of a grandparent, uncle, or aunt. The tradition was apparently honored among the whites as well. Many of the members of Rev. Howell Taylor's family were also named for blood relatives. Ora carried on the tradition by naming her first son, Walter Howell, for his father. When her first child was born in February 1903, she named the child for her grandmother Tamar.

At seventeen, Tamar was a tall, slim young woman with long thick black hair. She had a small face that was a light brown complexion. Most people considered her nice looking. By early 1920, Tamar had decided that she would marry a local boy named Dan Hafford. Grandma Tamar found the young man to be acceptable, so she gave her permission for them to get married. After all, she was acquainted with the young man's family. Dan Hafford was first cousin to Al Rawls, whose family was well known in the community.

Together Tamar and her grandmama made plans for the wedding. The ceremony was to be held at home, and they were inviting many people. Just the Taylor cousins alone would fill the house. Grandma Tamar cooked all of her favorite recipes. She prepared an entire wedding dinner with chicken and ham, several different vegetables, rolls, and a big wedding cake to go with her homemade grape wine. After all the cooking, cleaning the house, and securing extra chairs, everything was finally ready.

Tamar in her white dress made a beautiful bride, while the groom, a young man with a stocky build, looked nice in his dark suit. In the late afternoon of February 22, 1920, Tamar Taylor and Dan Hafford were married. All the family and neighbors enjoyed the occasion. They talked and ate, laughed and toasted the young couple. The celebration continued on into the night. Before it was over, the white people who lived nearby walked down. Macon Thornton, one of seven prominent brothers in the county whose mother was the granddaughter of Rev. Howell Taylor, brought a guest with him. He knew Grandma Tamar's reputation for being a good cook, and with a wedding going on, he knew there was going to be food. They all showed up at the back door and came in the kitchen. Grandma Tamar served Mr. Macon and his guest in the kitchen, because that was as far as they chose to go. Macon Thornton thought her cake was so good that he kept repeating, "Thank you, Tamar. Thank you, Tamar."

With the wedding behind them, Grandma Tamar followed a custom of the time: she provided the newly married couple with household items for their new home. Since most of the newlyweds got married at a very young age, they had not worked enough to have any savings. They started their life together with little money. With the meager wages most made farming, it would take some time for them to purchase the things they needed. When Tamar and her new husband moved out on their own, Grandma Tamar gave them a bed, linen, dishes, cooking utensils, a coal oil lamp, meat, and canned food to set up housekeeping.

Tamar left three sisters still at home. Like most children their age, the two older girls, Cloria Vean and Arizona, thought they were too grown up to play with Opal. They spent all their time talking to each other. They would talk about boys, who liked whom, or who had recently married. When Opal tried to listen to their conversations, they suddenly stopped talking. Opal found herself playing alone most of the time. She made little clothes for her dolls, wove blades of grass into tiny baskets, and read. The Bible was her favorite book. Her Mama Ora had bought the really large Bible shortly before she died. Opal would place the Bible on the floor in front of her and then lay on the floor for hours reading it.

Taylor's Chapel Church doubled as the school for the Negro children in the community. All eight grades were taught in one small room. This was the first school that Opal and her sisters attended. Since moving, they had been walking a short distance up the road to the church. Opal enjoyed learning, and she also liked the fact that at school she had lots of cousins to play with. One of these cousins, Lizzie Hess, was almost like a sister. Their other cousins, Ray, Ora, Daisy, and Octavia, were also at the school. Other children at the school were Dick Williams and his sister, Julie, and a boy named Gill Hess. Opal thought Gill was a "little runt," but he was always at the head of the class.

The children were required to stand in order based on who was the best speller. Since Opal could never beat Gill at spelling, she stood second in a line that stretched across the church. Julie was a few years younger than Opal and Gill, and Opal looked out for Julie because she always cried whenever the teacher moved her down in the line. One time Dick asked Opal to write a "love letter" for him to a girl named Alice. Since Opal was left handed, Alice recognized her handwriting. Dick wrote the next letter, but he still asked Opal what to write.

When lunchtime came, they all pulled out their lunches brought from home. Opal loved her biscuits and the homemade sausage and pear preserve that her grandma made. When it was recess, Opal, her cousins, and all the other children ran around playing games. Later as Opal and Lizzie walked home from school, they pulled plums and grapes from the bushes growing on the side of the road and ate the fruit as they hurried home together.

Lizzie's mother, Beulah, Ora's only sister, had moved back home with Grandma Tamar. Aunt Beulah had married a man named Alex Hess. Ever since Aunt Beulah and her husband first split up, she and her five girls had been living with her mother. In addition to Lizzie, there was Florida, Ruby, Daisy, and Octavia, her oldest daughter by her first husband. Since Opal's mother was dead and the children were living in the same house, people naturally assumed they were all sisters. The girls did not lack for male cousins, though. Uncle Tom had married a young woman named Priscilla

Wills. Uncle Tom and Aunt "Prissy" had all boys: Lewis, James, "Meedie," Clarence, Leonard, Vernal, and Eldred. Uncle Alonzo, who all the children called Uncle "Son," married Vera before marrying his second wife, Susan. Uncle "Son" and Aunt Susan had Ora, Ninnie Mae, Ray, Fred, Erma Lee, and Alonzo Jr. Uncle Clifton married Amelia, and they had one daughter, Josephine. Uncle Dempsy and Aunt Betty had Mattie Ray, Dempsy Jr., May Anna, and later, Albert, Selma, and Robert.

When Beulah moved back home, there was a lot of talk about why she had left her husband. For a long time, the family chose not to acknowledge the rumors that had spread throughout the community. After all, the infidelity of one's spouse was not that common. And, in instances where it was found, the accused was looked upon with disdain, especially in a small town steeped in the tradition of the church and Christian principles. But one of Polk's daughters by his first wife had a teenage daughter that lived in the community. The young girl had apparently been spending time with Beulah's husband. When it was discovered that the young girl was in the "family way," there was much speculation about the father. Beulah, feeling hurt and betrayed, took her children and left, and people figured they had their answer. The children, not knowing the circumstances that brought them to their grandma's house, just enjoyed being with their cousins. For a while, they lived across the road from Uncle Tom and played with his boys, too. Growing up, there was never a shortage of cousins around.

Uncle Tom was the son Grandma Tamar relied on to help her with the farming. Although she had sold Polk's equipment, she continued to farm. When Tom rented a farm on the road that ran from the church to Allens Station, she had him rent enough land to plant crops for both of them. In the spring, Uncle Tom hitched a mule to the plow and made the rows to plant cotton. Then he would "drag the cotton" to level the rows. This process involved attaching two long boards to one mule, with the mules pulling the boards over the rows. Uncle Tom built a seat on the drag so his son Clarence, who was a young boy, could sit while working. Opal sometimes sat with Clarence as he held on to the plow lines guiding the mule. Next, Uncle Tom planted the cotton. Later, all the cousins worked in the field together, chopping and picking cotton.

In the fall, when it was too wet to pick cotton, Uncle Tom took his mother and the children down to "Buttermilk Bottom." Grandma Tamar put her big tubs in the wagon and they rode out Highway 54; then they turned west and went across a bumpy "field road" to reach the bottom. The wooded area was near small streams, like the Little Slew and the Big Slew that flowed into the Forked Deer River. Once there everyone got busy filling the tubs with walnuts and "scaly barks," nuts similar to English walnuts.

During the winter, Grandma Tamar's sons would come to visit and they would sit around the fireplace at night telling stories and eating scaly barks. There would be Uncle Tom, Uncle "Son," Uncle Dempsy, and Uncle Clifton, who lived nearby, and Uncle Bishop, who lived in town. Sometimes Grandma Tamar baked sweet potatoes in the hot ashes. The children took the popcorn they found growing in the fields with the cotton and popped it over the open fire in a long-handled tin pan. Opal especially liked it when Uncle Tom came by, because he would eat roasted sweet potatoes and scaly barks while she "went to work on his head." Opal thought Uncle Tom was nice and patient and had a "good, thick head of hair."

The last week of August 1922, Grandma Tamar took a break from the fields to cook at the white church. Tabernacle United Methodist Church had been the home for Rev. Howell Taylor's family for close to one hundred years. When Richard Taylor first built the church in 1826, it was a little log building in the grove of his home. He called the church New Hope. In 1832, his family constructed a new building some four hundred yards from the old location. Rev. Howell Taylor renamed the church Tabernacle, the name of his church back home in Virginia.[27] Surrounded by large oak trees, with the largest in the front lawn, the church is now exactly 1.8 miles off Bells Highway. Taylor's Chapel Church, where blacks worship, is located about a mile further up the road.

At the New Hope Church in 1826 the Taylors started the first camp meeting in Haywood County. They decided to hold camp meetings on the church grounds, for convenience, because of the bad travel conditions during that time and because they sometimes had five church services in one day. The Taylor family used cloth tents until the early 1890s, when family members built cabins on the church grounds. The first cabins amounted to little more than shacks made from logs that had been sawed and then roughly put together. Later, they built some much larger cabins, having two bedrooms, a dining room, kitchen, and shed. Families built rows of small cabins by the road on the south side of the church.[28] In late August or early September, generations of Taylors from all over the county and other areas converged on the Kinfolks Camp Meeting. They came to hear the preaching, enjoy their relatives, and partake of the hospitality and the food. For a week and sometimes longer, they experienced what they referred to as a "love feast."

People packed the church so full they barely left any room to stand. They had to lock the doors so no one else could enter. Lines of churchgoers stood leaning against the walls in a semicircle around the pews. Everyone could feel the beads of perspiration soaking through their clothing, and they pulled the damp, sticky clothes free from their bodies. The minister preached for more than thirty minutes, and people clapped their hands, shouted, and praised the Lord. When the preacher finally took his seat, everyone stood and sang "Amazing Grace." They closed with the singing of "On Jordan's Stormy Bank I Stand." All those who had not been able to get inside the church gathered outdoors under a bush arbor to hear a different minister preach the gospel.

Kinfolks Camp Meeting would not have been successful without the food. The white Taylors and other camp regulars liked to brag that their Negro servants cooked some of the best food around, right there on the campgrounds. Newcomers to the camp voiced amazement at the "collection of Negro cooks and serving men."[29] Grandma Tamar cooked at the camp meeting, just as she had done every year since 1898. Her sister Nora had cooked at the campground until her death on October 6, 1897. The following year, Grandma Tamar replaced Nora as cook for William and Hattie Taylor.[30] William was the son of John A. Taylor, the grandson of Richard Taylor, and the great grandson of Rev. Howell Taylor.

About the middle of the week, all the families started to move their things into the living quarters on the churchgrounds. People filled the campground by the time that Friday came. Entire families arrived for camp: the men, their wives, teenagers, and small children. Amidst the heat, haze, and dust, you could hear the sounds of laughter and kinfolks greeting each other. The men talked about the crops, their business, or politics; the women fretted over their guests; and the young girls talked about boys and dating. The sounds of dishes clattering, pans rattling, and pot lids banging emanated from inside the cabins. All the cooks worked in their respective kitchens. They all fixed fried chicken, crisp and greasy; smothered chicken; hams and lamb; corn puddings, baked apples, black-eyed peas, butter beans, and other vegetables; and they baked caramel and chocolate cakes and sweet potato and egg custard pies. Grandma Tamar always took great care to make sure that she prepared every one of her dishes just right. She knew how much everyone at the camp enjoyed her cooking.

At first daybreak, Grandma Tamar fired up the old wood-burning stove. To help prepare the meals, she had a big bowl of eggs, a twenty-five pound sack of flour, a barrel of sugar, a stand of lard, and plenty of butter that she had freshly churned and shaped with her callused hands. In minutes, she had thick slices of ham frying in the skillet, buttermilk biscuits baking in the oven, and jars of homemade jams and preserves on the table. With breakfast over, Grandma Tamar moved on to the rest of her cooking. She prepared the ham and fryers for cooking before the early prayer service had even started. While campers enjoyed their "love feast," her cakes cooled on the table and her pies cooked in the oven.

Everyone loved Grandma Tamar's spice cake. It consisted of three layers filled with spices and covered with white icing. She made the best sweet potato pies on the grounds, using the first sweet potatoes of the season. As the campers greeted relatives and socialized, Grandma Tamar put the pot on for the crowder peas and got ready to cut and scrape corn off the ears for her corn pudding. By the time the morning service ended, she had prepared the entire noon meal.

A male camper blew the horn to tell everyone that it was dinnertime. Upon hearing the summons, all the families, accompanied by their guests, filed into their cabins for the main meal of the day. Grandma Tamar's granddaughter, Opal, helped serve Miss Hattie and the rest of her family. Opal had been to the campground on a few other occasions. Most of the time she came for the company of her grandma. This time she helped prepare the vegetables, pumped water from the well, and served the food. She and her grandmother made several trips from the little kitchen to the adjoining shed room, where a long table stood covered with food. Through all this cooking, in the hot August heat, Grandma Tamar never complained. She enjoyed having all the white folks praise her for being such a good cook.

Grandma Tamar wore her wig for the occasion since all "her white folks," some she had not seen for a year, were at the camp meeting. Opal stood over the table fanning flies with a small branch that she broke from a bush just outside the cabin. Everyone at the table talked as they ate. Miss Hattie said again that she just "could not camp without Tamar." One of the guests tried to join the conversation. The old white man looked at Opal then said, "Might nigh all niggers got old piece a cars. Ever' time ya see 'em, they settin' by da side of da road and ever'body passin' by 'em just a flyin'." Obviously pleased with himself for having made this observation, he looked around and laughed. But no one at the table said a word. Opal thought he looked like an old poor cousin just happy to be there. Finally, Miss Hattie's son, Edmund, said, "yes, a lot of them about broken down when they get them, alright." Opal almost got tickled herself when no one joined in and laughed at the old man's attempt at humor, which she was sure had been designed at her expense.

Darkness fell before Grandma Tamar and Opal began walking home. After the noon meal, they served supper, washed the dishes, and prepared a large platter of food for the men to take around after the evening service. As they walked past the white folk's cemetery, they heard noises coming from inside the grounds. Late at night, after the last service of the day, you could often hear noises coming from the direction of the cemetery. Opal was not sure about the source of the noises, but she had seen young couples emerge from the cemetery looking flushed. Grandma Tamar had heard that the young people supposedly went courting in the cemetery. She also heard that one of the ministers had called all the young people together for a special sermon designed to keep the teenagers out of the cemetery at night. However, according to the campers, a lot of them that were now married had gotten together right there in the cemetery.[31] This was the third thing for which the Kinfolks Camp Meeting had acquired a reputation. Grandma Tamar thought that her grandchild was not yet old enough to understand. There were some things that she just did not care to talk about with the young girl; she would find out soon enough. As they walked on past the home of Miss Emma Taylor, she decided it was best that she did not try to explain. The long day had taken its toll.

Miss Emma Taylor's house was positioned between Grandma Tamar's house and Tabernacle Church, with all the buildings within walking distance of the other. Grandma Tamar always sent Opal to take something down to Miss Emma. Most of the time, Opal took the old white woman vegetables that her grandma picked from the garden. The tall, white-haired woman lived alone and usually appeared lonely. She developed the habit of starting a conversation whenever Opal came around. On one occasion, she asked Opal to bring her mail. After Opal returned with the mail, Miss Emma asked her how Dempsy was doing. Opal said Uncle Dempsy and Aunt Betty had talked about moving to Michigan. Miss Emma said, "I always liked Dempsy. I used to call him my boy." She added, "You know, all the Taylors are kin anyhow."

The fall of 1922, following the camp meeting, Grandma Tamar was busy again picking cotton and putting up food for the winter. She canned everything from peaches, pears, and tomatoes to jars of lima beans and okra. She also prepared apples, and she fixed them every possible way one could imagine. Miss Hattie had someone bring Grandma Tamar a flatbed full of apples. She made apple jelly, baked apples, and apple pies. Then she sliced and dried lots of apples, some of which she later used for fried apple pies. She even used the peel from pears to make wine. The wine had kind of a whisky color and tasted good. She also made grape wine and muscadine wine. When Uncle Tom or one of her other sons killed hogs or a cow, they always killed enough for Grandma Tamar. She made her own sausage by running pieces of pork through the grinder and adding lots of seasoning, and she put up her other meat for the winter. She believed in keeping plenty of food around. Her grandchildren never went hungry. Once again, Grandma Tamar had all four of Ora's daughters living at home.

Young Tamar's marriage to the Hafford boy did not work out. Grandma Tamar said that it seems no matter how respected a person's family is, sometimes the person just does not turn out the same. Tamar and Dan had moved to Memphis after they got married. She did not know what had happened to cause the marriage to break up. She thought that it could have been living in the big city. There were a lot of things in Memphis to tempt a young man, and she knew what people said about Dan having a reputation for being rowdy.

It was not long after Tamar returned home that she began to feel sickly. By December, she had been feeling poorly for a few months. Although she was not completely well, there did not seem to be any one problem. At times, she did complain of her stomach hurting. She had a small frame and looked a little frail, but Tamar was only nineteen. Her grandma thought she would soon get over whatever bothered her, so she never called the doctor. On December 17, 1922, Tamar Taylor died. The cause of death was listed as unknown. But the family knew that the influenza outbreak had been bad throughout the country in recent times.

Two weeks after Tamar's death, Cloria Vean married Claiborne Taylor and moved away from home. The following year, on November 11, 1923, Arizona married Joe Taylor and also moved out on her own. That left just Grandma Tamar and Opal at home. Grandma Tamar did not think it was a good idea for the two of them to be living alone. One day she asked Opal whom she would rather live with, Uncle Dempsy or Uncle Tom. Opal chose to stay with Uncle Dempsy, since he was living with them when her parents died. Grandma Tamar moved in with her daughter Nancy, who lived in town.

On Springfield Road

Revival Sunday, August 1925, had arrived, and the little frame church was packed to capacity. Folding chairs lined the aisles and filled every available space. The temperature outside had climbed steadily since morning, and the old deacons and overweight sisters felt its effects profoundly. The preacher took his seat after inspiring at least three of the sisters to shout, and someone on the front row sang out, "Before this time another year I may be dead and gone." The whole congregation joined in at, "In some lonesome graveyard, oh Lord, how long." After they finished singing and extended the invitation to join the church, several deacons representing visiting churches assisted in passing around plates to take up the collection. But first they commented on how much they enjoyed the service. Opal sat on the pew, squeezed between two middle-aged ladies, wondering whether each deacon had to speak. She wanted services to be over so she could talk with Lizzie.

Snipes Grove Baptist Church was located less than a mile from Bells Highway, down Taylor's Chapel Road. The church stood in a clearing surrounded by wide-open fields, a short distance up from the narrow road leading to Taylor's cemetery. First-time visitors to the church were surprised to find the large area of cleared land just beyond the woods. This revival Sunday, as usual, brought people from all over the county. With the morning service finally over, men unloaded boxes from cars and wagons, while the church ladies spread tables with home-cooked food. Women brought packed boxes with fried chicken, ham, potato salad, and an assortment of breads, cakes, and pies. Men who worked in the fields all week seldom had the opportunity to socialize; they used this time to gather at the back of their wagons and eat, talk, and enjoy themselves. Women served and little children ran around in their Sunday best. Most people piled their plates high with more food than they could eat, and some even carried one plate in each hand. Opal, along with Uncle Dempsy and Grandma Tamar, had visited the church on revival Sunday for years. She and Lizzie found a big tree, in a futile attempt to find relief from the sun, and got caught up on recent news.

Opal was tired of people always coming up to her saying, "I know you're gonna to be next," or, "I know you're gonna get married now." Both of Opal's sisters were married, and Lizzie married Harrison Taylor last year at fourteen. Now everyone assumed Opal would soon marry too. As Opal and Lizzie talked about her new life, they were approached by two young men. The shorter of the two said his name was A. D. Springfield, and he wanted to introduce the girls to his cousin. They appeared to be close to the same age, but the cousin had a darker complexion with a stocky build and a nose shaped like that of an Indian. Opal and Lizzie said hello and walked away.

Later they saw the two young men mounting their horses. Obviously, they did not plan to stay for the afternoon service. Opal said she was not interested in them, but she noticed that the cousin looked rather striking in his dark suit and white shirt. Sneaking another glance as the young man prepared to leave, she observed that the horse he called "Old Hubbard" was not bad either. His horse was big and black with a long, pretty black mane. It was larger than the brown horse A. D. rode. She thought that not very many young men owned a fine-looking horse like Old Hubbard, and she could see the owner looked quite proud of it. Lizzie pressed Opal about her feelings for the young man, but Opal repeated that she was not interested. She said that she had never heard of the Springfields before, and, anyway, she thought "Tinnie" was a funny name.

Summer turned quickly into fall, and winter was just a few days away. The last of the cotton had been picked for the year. Now fields stood virtually bare, except for hundreds of pieces of dirty white cotton hanging from bows on broken stalks. Everyone's attention had turned to Christmas as people prepared for the holiday season. Stores in town put out their Christmas decorations and lampposts were adorned with cut greenery. The aroma of pine and cedar and goodies baking in the oven filled homes. The men at Taylor's Chapel Church cut a large cedar tree and placed it at the front of the church near the altar. The church's young people decorated the tree with homemade ornaments and strings of popcorn. Church members prepared for the annual Christmas party. They sent invitations to other churches in neighboring communities and carefully planned good wholesome fun for everyone.

Although Opal no longer lived with her grandma, she was still expected to abide by Grandma Tamar's strict standards. Grandma Tamar approved of church entertainment, but not house entertainment. These were "good time" or "shake down" houses, where people went for fish fries, drinking, and playing cards. No respectable young lady would think of being caught in such a place, not if she wanted to find herself a decent young man to marry. She went to church so she could find a mate from a "good family." Opal had been looking forward to the Christmas party all week. The night finally came, and she was going to the party with Uncle Dempsy in his Model-T Ford.

For the occasion, coal oil lamps in racks hung all around the wall, and one big lamp sat in the middle of the room. The presents, many small and crudely wrapped, spilled out from under the Christmas tree. In accordance with tradition, party goers brought a gift for someone and place it under the tree. The ladies of the church brought cakes and cookies and punch. The small church became crowded early, and Opal sat on a bench with a girlfriend and a boy name William, who they persuaded to get them punch. A lady called on people to get their gifts, and Mattie Ray assisted by handing her each present. Opal did not expect a gift, so she continued talking with her friends. Then, as Mattie Ray gave the woman the next small box, she called out "Opal Taylor," then she repeated it louder: "OPAL TAYLOR!"

Opal retrieved the box and returned to her seat, not knowing who could have bought her a gift. Neither of her friends had any ideas, either. As she began to unwrap the paper, the young man with the straight nose came over and squeezed in the small space between Opal and William. Tinnie had come to the party with his brother Brown. The two often rode their horses to different churches looking for suitable young ladies to date. Sometimes their cousin A. D. joined them. On more than a few occasions the young men had been successful. At twenty-one, Tinnie, and Brown who was two years younger, were serious about finding the right girl to marry. Tinnie did not say anything as Opal removed the wrapping paper and opened her gift. Inside the box she found two little vases. She thought they were pretty and dainty, and they were blue, one of her favorite colors. Opal had not seen Tinnie since revival Sunday, so she could not believe he had bought her a present. Though she quietly mumbled "thank you," Opal considered the gift one of the nicest things that anybody had ever done for her.

When May of 1926 arrived, rain had been falling for days. Men were ready to get back in the fields, for they knew too much rain could be just as bad for crops as too little. Haywood County's road supervisor, who was in charge of the building and maintaining of roads, expressed concern about the dirt roads in the county.[1] Throughout the county, wagons and buggies fought the mud. Opal wanted the rain to stop for another reason. In just a few more days, she was getting married.

Tinnie and Opal had been courting since the Christmas party. On Sunday evenings, he came to Uncle Dempsy's, where he and Opal would sit in the house "keeping company." When the weather got warm, they sat outside on the porch and talked until it was time for Tinnie to leave. Sometimes he and Opal went to church suppers at Taylor's Chapel. Ladies in the church packed shoe boxes with chicken and biscuits or rolls, slices of cake and pie, and pieces of fruit. Young men would then buy the boxed meals. The activity served as a fund-raiser for the church, while young couples could enjoy their supper in an approved setting. It did not take long for Tinnie to decide Opal was the one he wanted to spend his life with.

Uncle Dempsy picked up Grandma Tamar for her visit, as he did almost every Sunday after church. That evening they gathered in the front bedroom, which also served as the family sitting area. Opal and Tinnie sat next to each other in separate straight-back chairs, and Grandma Tamar sat nearby in her more comfortable chair. Grandma Tamar knew there was a reason why she had been summoned this time. Before Tinnie began to speak, she asked Opal to leave the room. Tinnie did not feel too nervous; he thought of this as a formality. He knew other young people who had run off together and married. But, his upbringing dictated that he do the decent thing. According to custom, the boy was supposed to ask the girl's parents for permission to marry their daughter. Since both Opal's parents were dead, he had to address her grandmother. At her age, Grandma Tamar still sat very erect, dressed up in her church clothes. She did not believe in any nonsense, and some said she could "get hard" when she wanted to. One time, a woman Grandma Tamar did not think was living right came to visit; Grandma Tamar asked the woman to leave her house. She never believed in "throwing a rock and hiding her hand."

After a brief pause, Tinnie said, "Opal and I have decided to marry." He added, "We'll like to marry if you have no objections." Grandma Tamar had already done her homework. She had asked around in the community and learned that Tinnie's father owned his own home and farm, and that he and his family were members of Willow Grove Baptist Church. Grandma Tamar had been Methodist all her life, but she was satisfied knowing the Springfields were good Christian people who believed in God and the church. Opal stood just outside the door, straining to hear. She thought tradition said nothing about whether or not she could listen, so she learned the same time as Tinnie that Grandma Tamar gave them her blessings.

In 1926, Memorial Day fell on a Sunday. Opal had been busy all day, though she had not missed going to church. In one bag, she packed everything she was taking with her. Opal was leaving Uncle Dempsy's to start a new life as a married woman. She had learn to cook some from spending time in the kitchen with Cloria, who was a good cook. From talking with Cloria and Lizzie, she also learned a little of what to expect from married life. Neither Grandma Tamar or Aunt Betty offered any particular advice. Tinnie waited outside in his buggy to pick up Opal for the ride to the preacher's house. After all the packing and good-byes to Uncle Dempsy, Aunt Betty, Mattie Ray, Dempsy Jr., and the other children, they got started later than they had planned.

The Reverend O. W. Wade lived on the same road as Uncle Tom. Tinnie and Opal arrived at the reverend's house late in the afternoon. In his pocket, Tinnie had the marriage license for the minister to sign, date, and file with the court clerk. He had gone into town the day before to pick it up, and Jack Averyheart, who was married to Tinnie's first cousin, Ada Springfield, signed with him to get it. The ceremony was brief. There was no music, no singing, and no wedding march. Only Reverend Wade and his wife were present. After saying "I do," Tinnie and Opal set out for his parents' home. Opal felt strange going to a home she had never been to before. Although she had met Brown and Tinnie's father, Jim Springfield, she had not met anyone else in the family.

Opal thought they would never get to Tinnie's home. It seemed like they had been riding in the buggy for an hour. Jim Springfield and Brown, who had arrived at the ceremony just as it ended, rode behind them. Tinnie's mother sent them because it was getting late, and she wanted to make sure nothing bad had happened. Since the night was warm, it made the trip more bearable; and the roads had been dragged, so they were in good condition. Opal thought if her mother were alive, she would have been at her wedding. In the dark, she tried to visualize her mother's face, but she could not even remember how her mother looked. Opal and Tinnie continued riding along in front of their escorts, not doing much talking, just listening to the steady clop, clop, clop sound of the horses.

On Springfield Road

Opal looked nice for her wedding day. At sixteen she had grown into a nice-looking young lady. People often complimented her, telling her how pretty her complexion was. The ones who knew her parents told her she resembled her mother. She had her mother's coloring and looked more like her sister Tamar than her other two sisters. For the occasion, her long black hair had been freshly hot combed. She wore a sky blue dress that had little white birds printed on the fabric; it was trimmed with white lace on the front, and it had a flare skirt and two belts on the side that tied in the back. Grandma Tamar bought the dress for her from Felsenthal's Department Store, one of the oldest and nicest stores in town, which had a separate floor for blacks to do their shopping. The dress was the style all the young girls were wearing at the time, and it was almost new.

The moon was out, but darkness had not completely fallen. Opal had heard that horses know the road, and that if you just head for home, even though it is too dark to see, the horses will take you home. The horses turned left on Springfield Road, and after going a short distance, past the little narrow road on the right, they turned onto the long, tree-lined drive leading them to Opal's new home.

The big white house, facing east, with the moon reflecting off its green roof, was surrounded by trees in their magnificent green springtime color. Big oak trees spread their long limbs across the large front yard, partially encircled by a white fence. Also in the front yard was a garden with several tomato plants; another garden, on the south side of the house, had cabbage, snap beans, English peas, butter beans, green onions, beets, carrots, Irish potatoes, and greens. On the north side of the house was a big orchard with peach, apricot, and apple trees. Several large pear trees lined the fence row in front of the house, and full-sized apricot trees stood on each side of the walkway leading to the front steps of the long front porch.

Behind the house sat the smokehouse, where fresh meats were salted down and kept. On the right side was the hen house, where, late in the evening, the chickens roosted. To the left stood the little outhouse. On the right side of the hen house, the fenced-in pigpen had hogs of all different sizes, including sows and their baby pigs and some hogs fattened for the kill. A wood trough on one side of the pen was used to pour slop for feeding the hogs. Two big red barns stood farther back behind the house in a pasture that extended all the way around to the south side of the house. There were several horses and cows in the pasture. The buggy shed on the north side of the house, just left of the orchard, housed the family's two buggies.

The front room was Tinnie's parents' bedroom, which doubled as the family sitting room. Steps near the front door led up to one large room where all the boys slept. Standing in the front room, they could look straight back through the little hallway to the second and third bedrooms. Two doors at the far end of the narrow hallway opened to the porches running along the north and south sides of the house. The third bedroom also had a door that exited to the south porch. To reach the kitchen, the family had to walk across the south porch to the room on the back end of the house. Part of the south porch had been screened in for use as a dining area, and a large wood table surrounded by cane-bottomed, ladder-back chairs sat in the center of the room.

When Tinnie and Opal arrived, everyone finally gathered into the dining room, where dinner had been waiting for some time. Sunday dinner was usually a big meal for the Springfields, but they took extra care to make the meal special on an occasion when they expected company. In the middle of the table was a large dish of chicken and dressing surrounded by bowls of black-eyed peas, greens, candied yams, beets, and a plate of cornbread. For dessert, Tinnie's mother made a big chocolate cake. Before the family could eat, they all had to bow their heads and close their eyes because Jim Springfield had to "turn thanks" for the food.

Opal did not think she had ever seen so many little children in one family in her life. In addition to Tinnie and Brown and the two older girls, Cherry and Mary, who everyone called Meg, there were Dan, Charles, Lee Arteen, Vernise, Louise, and the youngest, Ada and Avery, twins who looked to be about three. Opal and Tinnie sat at the table with his mother and father, all his brothers, and the smallest children. The girls waited to eat last. Jim took charge of the conversation once dinner was under way. Opal felt very uncomfortable in the midst of her new family, who were mostly strangers. She sat quietly, trying to get through the meal without talking. After a while, Jim began asking her questions. When he discovered she was shy, he decided to tease her. By the time dinner was over, Opal hated him.

Jim Springfield was born in Haywood County in 1880 to Dan and Eunice Springfield. Dan had one brother, Dave, and one sister, Mariah. Dan, Dave, and Mariah were born to former slaves, Freeman and Abbie Springfield. Dan and Eunice had Jim; his two brothers, Frank and Johnson; and his sister, Emma. Jim and his siblings lost their parents when they were young children, and they were raised by their grandparents, Freeman and Abbie. Dave was Jim's uncle, but they were close to the same age and grew up in the same house as brothers. Jim would always say that because Dave was his parents' baby, they never made him do much work. While Jim, on the other hand, without a mother or father, had learned the value of hard work at an early age. By the time he decided to get married, Jim had already become a hard-working, responsible young man.

Jim and Dave married sisters. In the mid-1890s, Dave Springfield married Lula Shaw, and they contributed to the Springfields' reputation for having large families. By 1926, Dave and Lula had eleven children; they were Herman, Gardner, A. D., Sam, Ada, Ethel, Gentry, Alice, Lucille, Lula (called "Candy"), and David (called "Buddie"). On February 24, 1902, Jim Springfield married Ada Shaw. By 1926 they had also produced eleven offspring. Jim Springfield was a good provider for his large family. He farmed many acres of land, growing big crops, and raising farm animals. In return, he demanded hard work and respect from his children, and they complied. When dealing with matters concerning his home, there was no question that Jim was master of his domain, and he ruled his family with a stern hand.

Jim Springfield was a big, ruggedly handsome man who stood over six feet tall. He had a light brown, ruddy complexion; a thick mustache that hung down over his top lip; and eyes that held a mischievous twinkle. The latter could perhaps be attributed to his pleasant disposition. The only time he ever looked unhappy was when he was hungry, and that could be because he was diabetic. As soon as Jim began to eat, he was a new person, entertaining those around him by telling one joke after another. He kept everyone laughing for hours. But Jim Springfield was an interesting dichotomy. No one who knew him would ever think of describing Jim Springfield as obsequious. The joking he did was reserved for family and friends. When time came to deal with the white man, he did not shift his eyes or scratch his head. Instead he was a shrewd business man. The strength exuded in his carriage and the confident manner in which he conducted his business belied his lack of formal education beyond grade school. His business acumen allowed him to become one of the few Negro landowners in Haywood County and earned him the right to be proud.

In 1925, Negroes in Haywood County made up almost 70 percent of the population, but only 8 percent of the farmers owned land in the county.[2] Most Negroes in the county were either tenant farmers or sharecroppers, with many of them working on the half. Under either system, the colored man and his wife and children lived in small shacks on the white man's land. He was allowed a certain amount of seeds and plants on credit to grow his crops. At harvest time, he had to give the white man half of the cotton, corn, vegetables, and half of everything else that he grew on the land. Most tenant farmers and sharecroppers considered themselves lucky at the end of the year just to break even and not have any debts carried over to the next year. It was a vicious cycle from which few ever broke free. Jim Springfield's determination not to be part of such a system motivated him to buy his own land. He was one of only 359 Negro landowners out of a population of more than 17,000.[3] He managed his business so that his sons could avoid the cycle of sharecropping. He was able to stay afloat even though farm prices had been steadily dropping for the last three years.

The 1920s had brought a new era of abundance and prosperity in the country as the stock market soared to unprecedented heights and the value of urban land increased; however, this abundance was not enjoyed by everyone, especially those working in agriculture.[4] Haywood County had always been an agricultural area where Negroes continuously worked close to the soil.[5] For many of the people involved in the system of sharecropping and tenant farming, the depression had begun for them early in the 1920s.[6] Records showed most Negro farmers in Haywood County and the rest of west Tennessee earned their living primarily from cotton. Since prices for the staple had been declining since 1923, they were already in a very weak economic position.[7] Thus, in 1929, when the stock market began its rapid descent, it initially brought about little change for the majority of Haywood County citizens.[8]

Strained economic conditions already experienced by most Negroes spread throughout the country after October 29, 1929, when prices on the New York Stock Market fell drastically. The previous day, 9.9 million shares of stock were traded for a loss of $14 billion. By the afternoon of October 29, 16.4 million shares had been traded for a loss of $15 billion.[9] The crash touched off the worst depression in the history of the nation. Millions of people lost their jobs as factories either cut back production or closed completely. Thousands of businesses failed. Tennessee banks, much like those all across the country, closed, and families lost their life savings. In nearby Memphis, black-owned banks filed for bankruptcy.[10] All Americans were victims of the depression, but the group that suffered the most were the Negroes.[11]

The black farmer in Haywood County experienced some of the same problems as those in other parts of the South. Tenants, especially the Negro sharecroppers, had their own unique set of problems. Many who worked on large farms were not allowed to sell their crops; instead, the landlord did the selling and credited the tenants with the proceeds.[12] Under these circumstances, it was not unusual for the landlord to give the tenant credit for the cotton at the lowest price of the season, when in fact the crop had been kept off the market until conditions were better and the price was higher.[13] There was also unfair treatment and outright cheating in many instances when time came to "settle up" at the end of the year. Not able to do anything to prevent such tactics, the tenant farmer was at the mercy of his landlord.[14] Few black farmers were fortunate enough to have family members they could work with for a period of time. However, during the troubled times of the Great Depression, the members of Jim Springfield's family never suffered.

Tinnie and Opal spent the first months of their marriage staying with Tinnie's family. While Tinnie continued to farm with his father, Opal did the same work as his sisters. When Cherry and Meg had to cook, Opal was in the kitchen cooking with them. When it was time for everyone to chop cotton and pick cotton, she went with them to the fields and worked alongside the other children. She actually enjoyed spending time with Cherry and Meg since they were close to her age. When the fruit ripened and the vegetables were ready to pick from the vines, they filled basketloads. Then they peeled and cut and chopped until the shelves were lined with all different kinds of canned fruits, vegetables, preserves, and jellies for the winter. Fall brought with it cool weather and hog-killing time, when the family prepared meat for winter by cutting the shoulder and bacon meat, shaping the hams, cooking the lard, grinding the sausage, washing the chitlins, and salting the meat. Then the leaves on the trees turned bright yellow, red, and gold before they slowly disappeared.

With the arrival of winter, Tinnie and Opal began thinking about getting their own place. They settled on a small house down across the field behind Tinnie's home place. The little house had just two rooms, with a porch that separated the kitchen on one side from the bedroom on the other. They had to walk across the open porch to get from the bedroom to the kitchen and then back again, but it was their first home together. After they moved, Tinnie and Brown drove the wagon to Uncle Dempsy's house to pick up the household items Grandma Tamar was giving Opal, just as she had done for Tamar, Cloria, and Arizona. They loaded up a bedroom suite, quilts, pots and pans, bed and table linens, dishes, and glassware and crystal. Grandma Tamar wanted to help Opal "set up housekeeping."

In February of 1927, Tinnie and Opal were settled in their little house.

They had moved out on their own just in time. On February 28, Opal gave birth to her first child. It was a baby boy. She maintained the long-honored tradition of naming firstborn males after a family member. Opal named the child Jim Howell, for both his grandfathers, Jim Springfield and Howell Taylor.

In the summer of 1928, several families in the community cut their sorghum and brought the cornlike stalks to the mill for cooking. The sorghum mill consisted of two big iron barrels, set on a wood structure connected to a long, thick wooden tongue. The tongue was similar to a wagon tongue, but bigger and longer. Two mules, one attached on each side of the tongue, were used to drive the mill. The mules walked in a circle, which rotated the large iron barrels in opposite directions. An elongated aluminum-like contraption extended from the barrels to a big pan about the length of two tables and wider than the average table. This pan was divided into sections, and a wood fire burned in a hole dug beneath it. Once the mill was set up, the sorghum cooker fed the mill by placing sorghum stalks between the two barrels. As the mules circled, the stalks were drawn between the barrels. The barrels squeezed the stalks, causing juice from the stalks to run down the elongated contraption into the big pan.

"Old man" Henry Averyheart, father of Jack Averyheart, was the sorghum cook. In addition to feeding the mill, he moved the juice from one section of the pan to the next. This kept the fresh green juice from the cooked juice. Using a long-handled paddle, the cook constantly stirred the juice to keep it from burning. When white foam developed on top, he used a different long-handled flat dipper scoop to lift off the foam. When the fire got low, the cook added more wood. When the juice reached the last section of the pan, the cooking process was complete. The cook then removed the stopper at the bottom end of the pan to allow the thick brown molasses to flow into a big lard can under the pan. Other workers then transferred the molasses to large sorghum barrels and gallon cans, which were sold. Sometimes it took close to a week to cook sorghum for one family. The family whose sorghum was being cooked on a certain day provided dinner for the mill workers.

When Opal first married Tinnie she had never seen anyone eat molasses like Tinnie and his brothers. First, they would pour red-eye gravy in the plate, then they poured molasses in the middle of the gravy until the molasses spread across the plate, pushing the gravy around the rim. They set their biscuits around the edge of the plate and sopped the thick, sweet syrup. Grandpa

Jim had to keep a large barrel of molasses in the smokehouse to keep his family well supplied. He did not mind sharing it with company, though, and actually got a kick telling about a man they called "Lump," who once happened up to the house at supper time. Grandpa Jim and the family were eating in the screened-in area while Lump sat on the porch. Lump declined the offer of supper until Grandpa Jim said, "I got some fresh molasses in here." Lump said he would "taste" some so Dan took his plate out for the old man to taste the molasses. Lump kept "tasting" and "tasting," while Dan stood waiting for the return of his plate. Finally Lump said, "you can go on back now, I'll bring the plate in."

One morning, Tinnie answered a knock on the kitchen door. Miss Laura Hunter brushed past him and began telling her story. Miss Laura, a middle-aged, short, dark-brown-skinned woman, who was one of the local midwives, was suppose to feed the mill that day, but she did not have enough food to fix for the workers. She told her husband, Frank, that all she had was some black-eyed peas and meal. Frank said, "That's enough," and Miss Laura "walked out the house and kept walking." She laughed in a real high-pitched voice, then said, "I told him I can't go struttin' up to that mill with just some peas and cornbread." She said, "I can't do it. I can't do it. I just can't do it." Miss Laura said, "I need some sugar. I need some flour. I need a piece of meat." After giving Tinnie the list of food items she needed, she said again, "I can't just take 'em no peas and cornbread." Then Miss Laura laughed and said, "I can't do it, Tinnie. I can't do it, Tinnie. No I can't. No I can't."

Opal was lying in bed in the other room. She and Tinnie were in a different house now. It was a big old house that had been whitewashed, but the white had just about worn off. There were two bedrooms, a kitchen, and another room that could be used as an extra bedroom. That fall Tinnie let his cousin, Lee Andrew Perry, use the room so he could raise a crop with Tinnie. Lee Andrew's mother and Tinnie's mother were half-sisters. Tinnie helped his cousin to get started farming. Opal did not think she really needed to have a third bedroom for her family anyway, since it was just her, Tinnie, Jim Howell, and a new baby. On July 20, 1928, Miss Laura had delivered Opal's second child, another boy, named Aaron. Opal had chosen the name from the Bible.

Opal could not help but hear Miss Laura explain her predicament. She felt glad that Tinnie was a good provider, like his father. With times being as hard as they were, a lot of women not as fortunate were suffering. If a woman married a man who did not want to work, which is what was said about Mr. Frank, it made things much harder for the woman and her family. Taking care of a wife and children required hard work. One thing Opal could say about Tinnie was he did not mind working. Although she thought he had a "high temper" and quickly got angry if someone crossed him, Opal always said he had a good heart. She knew he would get together everything Miss Laura asked for and give it to her. Tinnie always believed in helping anyone in need. As she lay there with Aaron, listening to the conversation coming from the kitchen, Opal thought if she ever heard anyone who had to laugh to keep from crying, it was Miss Laura.

Tinnie rented his new place from Mr. Aaron Sternberger, a lawyer in Brownsville who had moved to Memphis. Renting the land did not require Tinnie to divide his crops by the "halves" or the "thirds." All he had to do was pay a fixed amount of rent, then he could do with his crops as he pleased, but he was in the minority. By 1930, the number of Americans experiencing tremendous suffering had increased. Low prices for farm products and poor agricultural practices impacted the nation's farmers as a whole, and it had forced more and more Negro farmers into tenancy.[15] This exacerbated the problems for black farmers. Over half of the Negroes in the country lived in the South. Out of the 97 percent of black farmers living in the South, only 20 percent owned their land.[16] Thus, 80 percent of Negro farmers were tenants. The number was roughly the same for Tennessee, and it was even higher in Haywood County, where most sharecroppers lived in poverty and a sizable number of tenants earned less than one hundred dollars a year.[17]

Although President Herbert Hoover and the more fortunate continued to proclaim "No one has yet starved," the plight of many white and Negro tenant farmers in Haywood County had them singing the words of the Populist song of 1896: "Oh, the farmer is the man, the farmer is the man. Lives on credit till the fall. With interest rates so high, it's a wonder he don't die. For the mortgage man's the one that gets it all."[18]

The conditions in Tennessee and the nation continued to worsen as the 1930 drought created even more problems for the Great Plains, the Midwest, and the South. Tennessee's western neighbor, Arkansas, was hit extremely hard. Drought recognized no color line in the heat-ravaged Arkansas Delta, where it was reported that several straight days of rain had not "been enough to wet a man's shirt."[19] The poor white man and the poor black man suffered equally. In August 1930, southern states were seeking federal aid for the drought-seared regions. President Hoover announced the drought situation was the subject of several conferences and the Department of Agriculture had undertaken a detailed survey. Locals realized, just as everyone else, that large measures were required to assist people in the region since no prospect for relief from the dry weather was in sight. Negro farmers were desperate, facing terrible conditions where thousands were thin and hungry, with no meat or bread.

Conditions in the state and other parts of the country did not go unnoticed by Grandpa Jim and the rest of the family. Whenever Grandpa Jim and Tinnie went into town on Saturday, they always spent time talking with the store owners after doing their business. These were usually the same storekeepers, which included Mr. Rothschild, Mr. Sternberger, and Mr. Tamm, where Tinnie bought material for Opal to do her sewing. The owners voiced obvious concern over the fact that stores were not receiving the same amount of supplies and the quality of shipments were down. Because Tinnie was a good customer, Mr. Tamm, who knew what Tinnie usually bought, held fabric for him. This was the only way Opal could get material to make pants for the boys. It did not appear things would improve anytime soon. They all had heard the reports that everywhere breadlines had lengthened and apple vendors were multiplying. In New York City alone there were as many as six thousand apple vendors, and pawnshops continued to swell with used clothing and furniture.[20] During this same period, earnings of the local and other Negro landowners, cash tenants, sharecroppers, and wage laborers all continued to drastically decline.[21]

The depression did not change some things. Every second and fourth Sunday, Tinnie took the family to church. Willow Grove Missionary Baptist Church was sat on a little hill on the side of the road about seven miles east of town. It was located on Highway 70—or Jackson Highway, as it was called by the locals, except for some blacks who called it Willow Grove Road. Services were only held twice a month. Opal had joined Tinnie's church, but on the Sundays when Willow Grove did not have services she sometimes went back to visit Taylor's Chapel. On Sunday afternoons the family often gathered at Grandpa Jim's and Grandma Ada's for dinner or just to visit. Sunday dinners were still a big meal, since the family produced almost everything they ate—meats, vegetables, milk and butter, eggs, lard, and corn meal. Most of the time the only things they bought were sugar and flour. A ten-pound sack of sugar cost not much more than fifty cents, while a twenty-five-pound sack of flour cost about a dollar. There was plenty of food, and the family continued to enjoy Sunday gatherings, where they laughed, talked, and shared more than the food.

Since Grandpa Jim had no radio, conversation was the only source of entertainment, and it was always lively. In addition to the family members still at home, the crowd included Tinnie's brothers and their wives. In 1929, Brown married Crettie Mae Bond. Later that same year, Dan married Lucille Rainer. And the number of children continued to increase. Opal and Tinnie had two more boys: Tony, who was born January 11, 1930, and Salathiel, born September 28 the following year. Crettie Mae had two children: Lydia Mae, born the same month as Tony, and James Edward, born the day after Salathiel. Grandma Ada's baby boy, Lawrence, was born in May of 1928, one month before Aaron. The adult conversations were usually about what was going on in Brownsville and other places. With the presidential election just months away, the discussion naturally turned to the candidates.

As the 1932 election approached, most Negroes rallied around the slogan "who but Hoover."[22] Despite the severity of the Great Depression, they considered the Republican candidate more attractive. Most continued to support Hoover despite his belief that the federal government had no business aiding the millions of indigents, and the majority of black newspapers and magazines also stayed Republican.[23] The NAACP monthly magazine, *The Crisis*, printed an article entitled "Why the Negro Should Vote for Mr. Hoover," charging that a vote for Franklin Delano Roosevelt was a vote to extend segregation.[24] According to an article in *The Chicago Defender*, the most widely read of the nation's black dailies, "The future of the black man, so far as his civil rights are concerned, is at least safe in the hands of the Republican Party."[25]

While the Negro press continued to criticize him, the governor of New York did nothing to warrant better treatment. Roosevelt, after purchasing property in Warm Springs, proclaimed himself an adopted son of Georgia and never commented on the segregated practices of the state. Roosevelt was a loyal Democrat, and at the same time a northern politician in a party that was overwhelmingly southern. Many Negro leaders correctly pointed out during the course of the campaign that Roosevelt had ignored the Negro in legislation and appointments. Despite the cries of the black press and the efforts of the NAACP, Roosevelt remained silent on the rights of blacks. During the Democratic national convention at Chicago, his aides rejected the NAACP's request that he endorse a civil rights plank for the platform.[26]

Grandpa Jim made sure he kept abreast of the news concerning the candidates and their campaign. He was not a big Roosevelt supporter, but he said Hoover was a sorry president. Tinnie and the rest of the family agreed. They knew of several people who were wearing rags for clothing, living in shacks, and going hungry. Someone told them that the worn, tattered clothing of a poor person had even been sent to the president to dramatize the nation's ills. In their opinion, a vote for anyone else was preferable to a vote for Hoover. Grandpa and the others discussed the issues important to them, although they knew their views would not matter much in the election. Black people in Haywood County had not voted since Reconstruction.[27]

The attention of the country focused on the election news for weeks. While two-thirds of the Negro vote in the 1932 election went to the Republicans, a higher proportion than in 1928, the Great Depression allowed the Democrats to sweep the nation.[28] Roosevelt carried forty-two of forty-eight states and received 472 electoral votes to Hoover's 59.[29] The popular vote in Tennessee registered 74,535 for Hoover and 115,915 for Roosevelt.[30] With a new leader in charge, the Springfield family, the people of Haywood County, and the rest of the country waited to see if this change would bring them a better deal.

4.

Sweet Gum Trees

In early March 1930, President Hoover announced to the country, "We have now passed the worst." Three years later, when Franklin D. Roosevelt was inaugurated as president on March 4, 1933, the economic life of the nation was at a standstill.[1]

Speaking before an estimated crowd of 100,000 at the Capital Plaza in Washington, D.C., Roosevelt delivered his inaugural address to the nation. Hundreds of thousands of people listened to the radio in their homes or place of business as Roosevelt addressed problems that by now were familiar, stating, "farmers find no market for their produce; the savings of many years in thousands of families are gone." He added that more important, "a host of unemployed citizens face the grim problem of existence, and an equally great number toil with little return. Only a foolish optimist can deny the dark realities of the moment." He promised to ask Congress for unprecedented broad powers to "wage a war against the emergency," but what was perhaps remembered most from the address were the president's first words. Before he mentioned the litany of problems facing the country, Roosevelt stated that "the only thing we have to fear is fear itself."[2] Many would have to be convinced to adopt such belief.

During the months between the November election and the inauguration, things had grown increasingly worse instead of better. In the first few months of 1933, over four thousand banks failed and $3.6 billion in deposits were lost. By March, between 13 and 14 million Americans were out of work.[3] Agricultural prices were less than half what they had been four years earlier, and industrial production had declined by more than half. Cotton that had been selling for eighteen cents per pound in 1929 brought less than six cents per pound by 1933.[4] Several urban centers had 40 percent of the Negro population on relief, while in some southern cities like Atlanta and Norfolk, the number was as high as 65 to 80 percent.[5] In rural areas like Haywood County, most Negroes and poor whites lived in abject poverty.

Opal had no way of hearing the inaugural speech since her family did not have a radio. She later read the published account from a paper that Tinnie brought home. She also read newspaper articles about the new first lady, Eleanor Roosevelt. Opal even suggested to Crettie Mae that she should name her next child Eleanor. Opal and others in town were concerned about what was going on in the nation, but other than the initial discussions of Hoover's defeat, the new president in Washington generated little hope for change. People who had lived in Brownsville all their lives had learned not to expect much change with the inauguration of a president. It was not that the people were apathetic; the system had snuffed out expectations and did not tolerate challenges to the status quo. Living and dying were the primary concerns.

In November of 1932, when Roosevelt was elected to his first term, Grandma Tamar still worked. Although up in age now, she had once again cooked for the Kinfolks meeting at Tabernacle Church in August. The crowds were larger now, with people coming from all over the country. Grandma Tamar's regular job was working for a white woman called Miss Louise. Grandma Tamar took care of Miss Louise's son, who she described as "not quite right in the head." She was actually paid to care for the young man to make sure he did not hurt himself. Miss Louise did not live too far down the street from Aunt Nancy's house. Grandma Tamar always got up early and without taking the time to fix a hot breakfast, she walked to work. Two weeks after the election, she was walking to work when all of a sudden she started to feel "funny" in her chest.

Aunt Nancy was inside the house with her daughter Mary. She thought she heard a faint noise. Although not sure of the sound, she said to Mary, "I think I hear something outside." Aunt Nancy went to the door to investigate. There on her knees on the top step was Grandma Tamar, clutching her chest with one hand and reaching for the screen door with the other. Aunt Nancy got her mother to bed and called the doctor. By the time the doctor arrived, Grandma Tamar was already dead. Tamar Taylor probably could have gone on working for a few more years, but on November 24, 1932, at age eighty-one, her heart failed.

Nature has a way of insulating grief when the pain is too much to endure all at once. By focusing on things of little consequence, dealing with a loss can be delayed until the system is ready to cope. It is this coping mechanism, for instance, that allows a person attending the funeral of a loved one to think about something or someone other than the deceased. The preacher had nothing but good things to say about Grandma Tamar. He told the family that she was a woman whose whole life had been hard work and clean living. Kissy Green, a young teacher in the Taylor's Chapel community, had some nice words to say too. She spoke of how Grandma Tamar always made her living with her own hands and by the sweat of her brow. Opal sat with the other family members, listening to the eulogy. She did not like what she heard the young woman saying. Opal thought Kissy made Grandma Tamar appear more like a "slave woman." While she did not want to admit feeling this way, it actually made Opal angry to hear the young woman speak about her grandmama. She was glad when Kissy finished what she had to say and took her seat.

The weather was cold and light snow fell as Barlow Funeral Home out of Stanton prepared to take Grandma Tamar's body to Taylor's Chapel Cemetery. The procession included wagons and a few cars. Opal and Tinnie rode in a car furnished by the funeral home. Tinnie's sister Louise was staying with the children. They drove past Tabernacle Church and turned right at Kinfolks campgrounds. The route seemed fitting, since the camp had been a part of Grandma Tamar's life for thirty-five years, beginning before the turn of the century. They passed the white folks' cemetery, where Miss Hattie Taylor, the woman for whom Grandma Tamar cooked at the camp meetings, had been buried earlier that same year. As fate would have it, Miss Hattie never had to worry about what she "would do without Tamar." As for Grandma Tamar, she wore a white dress and was "fixed up" to look nice one last time.

In the spring of 1933, the Springfield family, like the country, focused much of its attention on the first "hundred days" of the Roosevelt administration. They were particularly interested in the introduction of the first of the New Deal programs, designed to solve the nation's economic problems. The Roosevelt administration enacted two major pieces of recovery legislation, the Agricultural Adjustment Act (AAA) and the National Industrial Recovery Act (NIRA), which were at the heart of the new administration's effort to revive the economy. The AAA established a national agricultural policy that paid farmers for removing their crops from cultivation. The NIRA, in addition to providing for a system of industrial self-government, provided over $3 billion for the Public Works Program (PWA).[6] Other New Deal programs included the Federal Emergency Relief Administration (FERA) and the Civilian Conservation Corps (CCC). Many Tennesseans were employed under or received aid through these federal relief programs, and thousands of farmers in Tennessee participated in the AAA land removal program.

By June 15, 1933, the president and Congress had set a record for legislation passed. At least sixteen new programs were in place to restore America's confidence. The questions facing most Negroes, however, was whether they were among the people who would reap the benefits of the New Deal programs. There was little question that relief under most of the federal programs was not administered fairly.[7] In July it was reported that vociferous opposition by local whites had dashed Negro hope for equal treatment by the Tennessee Valley Authority. The TVA site at Norris, Tennessee, employed no Negroes in either office positions or in the job of foremen, and the city was still all white. Local TVA officials not only denied the Negro his proportionate share of jobs, but assigned him to the least skilled, lowest paid work, which resulted in Negro workers receiving less than 1 percent of the TVA payroll.[8]

Negroes in Tennessee and other places also complained of the treatment they received by the Civilian Conservation Corps, being that they constituted only 5 percent of those enrolled. Local officials who selected CCC enrollees repeatedly gave preference to whites, although Negro males had twice the unemployment rate of their white counterparts.[9] The plight of the Negro was also desperate under the AAA. It was estimated that the number of Negroes driven out of cotton production by the AAA 40 percent in crop reduction acreage was as high as half a million. This was one-third of the total number of Negroes engaged in farming in 1933.[10] Most Negroes could not find economic relief in industry or farming.

When the director of the AAA activities in Tennessee urged more farmers to join President Roosevelt's cotton reduction program, Grandpa Jim decided he would sign up along with the other Haywood County farmers. He was persuaded by the director's statement that the future of cotton prices was at stake. The director told farmers that the cotton "plow-up" campaign was designed to prevent another production of cotton being piled up on the surplus already in existence. The AAA sought the 40 percent reduction in acreage throughout the cotton belt. Grandpa Jim and most other cotton growers knew that the depression had resulted in less use of cotton and that the production of the staple remained far in excess of its annual consumption.[11] They thought the reduction campaign would remedy this situation.

Grandpa Jim and other local farmers liked one important feature of the program, it aided them in getting on cash basis the money for withholding a portion of their land from farming. They received the rental payments for reducing their acreage in two equal installments. The first payment was made between March 1 and April 30, in time to help most of the growers plant their crops. The second payment was made between August 1 and September 30, when they needed money to finance cotton picking.[12] Most black farmers in Haywood County worked the white man's land, depriving them of receiving any of the $20 million paid to Tennessee farmers under the AAA, since the money was allocated based upon land ownership.[13] Grandpa Jim counted himself fortunate to be one of the few Negroes in the county to reap the program's benefit. Tinnie had not participated in the program because as a new landowner, he was not yet convinced of its advantages.

In 1933, at a time when the Negro in Haywood County and the country was facing the worst economic and social outlook since slavery, Tonnie Springfield became a landowner. An old black man, "Uncle" Jim Bond and his wife, "Aunt" Liza, owned land off Poplar Corner Road in Haywood County. Poplar Corner Road, located between Jackson Highway and Bells Highway, headed east out of town, parallel to the two highways. Uncle Jim had a reputation for being stingy. He and Aunt Liza, who was a big woman with wide hips, could often be seen out in the fields plowing together. While most people used a single plow, they used a double two-horse plow. They had several acres of land to plow, and it was just the two of them—they never had children.

Tinnie was not related to Uncle Jim and Aunt Liza. He called them "aunt" and "uncle" as a matter of respect, but he had learned not to use the terms loosely. During the summer months, Tinnie often took fruits and vegetables to town to sell. On one occasion, he took a wagonload of watermelons into town. He saw an old man he knew sitting in front one of the stores. Tinnie yelled, "Hey, Unc, you want to buy a watermelon?" The old man was a sharp dresser and apparently did not view himself as one of the town's senior residents. He responded, "When I get old enough to be your uncle, I'll let you know." Tinnie knew the man was old, so he was not bothered by what the man said. Uncle Jim and Aunt Liza appeared to enjoy the kin titles, especially since they were an old couple who lived alone.

The fact that the old couple lived alone proved to be unfortunate. As the story goes, some white people went out to the farm and robbed Uncle Jim and Aunt Liza. The white men locked the old couple up in the crib and left them there. Then they ransacked the house, apparently thinking the old people had money hidden somewhere. They did so much damage that neighbors who later went by the house and saw things strewn around said it looked like someone was just moving in. Those responsible were never found and made to pay for their crime. Uncle Jim did not live long after the incident. After he died, Aunt Liza sold part of the land. Tinnie changed his name for business dealings, so it was Tonnie Springfield who bought his first fifty-acre farm.

Owning land had always been important to Tonnie, just as it had been to Grandpa Jim. He was aware of the bleak conditions for the nation's farmers. After all, this was a period of extreme economic strife that reached millions. He probably could not have chosen a worse time to try to make a living from the soil. However, given any of the choices as a tenant farmer, he thought he could better provide for the family as a landowner. Tonnie did not have to worry about having help to work the land. He had five boys who would soon be old enough to help with the farming. The number had just increased in the spring, when the fifth son, Lee Arthur, was born on April 2. Like many who hoped the economic policies of the new administration would aid their recovery, Tonnie shared this hope for his growing family.

Tonnie and the family soon found their lives affected by the New Deal programs. One such program, the Public Works Administration, was more solicitous of the needs of Negroes than any of the other industrial or agricultural programs established in the spring of 1933; its purpose was twofold: build useful projects and give employment to those who needed it.[14] In the mid-1930s, with intense competition for every available job, the giving of jobs to the unemployed presented a problem for the Negro. However, Negroes benefited from the projects to build roads, dams, post offices, and other government buildings. In Haywood County there were still many dirt roads. The county required the men to donate time each month to working on the roads. Tonnie and other men worked on clearing the roads, cutting bushes along the roadside, and keeping the roads clean.

The National Youth Administration, which hired thousands of young people, paid Tonnie's sister Louise to cook lunch for the children at Springfield School, where she was also a student. The government provided all the food that had to be picked up every week. Grandpa Jim drove his wagon into town to receive the loads of cabbage, onions, potatoes, apples, flour, sugar, cornmeal, and a big piece of fatback meat. He kept the food stored at the house and carried it down to the school as needed. Louise went to classes for part of the morning, then she cooked a big pot of cabbage with the fat meat, a big pan of corn bread, and an oversized apple cobbler. When she served the meal, the children ate as if they were starved. Louise received twenty-five dollars a month, which she considered "good money." Each month she gave a share of her earnings to her mama and papa.

In rural areas such as Haywood County, Negroes had difficulty getting jobs under the Works Progress Administration (WPA). Still, more Negro workers were assigned to WPA projects in part due to pressure exerted by the central administration on local authorities to give jobs to the needy regardless of race.[15] In instances where some found employment, they were faced with the WPA attempting to placate southern whites by releasing Negro workers from government jobs during harvest time. This forced black workers to continue in the low-paying seasonal jobs in the fields, where the standard wage for picking cotton averaged around fifty cents per day. Those who did work WPA jobs usually made more money than they would have received in private employment.[16] But Tonnie never sought a job through the government programs. He preferred to continue farming.

While waiting for the house to be built on Poplar Corner Road, Tonnie, Opal, and the children moved to another house near their new place. They rented the house from a white man in town, but Tonnie farmed his own land. The family stayed in the rented house for one crop season. During that year, on November 3, Opal gave birth to another child. This time she finally had a little girl. She named her Asalean, but after five boys everyone called her "Sister." It was a tradition in Negro families to call the first female child in the family "Sister" and their son "Bubba." Everyone referred to Tonnie's third boy, Tony, as "Bubba."

In 1935, Tonnie and Opal moved into their newly built house. The new house was small, with two bedrooms and a kitchen, but now they were homeowners. The other buildings constructed behind the house included a hen house, a outhouse, and a smokehouse. A distance back from the house, the barn was already half filled with corn and hay for the animals. Tonnie placed his wagon and farm tools, including his new plow, under the shed. The family settled into what seemed like an endless routine. Tonnie plowed the fields for planting corn and cotton, and he planted vegetables in the garden near the house. Opal spent long hours cutting corn and tomatoes and shelling peas and beans to can for the winter. Tonnie carried bushel baskets of vegetables into town to sell to the stores. Sometimes he stopped his wagon on the street and sold to the white town people. When Tonnie was away from the wagon, Jim and Aaron sold the potatoes, greens, peas, beans, and tomatoes. Most of the time, the white people gave only nickels or dimes for their purchase. Jim and Aaron used their small change to buy pieces of candy when Tonnie stopped at the store before heading home.

In the fall, Tonnie and Grandpa Jim frequently hunted, but only during the day because Grandpa Jim did not like to hunt at night. Tonnie went with other men in the community to hunt at night. He brought home rabbits, squirrels, coons, quail, and possum. There was a period when Tonnie hunted so much that Opal would get angry when he picked up his shotgun. One thing Opal liked, though, was the sound of the coon dogs barking at night. Late at night, after the children were asleep in their bed, she sat up quilting and listening to the dogs running and barking. Sometimes the white men fox hunting on Mr. Harbert Thornton's place would ride across a portion of Tonnie's land, with their dogs barking ferociously on the scent of their prey. When Tonnie was hunting, Opal was content to hear his old coon dogs barking. This meant he was somewhere nearby.

On Saturday mornings, Opal got up early and carried buckets of water from the well to the large black kettle in the backyard. She hauled bucket after bucket until the big kettle was full. After starting a fire under the kettle, Opal put in Tonnie's work clothes and some of the badly soiled children's clothing. She allowed them to boil until most of the dirt soaked out. Then she placed the clothes in a tub, where she used a washboard and a large piece of brown cake soap to scrub the clothes clean. After the first load was hung on the clothesline to dry in the hot sun, she continued her washing. Opal washed by hand all the bed linen, towels, dresses, undergarments, and children's clothes. For years Opal did all the washing by herself, since Tonnie worked in the fields from sun up until sun down. But, she did not expect a man to help with this kind of work. The older boys were now big enough to use the washboard to scrub some of the clothes. She decided to use the boys' help until they thought they were too old for such work. Saturday was wash day; and even with help, laundry was an all-day job.

Sometimes during the week Opal's new neighbor, Miss Winbush, dropped by to visit. A poor white woman, Miss Winbush lived with her husband on

Mr. Harbert Thornton's place. Mr. Harbert owned much of the land on Poplar Corner Road, part of which was right across a little road in front of Tonnie and Opal's house. Since Miss Winbush did not have any white neighbors, she often walked through the pasture to reach the house, where she sat and talked to Opal. She was a young woman, probably not as old as Opal, who enjoyed having someone to talk to. If Opal cooked, Miss Winbush usually did not turn down an offer to taste whatever Opal prepared. One day, as the young woman sat at the kitchen table eating Opal's blackberry cobbler and commenting on how good it was, Salathiel sat down at the table. All of a sudden, Miss Winbush quit eating and got up from the table. Opal thought it was mighty "funny" that this young white woman could sit there and eat her food but think she was too good to sit at the table with Opal's children. But the visits continued. Isolated out in the country, with the closest neighbors sometimes miles away, the two women formed a strange relationship, devoid of the usual bond of friendship.

In the summer of 1936, Tennessee experienced one of the worst early droughts in its history. It extended from the Great Smoky Mountains in the east to the Mississippi River, the "Father of the Waters" in the west. Crops of all kinds were severely affected. The drought also seriously injured almost all of the pastures and grain crops. This brought about a serious shortage of hay, wheat, and other grain crops. The city advised everyone that when a little rain comes, it "behooves us to put every effort in planting feed crops, hay crops as well as truck and garden crops for home use." Haywood County agents warned farmers to plant corn, hay, and all varieties of soybeans and crops for home and storage for winter, such as Irish potatoes, sweet potatoes, "bunch beans," pole beans, butter beans, tomatoes, collards, and cabbage. They also instructed farmers to prepare the land now for sowing turnips, mustard, carrots beets, and lettuce for fall. With such a severe drought, agents wanted the people to prepare as much as they could for possible additional shortages later in the year.[17]

That summer, Opal kept up a grueling schedule working in the fields all day. In the morning before going to the field, Opal milked the cow before putting on breakfast. She poured the milk that was not used for drinking through a cloth into a big jar to set until it turned sour. While the home made biscuits and sausage cooked for breakfast, Opal churned the milk that had already turned. Churning the milk, she worked the dash up and down through the milk until butter formed on top, then Opal scooped it off and washed it two or three times until all the milk was out.

After the washing she shaped the butter into cakes. She completed all these chores before one of Tonnie's sisters arrived to take care of the younger children so Opal could go to the fields. Opal left the field just before midday, came to the house and cooked dinner, then returned to the field and worked until suppertime. She worked like this all summer while she was in the "family way."

In June, the sun beamed down on Opal's head as she started in the direction of the house to put on dinner. She had been having difficulty with this baby and could hardly walk. Her legs were swollen all down to her ankles, and both her feet looked as though they were full of fluid. She had to cut long slits on the side of both shoes to get them on her feet. This day, Opal hurt so much, that the pain increased with every step she took. Finally deciding that she could not go any further, Opal sat down under a large shade tree. Sitting there, she thought about what an old lady once told her a long time ago about her mama. Upon learning who Opal was, the woman said, "I know why your Mama died. Having all them babies right together is what killed your Mama." Opal thought about being twenty-six and expecting her seventh child. She was about the same age Ora had been when her seventh child was born. Rubbing her legs eased the pain. She rubbed them up and down, up and down, running her hand over the scar that she had had since she was a young girl. Looking at the scar reminded her of her grandmama.

Opal knew that while Grandma Tamar had been born a slave, that did not define her. She was so much more. When Opal was sick with pneumonia, Dr. John Thornton gave her big white tablets to take. Opal could hardly swallow the pills because her throat hurt. Grandma Tamar whipped up the white of eggs and gave it to her because it was suppose to be good for her lungs. After drinking it, Opal got better. When she had her first child and her milk did not come down right away, Grandma Tamar told her about "sugar tit" and "catnip tea." She put a little butter and sugar in a clean cloth, then wrapped it in the shape of a nipple for the baby to suck. From a little green plant, she made the "tea" that she spoon fed the baby so it would have some nourishment.

Opal's thoughts returned to the scar on her leg. She was about ten or twelve that winter when her uncles were visiting Grandma Tamar and everyone was sitting around the fireplace talking and telling stories. She was heating water in a black tea kettle over the fireplace to wash dishes. Arizona and Cloria kept telling Opal to take the water off the fire and wash the dishes, but she was enjoying the stories so much that she ignored their repeated admonishments to take the water from the fire. Finally, Opal removed the kettle, took it to the kitchen, and, holding the aluminum dishpan in one hand, she poured the water into it. The water quickly heated the thin dishpan and burned Opal's hand. She drop the pan, spilling the hot scalding water on her leg.

When Opal pulled off her cotton stocking, the skin on the front of her leg came off too. Her left leg was burned so badly that Opal was home from school for over a month. None of the medicine the doctor gave her worked; her leg would not heal. Grandma Tamar took some balls from the sweet gum tree and burned them until they were reduced to ashes. She sprinkled the ashes from the balls over the sore on Opal's leg. A short time later, a scab formed over the sore and her leg finally healed.

Opal realized that her grandma had been the one who taught her everything she knew about being a decent person, one who devoted herself to family, church, and God. She also taught Opal to keep going even when she did not think she could make it any further. Regardless of how bad the conditions or how severe the blow life dealt, Grandma Tamar found a way to make everything better. Grandma Tamar actually believed it when she said, as she often did, that "God's always got a ram in the bush." Opal was glad that before her grandmama left this world, she passed on some of the things she had learned from Isabel, and Isabel had learned from her mother and those before. Opal thought it ironic that Grandma Tamar had been interred in the Taylor burial ground amid big sweet gum trees.

Opal sat there on the ground thinking about her grandmama until she stopped crying. Then she got up, because she still had work to do before she could quit for the day. The next month, on July 25, 1936, Opal gave birth to a healthy baby girl. She named the child Cloria Vean, after her sister, whom all the children called Aunt Clora. Now that she had a new baby, Opal stayed home from the fields for a while so she could nurse.

A few days after the baby was born, Tonnie came in and told Opal that Mr. Macon Thornton had died. Tonnie said Mr. Macon had been sick with cancer for a long time, so his death came as no surprise to his family. Opal thought it was interesting, since just last month Tonnie had come in with the news that lawyer Mann Wills had died suddenly at his home. His death had caught everyone by surprise. Just two months ago, in May, she learned "Old Man" Henry Averyheart passed. He had served for years as a steward at Taylor's Chapel Church, and Opal had known him all her life. Since

Opal did not get out of the house much, she mainly relied on Tonnie to tell her the news. Whenever she came across a copy of the local newspaper, *The States Graphic*, she liked to read about what was going on in Brownsville and other places. The paper had a special section called "With the Colored Folks," which reported on news in the black community. The paper was published only once a week, so by the time she read it, Tonnie had usually already given her the news.

At the beginning of the year, Tonnie told Opal about the terrible triple killing of some people who lived not far from their home. The man, named Julius, and his wife, Ollie, were living on the P. H. Bell farm, where a woman from Memphis had been staying with them. On this particular Sunday, the estranged husband of the Memphis woman was visiting, and he brought another man with him. Local people referred to the house as one of those "good-time" houses. True to its reputation, everyone sat around drinking and playing cards. One of the men in the community went to the house earlier in the day and was suspicious. Before he left, he warned Julius that the Memphis woman's husband and his friend were "up to no good." Julius went to the bedroom, got his gun out of the dresser drawer, and put it in his pocket, just in case there was going to be trouble. As they continued playing cards, the husband from Memphis did not let his wife out of his sight, setting her on his lap while his friend stayed close to Julius. After a while, the woman felt her husband pull a razor out of his pocket. She screamed, "Don't y'all let this man kill me." Ollie then broke for the bedroom to get their gun as she yelled out, "I'll die with you." The man slit his wife's throat while his friend attacked Julius, cutting him before he had a chance to pull his gun. After killing his wife, the man went to the bedroom and found Ollie looking in the drawer, not knowing Julius had already removed the gun.

The next day, Tonnie and Grandpa Jim went by the house to get a look at the site of the killing. Tonnie told Opal there was blood all over the house, especially in the kitchen, where Ollie had staggered before she collapsed and died. Tonnie said that some years ago he had been at that house when Ollie was down on her knees calling the Lord's name. He said she was singing the blues like she was singing a gospel song, while the people at the house were partying. The killings were the talk of the community for a long time. What happened to these people was held up as an example of why people in the community should not frequent such "good-time" places. The *States Graphic* ran a front-page story of the killings. It said that law enforcement officials never apprehended the husband and his accomplice, who ran from the house and were not seen again.[18] The reporter left out some of the details that Tonnie had shared with Opal. Still, the typical stories that ran in the paper were not nearly as sensational.

In the July 31, 1936, edition of the local paper, Opal read that the Public Works Administration had granted a request by Brownsville for assistance in building city streets. The program included plans to provide curbs, gutters, storm sewers, and sidewalks on all streets where necessary. Many of the streets in town still did not have sidewalks and curbs. The estimated cost of the program was just over $78,000, of which the federal government made an outright grant of over $35,000. The mayor said the city would have to sell bonds to provide the balance. The Emergency Administration of Publics Works had approved another grant for Brownsville city schools, authorizing approximately $17,000 for school building purposes. Opal was glad the city had used part of these funds to build an addition to Haywood County Colored Training School, the school for Negro children.[19]

October brought news from the U.S. Department of Agriculture that 95,000 Tennessee farmers would receive a total of almost $8 million as the 1936 crop and soil benefit payments. Specific payments were to be made to farmers for cotton and tobacco, making Tennessee's share of the payments as large as it had been under the AAA. The report said the average check for each local participant, which still included Grandpa Jim, was about $78.[20] In November 1936, the news came that everyone expected. Franklin Delano Roosevelt had been reelected as president of the United States.

On January 20, 1937, President Roosevelt entered his second term, taking the oath of office twenty-nine minutes late. John Nance Garner, the gray-haired Texan who moments before had taken office as vice president, sat near him. Thousands braved rain, sleet, and snow to gather at the Capitol Plaza to take part in the ceremony and to express their approval of the president's administration. In his inaugural address, Roosevelt renewed his pledge to the American people to carry on the fight to aid millions in need, saying the underprivileged citizen was a challenge to democracy. He assailed special privileges and bespoke America's desire that the New Deal would carry on its struggle for the common man. Roosevelt stood bare headed in the worst inaugural weather in twenty-eight years, refusing to disappoint visitors by holding the ceremony indoors, because he said, "If they can take it, so can I." The president pointed out that the nation's 130 million people "are at peace among themselves," but he barely touched on troubled conditions abroad. He concluded his address at 12:48 P.M. Rain-soaked microphones had carried FDR's crisp words into millions of homes.[21] This time, Opal and the family joined the rest of the nation in listening to the address, trying to garner some knowledge of what programs the president planned for the next four years. As they sat gathered around their new radio, Opal said it seemed just like the president was sitting right there in the room talking to them.

One day Tonnie came back from uptown, and along with his usual sacks of groceries he had presented the radio. Grandpa Jim already owned a radio, and other people were buying them, so Tonnie bought one for Opal. It was a unilateral decision. The radio was a table model that operated on batteries, which worked out fine, since they did not have electricity. Tonnie fiddled with his new purchase until he finally got the battery attached, then he tuned into a station, and the male voice emanating from the radio filled the room. Hearing the sound of this stranger inside her home for the first time, Opal was about as excited as the children. They were even more excited that Saturday night when Tonnie changed the stations on the radio and discovered the Grand Ole Opry, a program from Nashville, Tennessee. Listening to the Opry soon became a Saturday night family ritual. While Opal did her ironing, Tonnie and the children sat around the radio before they went to bed. Opal liked to hear Bill Monroe "pick his box" and sing, and she liked "Stringbean" and some of the other people who told jokes. One of her favorites was Roy Acuff, especially when he sang, "I heard a crash on the highway, but I didn't hear nobody pray." Even the children enjoyed listening to the Opry. For one night every weekend, the music and laughter provided an escape from the drudgery of work and the dismal news about hard times and the depression.

Despite the hard times, the paper ran full-page advertisements of Uncle Sam asking the public to buy government bonds. Urged on by the campaign, people of Haywood County made their contribution in record numbers. That January, Brownsville reported that the previous year its citizens had invested over $58,000 in government bonds. Locals had gone to the post office during 1936 and purchased bonds ranging from twenty-five dollars to one thousand dollars. Townspeople generally felt that the sale of these bonds to the citizens of Brownsville indicated the wholesome financial condition of the city and increased confidence in the return of normal business conditions. Many of the people who bought government bonds in large denominations could ill afford to do so. Although it may have seemed incongruous, that was their way of contributing to the recovery of the nation's economy.

Haywood County workers shared in the approximately six million dollars that workers in the state had earned as a result of WPA investments. Workers had put in more than twenty-four million man hours from the program's beginning in September of 1935 up to January 1937.[22] The men widened and reshaped roads, did cuttings and clearings, and ditched and dressed roads. The city built new roads, using workers to apply stone and gravel to over three million cubic yards of road. Workers used concrete and timber to build bridges, repaired and painted steel and concrete bridges, replaced pipes, applied tar and oil on roads, and replaced signs where needed.

Grandpa Jim decided that since gravel was being applied to lots of other roads throughout the county, he would go into town and speak with the county road supervisor about putting gravel on Springfield Road. Being a dirt road, it was difficult to travel whenever weather conditions were bad. He was tired of his wagon getting stuck in the mud every time it rained. On those occasions when he and the children were forced to walk to church, they carried their good church shoes in a paper sack and walked in their old shoes, which were covered with mud by the time they arrived for Sunday school. Grandpa Jim politely posed the question about putting gravel on his road. The white man gave the request little thought. Without even looking up, he said, "Why should we gravel it, don't nobody live out there anyway." Grandpa shared the news with the rest of the family at one of their Sunday gatherings. Seeing that they were unsuccessful in having something done about the road situation, the discussion turned to other problems.

Tonnie said someone was going to get killed if people did not stop what they were doing. For the last few weeks, some men had been sneaking onto farms during the night. They had gone out to "Old Man" Mullins place, but he had heard about the nocturnal visitors and was prepared for them. He ran a thin wire from the little building outside the house to his bedroom window; then he hung a cowbell on the wire and sat and waited. During the night, he heard the clinking noise of metal banging against the bell. Knowing the culprits had also been alerted, the old man, with his shotgun in hand, rushed out the backdoor just as the two men were running away. He fired his shotgun, striking one of the men in the leg. The

Sweet Gum Trees

wounded man fell to the ground, dropping his crocus sack, while the other man fled, leaving his sack behind on the ground. Opal said she hated to see anybody get killed for stealing some chickens, but thieves were about to take all of her good egg-laying chickens.

Grandpa Jim said there had been a rash of chicken stealing cases lately. The next morning after this latest incident, he and several other men were called over to the next farm to claim their stolen chickens. He told Tonnie that the two men had a busy night, because they left behind crocus sacks filled with chickens. Tonnie did not have any chickens stolen in this batch. The two thieves apparently had not reached his farm before the shooting interrupted their mission. About two weeks before, Opal had discovered some of their chickens missing. She noticed a couple of old hens "acting like they wanted to set." She marked a lot of eggs and took them to the hen house to place in the nest that she had made the previous day. This would make the baby chicks due about the time the weather turned warmer. When she got down to the hen house, she was surprised to find several of her chickens missing. She would have to mark more eggs the next time she set her hens in order to replace the chickens that were stolen. Still, she did not want to believe that grown men were running around in the community taking other people's chickens.

Tonnie had just bought an old rooster that might put a stop to anyone else going in the hen house. The rooster made people afraid to come in the yard, and he was getting meaner by the day. The last time Miss Winbush came to visit, she was too scared to come in the yard when she saw the rooster. Opal kept coaxing her, saying that the rooster was not going to hurt her. Although it was always fighting, the rooster had not attacked anyone before, and Opal did not think it would actually attack a person. At Opal's urging, Miss Winbush finally got up her nerve and walked across the yard, keeping her eyes on the rooster the whole time. She made it to the steps and almost onto the front porch. About the time she thought she was safe, the old rooster came flying at her, digging his spurs deep into her arm. Opal now believed the old rooster just might try to fight anyone who tried to come in their hen house at night.

Several months passed, and there had been no more reports of chicken stealing, at least not as far as Tonnie and Opal knew. Tonnie got up early one morning and, as usual, he headed for the barn. He was going to milk the cow before going to the field, but when he got to the barn, he looked all around, then looked around again. He could not believe it was not there.

Someone had stolen his Jersey cow, the only milk cow he had. Finding who had taken his cow became all Tonnie could think about. He talked to anybody who would listen, trying to find what happened to his cow. Pretty soon the news of his cow being stolen had spread around town, and he received word that a man called "Hosie" was the person responsible. Tonnie went straight to the police and had the man arrested, but because there was no solid evidence against the man, the police released him. Tonnie was not dissuaded; he was determined to find the guilty person and get his cow back.

On a Saturday afternoon, Tonnie sat in the living room of a stranger, waiting to talk to a woman he had never seen before. The curtains were drawn, but a stream of light filtered through the front door, which was slightly ajar. It had been a while since his arrival was announced, and he began to think he would change his mind and leave; then the woman emerged from a back room. Some man in town had told him about this woman over in Jackson who had a reputation for being good at what she did. Tonnie had never been to a fortune teller before, but the man said she could tell him what happened to his cow. He took in every word the woman said. She told him, " A colored man stole your cow, but he got it on a white man's place not far from where you live." She said, "You can get your cow back if you want to, but you've got to keep quiet about it." The woman added, "If you talk, your cow is gonna be sold and you'll never see it again." Tonnie left more convinced than ever that Hosie, who lived near him on a white's place, was the person who had his cow.

One morning not long after his visit, Mr. Grady Rainer came to Tonnie's door. He knew Tonnie because his daughter Lucille had married Tonnie's brother Dan. Mr. Grady, who lived on the other side of Jackson Highway, explained that he had been out walking early that morning when he saw what he thought was Tonnie's cow. He said he saw a "colored man walking with a rope tied to a cow, and he was pulling it toward a parked truck." When he got closer, he saw it was Hosie and some white man loading the cow into the back of the truck. The truck had a bed on the back, so he could not see the cow once it was on the truck. It was a light color Jersey just like the one stolen from Tonnie. After the men got the cow in the truck, they drove off and appeared to be headed in the direction of Memphis.

Tonnie had not kept quiet about his visit to the fortune teller. As soon as he left Jackson, he told everything that the woman said. The day before Mr. Grady made his visit, Hosie's father-in-law had come by the house.

The people in the community said the man was more "crooked than a barrel of snakes." Tonnie would not stop talking until he had told the man about the fortune teller, as well as his suspicion of Hosie. It was the following day that Mr. Grady saw the cow being driven out of town. Opal thought Tonnie had talked too much, now they did not stand a chance of ever seeing the cow again. At the same time, she knew he desperately wanted to get his milk cow back. They had a house full of little children and another one on the way.

On May 27, 1938, Opal gave birth to her third girl. She named the child Wallis. Opal had heard on the radio about King Edward VIII of England having abdicated the throne for Wallis Warfield Simpson, an American divorcée the British government opposed as queen. She had also seen a picture of Wallis Simpson and the king in a magazine at Aunt Cloria's one Saturday when visiting while Tonnie did the shopping. Opal thought it all very romantic hearing about royalty, although it was difficult to imagine how they lived, since farm life was usually so dull and predictable.

About three months after Wallis was born, Opal and the family were again at Snipes Grove Church for revival Sunday. Grandpa Jim, Grandma Ada, and Lawrence and the twins had come by in their wagon and picked up Tonnie, Opal, and the younger children for church. Opal had not been feeling well, and it must have showed on her face because one of the church ladies asked to hold the baby. She did not know exactly what the problem was; she just had a "funny feeling" all morning. The early service was over and they were waiting for the afternoon service to begin when Tonnie came rushing in the church and told Opal that someone had burned their barn.

Tonnie said two men who had gone out to Mr. Harbert's place to pick up some people for church had just arrived with the news. The men were passing Tonnie's farm when they saw smoke coming from the barn. They rushed to the barn and began taking out Tonnie's wagon, plow, and some smaller farm tools. They were also able to save all the animals, but they said there was not a thing they could do about the barn. It was completely destroyed. The biggest boy, Jim Howell, told them that he saw a man he thought he recognized running away from the barn about the time the fire started. The previous week, Tonnie had cussed out a neighbor for letting his hogs get in Tonnie's cornfield. It was not the first time the hogs had done damage, trampling down and rutting up stalks of corn. Tonnie found the man, Hosie's son, trying to round the hogs back in the pen. He knew immediately the identity of the person who burned his barn.

During these hard times, it was difficult enough for Tonnie to eke out a living from the land without having to replace a barn and stolen animals. Although Tonnie never seriously considered leaving the farm, black people were leaving the rural South by the thousands. With little hope of finding jobs in the city, the exodus continued as more and more Negroes quit farming. By the late thirties, the number of Negroes that had left the South was placed at about four hundred thousand. They persisted in blaming the AAA for driving hundreds of thousands of blacks from the land.[23] Upon arriving in the city, they quickly learned that menial jobs such as street cleaning, garbage collecting, and domestic work, traditionally known as "Negro jobs," were being filled by unemployed whites.

Some blacks in Brownsville, who opted for the city over doing backbreaking fieldwork all their lives, joined the crowd going up north. During this time, Uncle Dempsy left for Michigan; several family members, including some of Tonnie's sisters and brothers, left for Chicago and Decatur, Illinois, and New York. Many others chose to relocate to large southern towns. Tonnie and Opal had a few relatives who moved from Brownsville to nearby Memphis. Tonnie's cousin A. D. moved to Jackson. Tonnie was talking to a white man in town one day when the subject came up about the number of black people who were leaving town to go North. The man said, "I hope all the niggers leave, then our wives won't be ashamed to work."

Grandpa Jim and the family, like many other blacks, had become convinced that Roosevelt's policies for economic recovery had contributed to the Negro migration to urban centers. Much of the New Deal, especially during FDR's first term, was thought to discriminate against Negroes. In addition to blaming the AAA, they also criticized the NRA. Under the latter, 11,000 of the 13,000 Negroes on southern cotton mills were classified such that they were excluded from all NRA benefits. Because the NRA never promulgated codes to cover the majority of domestic and unskilled Negro labor, most remained as poor as ever. Employers often fired Negro workers rather than honoring NRA requirements and paying them the same salary as whites.[24] As a result of these practices, some black people, even around Brownsville, started referring to the NRA by such nicknames as "Negro Run Around" and "Negro Robbed Again."[25] Neither did the WPA escape criticism. Although more than a million Negroes owed their living to the program, those seeking WPA jobs found some southern newspapers openly offering whites higher wages than Negroes for doing the same work.[26]

Although some people thought Roosevelt's policies assisted the Negro in varying degrees, most had to agree with the overall conclusion that discrimination ran rampant through the New Deal. The newspapers and Negro magazines wrote that there was discrimination even in starvation, as some religious and charitable organizations excluded Negroes from soup kitchens operated to relieve suffering. In public assistance, white families received as much as six dollars more in monthly aid than what was given to black families. At a conference on "The Position of the Negro in the Present Economic Crisis," held in Washington in 1935, every New Deal program was damned as inimical to the black masses. Conference attendees generally agreed that "the will of those who have kept Negroes in economic disfranchisement has been permitted to prevail, and the government has looked on in silence and at times with approval."[27]

As a result of the economic crisis of the Great Depression, the National Association for the Advancement of Colored People changed its strategies and tactics and began to insist that civil liberties and basic economic securities must complement one another. As early as 1919, the NAACP adopted resolutions expressing its great concern over the status of Negroes, and it continued to express concern. Leaders of the NAACP called the New Deal programs blatantly racist and attacked them for their vicious discrimination. Advocating economic independence for the Negro, the organization proclaimed that "what the Negro needs primarily is a definite economic program."[28]

In 1939, a group of Negro citizens in Brownsville heeded the call of the NAACP. They had seen enough discrimination by local whites and thought they could help their people. The group began meeting at different locations around town to discuss forming a local branch of the national organization, holding some meetings at Willow Grove Baptist Church. Some of the local white folks had their own ideas about what black people could do, or, more accurately, could not do, in Haywood County. They began a reign of terror that would culminate in a killing and a hurried burial in Taylor's Chapel Cemetery, with no funeral or graveside service, just the workers doing their job in the summer shade of the sweet gum trees.

5.

Fighting Odds

"Look out, brown man!" Sherwood Anderson forewarned in the *Nation*. "These aren't good times for a Negro man to be proud, step too high. There are a lot of white men hard up. There are a lot of white men out of work. They won't be wanting to see a big, proud black man getting along. There'll be lynchings now."[1] Nine years later, in 1939, the warning was still as appropriate as ever.

Tennessee's earliest chapters of the NAACP were established in Memphis in 1918 and Nashville in 1919.[2] Twenty years later, on March 12, 1939, some prominent Negro citizens in town held an organizational meeting to finalize its application for a charter of the Brownsville branch of the NAACP. The organization required fifty members for a branch charter. The Brownsville group had fifty-two members who each paid one dollar dues before they submitted the application to the national office in New York. Executive authorization was granted on May 22, 1939, when the application was signed by the chairman of the Board of Directors, Louis Wright, and Secretary Walter White.[3] On July 20, 1939, the national office forwarded the charter to the new Brownsville branch of the NAACP, whose members stated in their application that "we believe our interests coincide with efforts for the advancement of colored people."[4] One of the first undertakings of the Brownsville branch was the effort to register blacks to vote in the election the following year.

The Ku Klux Klan had developed as a force in west Tennessee since the spring of 1868, with widely scattered reports of night riders, threatened Negroes, and Negroes' guns being taken away. Some people considered Haywood County a base of operation for a gang who conducted activities in several adjacent counties. This group, reported to have been in operation since early 1867, was thought to possibly represent a "Klan den" in the county.[5] The Klan was revived in Indiana in 1915, with slow growth until after the First World War, at which time they instituted a broad program for uniting against Negroes and any other group that were not "white Christians." Their actions appeared to reflect what was going on across the country during the first year of the postwar period, when more than seventy Negroes were lynched. Scarcely a day passed that some newspaper did not report that a Negro soldier had been lynched, several still in their uniform.

With the coming of the Great Depression, racial animosity intensified because of the increased competition for a share of the dwindling economic pie. In places like Haywood County, where the Negro population outnumbered the whites almost two to one, race always played a major part in local politics. One primary means of controlling the town's black people was to deny them the right to vote. The actions of some white citizens of Haywood County epitomized the view later expressed by U.S. senator and former governor of Mississippi Theodore Bilbo. In his campaign for reelection, reports quoted him as saying, "Do not let a single Nigger register and vote. If you let a few register and vote this year, next year there will be twice as many, and the next thing you know the whole thing will be out of hand." He added, "You and I know what's the best way to keep the Nigger from voting. You do it the night before the election. I don't have to tell you any more than that. Red-blooded men know what I mean."[6] Most people had little doubt about what he meant.

The NAACP served as a consistent force in protest of injustices to Negroes through its fight in the courts and agencies of the federal government. In 1919, the organization held a national conference on lynching, and three years later it placed a full-page advertisement in leading newspapers as part of its campaign to secure passage of the Dyer Antilynching Bill before the U.S. Senate.[7] The NAACP announced in 1933 that its main activity would be to concentrate on antilynching legislation.[8] It was a decade-long struggle. At the same time, the group continued its effort to secure basic civil rights for black people. Believing they were "safe under the wings of the National Association for the Advancement of Colored People," members of the Brownsville branch embarked upon their own campaign for voter registration. This would put them on a direct collision course with opposing forces.

The next few years marked one of the darkest periods in the history of Haywood County. For Opal and others living in the county during this time, the events that occurred were forever etched in their memories. They recalled a combination of actual participants' stories, accounts they read in newspapers, findings of outside investigations, and many rumors they thought reliable.

The knock on the door always came late at night. When the person inside the house inquired who it was, a voice answered, "Santa Claus." Hearing the familiar voice, the person inside opened the door and exchanged cash for merchandise. Major Hess delivered bootleg whiskey at night—but not because he was concerned about being discovered. Not only had Mayor George Reed been present on occasions when Hess was loading his liquor for delivery, but rumor had spread that Hess actually worked for the mayor of the town. Clarence Taylor, one of Uncle Tom's sons, was a friend of Major Hess. Clarence told people that since he was friends with "Santa Claus," who worked for Mayor Reed, the mayor looked out for him, too. He said the mayor helped him establish a franchise to sell beer. Clarence was the only person licensed to sell beer at the fairgrounds.

Clarence operated a little restaurant in town that did good business. With the help of his cook, Addie Mae Rawls, he sold barbecue, chicken, fish, hamburgers, hotdogs and cold drinks. Clarence married Alma Sloan, who ran the Negro cosmetology school and was a charter member of the Brownsville branch of the NAACP. Clarence did not know what to think when two officers pulled up to his restaurant one day around late spring 1940. The two men said they wanted to talk to him. With Clarence in the back seat of the police cruiser, the officers drove around town and out to the country. They questioned Clarence about the NAACP and their voting efforts. When the officers brought him back to the restaurant, Clarence removed the gun tucked in his belt under his apron, which he had every intention of using if necessary.

It was no secret that whites in Haywood County had long had a reputation for "running over" blacks. Some black people in town were determined to stand up to the whites. A big factor, however, was how many whites they had to stand up to at once. When Tonnie and the family were living on Poplar Corner Road, Mr. Harbert Thornton came by the house upset because Tonnie's hogs had gotten into his corn. Tonnie was out working in the field. When Mr. Harbert saw him, he started walking toward him, yelling that he needed to keep his "goddamn hogs put up." Before Mr. Harbert got very far,

Fighting Odds

Tonnie set out in the direction of Mr. Harbert, yelling and cursing back. Mr. Harbert never messed with Tonnie again.

Tonnie told Opal about separate incidents involving Mr. Harbert and two other black men. Once Mr. Harbert was at his gin settling up a crop with Harrison Taylor, who was married to Opal's cousin Lizzie. Mr. Harbert was obviously not satisfied with the amount of money Cousin Harrison gave him, so he started to close the door. Cousin Harrison, knowing what the white man planned to do behind closed doors, said in his soft, southern drawl, "Mr. Harbert, you might not wanna shut that door there, 'cause if you do, you or me, one, might wanna get outta here." The people at the gin that day laughed and said Mr. Harbert kept that door open. The other event involved Mr. Harvey Rice, who, like Cousin Harrison, was unassuming and did not talk very much. Mr. Harvey Rice was in Mr. Harbert's office to settle up for cotton grown that year. Tonnie said Mr. Harbert was not pleased about something, so he just "hauled off" and hit the black man "upside the head." Mr. Harvey Rice grabbed Mr. Harbert and put him in a "Nelson," which was a headlock. Then, he commenced to beating the white man "in the top of the head." He picked up Mr. Harbert and walked across the floor with him until others pleaded with him not to throw the beaten man out the opened window.

Grandpa Jim joked that after the incident that Mr. Harbert's wife, Miss Marie, asked him one morning if he wanted some rice for breakfast. Mr. Harbert said, "Hell naw, I don't want no damn rice." Even with the humor, everyone knew this was a serious matter. Harvey Rice was scared after beating the white man. For about a week, he and his brother lay out in the bushes near his home at night. They waited with their guns for the mob to come. Aunt Cloria told Opal that she knew why the mob never got Harvey. The mob had come by Mr. Harbert's house and asked him where Harvey Rice lived. Mr. Harbert, knowing what the mob intended to do, said, "I don't need all y'all to whip that little nigger. I can whip that little nigger by myself." Opal knew Mr. Harbert had a reputation for being mean, but she had never heard anything about him being part of the mob.

By June 1940, mob activities had intensified. Although the black people called them the "mob," they were the same group that called themselves the Klan. Whatever they were called, it did not matter to the people they targeted. The result was the same. Two of their latest targets were Elisha and Thomas Davis, who operated the Davis Service Station in Brownsville.

They were also charter members of the local NAACP. Tonnie and Opal knew Elisha, Thomas, their brother Cashier, and their mother and sisters because they were all members of Willow Grove Baptist Church. The Davis family lived not far from the church, just off Jackson Highway near Mulligan's Store, so Tonnie knew them well. Opal had met the family after she and Tonnie married, and she also knew Elisha's wife, Nan, from when she was a girl living in the Taylor's Chapel community. Cashier Davis's wife was connected by marriage to Tonnie's side of the family. Since they knew the entire Davis family, Opal was shocked when Tonnie told her what had happened.

During the early morning of June 15, 1940, at approximately one o'clock, Elisha Davis was awakened by loud pounding on his door. Upon opening the door, Tip Hunter, in full uniform, Albert Mann, and another man entered the house and ordered Elisha to get dressed. A mob of some fifty or sixty men were gathered outside in the street and around his home. Tip Hunter, the night marshall for Brownsville and the Democratic nominee for the office of sheriff of Haywood County, escorted Elisha outside. The men placed Elisha in the backseat of a waiting car with one Charles Reed, the town's night policeman.[9] Before they left, Albert Mann told Elisha's wife, who pleaded with them not to harm her husband, "You will never see this black son of a bitch again. We are going to kill him."[10]

The mob drove Elisha out of town to the Forked Deer River bottom. Once there, the mob ordered Elisha out of the car and surrounded him. In addition to Tip Hunter and Albert Mann, the farm foreman for Dan Shaw and president of the Brownsville Bank, Davis recognized Clyde Hopkins, highway commissioner for Haywood County; P. G. Farrell, a truck driver for the Brownsville Laundry; Elliot Hayes, a grocer; "Shorty" Smith, a WPA worker; Will Mann, a farmer and brother of Albert Mann; Albert Dixon, a mule trader for Dan Shaw; and as many as fifty other men he did not recognize. After the mob encircled Elisha, Albert Mann said to him, "We have brought you out here to kill you, but I ain't going to let them do it. They all want to know about that organization named the National Association for the Advancement of Colored People and who the members are of that organization and what you Negroes intend to do." When they threatened to kill him if he did not tell them what they wanted to know, Elisha told them the purpose of the organization and gave the names of several members. He also explained that at the organizational meeting of the NAACP branch some of Brownsville's most prominent white citizens were present and encouraged colored citizens to register to vote in the fall presidential election of 1940. The mob ordered Elisha to leave the county immediately and warned that if he ever showed his face there again he would be killed. They would not even allow him to go back home and get his clothes. Elisha walked eight or nine miles to Jackson Highway, where two strangers picked him up and drove him out of town.[11]

Tonnie said that same night they took another man, Jack Adams, out to the Forked Deer bottom. Adams was apparently a case of mistaken identity, though. The mob discovered he was not the person they wanted and released him when Elisha told them Adams was a "good boy."[12] Tonnie heard the only thing that saved Elisha was that Mr. Musgraves, who used to own the land by Mulligan's Store, where the Davis family lived, spoke up for him. Before the mob could harm Elisha, Mr. Musgraves said that he had known Elisha since he was a boy. He said, "we was raised up together and we ain't never had a cross word. If y'all kill that boy, you gonna have to kill me too."

Rumors around Brownsville abounded about the black people being "run out of town." Tonnie told Opal that the mob took one man thinking he was her cousin Clarence Taylor. He did not think the man was Adams, because this person was taken near Snipes Grove. The man told someone that when the mob got him to the bottom, a large crowd had already gathered. As soon as he stepped out of the car, a man in the crowd said, "You done took the wrong boy. That ain't Clarence Taylor. I know Clarence Taylor, and that ain't him." Some of the men in the crowd then hit him on the head a few times "just for meanness." Although he had to walk back to town, he was so glad they turned him loose that he left there running when one man shouted the order, "get that nigger outta here." According to Tonnie, this man said the same thing that Elisha said about people in the crowd. When Elisha called his mother, he told her, "You would be surprised at some of the people around Brownsville who were part of the mob."

The mob was the main topic of discussion at family gatherings after church on Sunday. Grandpa Jim asked Tonnie if he had heard about what happened with Buster Walker. He was a local minister, but most of the people who knew him just called him "Buster." He was also a charter member of the Brownsville branch of the NAACP and president of the organization. In May, Buster, John Lester, John Gaines, Taylor Newbern, and Elisha Davis had gone to County Registrar Mann's office to inquire about how they could qualify to vote in the 1940 presidential election. Mr.

Mann sent them to City Judge Pearson, who asked them, "What committee is this?" When the men explained that they were seeking information concerning voting, Judge Pearson referred them to Jonas Steinberger, a cotton buyer who was chairman of the Elections Committee. Since Mr. Steinberger was out of the city and the men had learned that the registration booths would not open until August, they decided to let the matter rest. But their inquiry put the whites in town on notice. The next day, Deputy Sheriff T. Bolden went to Buster and threatened him, saying that he had better "drop encouraging Negroes to vote or there will be trouble." As if doing him a favor, he added, "Don't say I didn't warn you."[13]

About two weeks later, an unemployed white man named Strauss Drumwright went to see Elisha Davis at his filling station. He said he heard Elisha was "a member of some organization getting Negroes to vote." He warned, "Let that thing drop or Negroes will get into some serious trouble. The people down at the courthouse say they will run you and Walker out of town if you try to vote." Later, Buster was present when George Reed and Erma Drake, a city policeman dressed in uniform with his badge and gun, paid a visit on Elisha. They asked if the Negroes were still planning on voting in the presidential election. When Elisha said they did, George Reed asked him not to encourage the Negroes to pay their taxes and vote. If he would "stop the Negroes," they promised to give him anything he wanted. "The last time the Negroes tried to vote in the presidential election," Reed said, "many a Negro was killed and thrown in the river." The men warned, "if they tried in 1940, there would be a many more Negroes killed and thrown in the river again."[14] Grandpa Jim said the threat was delivered by the same George Reed who had served as mayor of Brownsville.

Tonnie heard that several of Brownsville's black citizens with ties to the NAACP had left town and were in hiding. Buster Walker was the latest victim. Tonnie said A. D. Springfield told him that Buster called him and said the mob had come looking for him and met him leaving town on foot. Not recognizing Buster, who had disguised himself, one of the men yelled, "We looking for a nigger called Buster Walker. Do you know where he stay?" The minister had turned and pointed behind him and said, "Yessuh, yessuh, yessuh, he stay right down the road there." He said the cars were loaded with white men who were cussing as they sped off in the direction he indicated. Buster quickly made his way out of town. After walking for some distance, a motorist picked him up and drove him to Jackson and safety. Buster had left Brownsville like all the others who had been run out of town as part of the mob's "fear campaign." They had a good laugh at how Buster was able to trick the mob.

On Thursday evening, June 20, 1940, thousands of people across the country sat glued to their radios. Out on the farm, Tonnie, Opal, and the children tuned in. At the Service Sundries Drug Store and Ice Cream Parlor, Brownsville's first and only black-owned drugstore, a group gathered to listen: Miss Maude Rawls, the store owner and wife of Al Rawls; Miss Willie Bell Rawls, who was married to Al's brother, George "Buddy" Rawls, also present; Aunt Cloria, now married to another one of the brothers, Dan "Boy" Rawls; "Babe" Vance, the pharmacist; and several other locals. Before a crowd of 28,000 at Yankee Stadium, Joe Louis was defending his title against Arturo Godoy of Chile. When Joe Louis knocked out his opponent in the eighth round, the crowd at the drugstore began clapping their hands, cheering, and celebrating. At the same time, Aunt Cloria and the other women were a little nervous about a small group of white men who were watching the celebration from across the street in front of the Billy Cox Funeral Home. When Buddy drove Willie Bell and Maude home, sometime between ten and eleven o'clock, they noticed a car "hogging" the road in front of Elbert Williams's home at 210 Bradford Street. A policeman got out of the car and went to the door. Maude said the man driving the car looked so mean she would remember that look the rest of her life.[15] Soon details of what happened that night began to emerge.

Elbert Williams worked at the Sunshine Laundry and was a charter member of the local NAACP. He and his wife, Annie, had just finished listening to the fight and were getting ready for bed when someone knocked on the front door. Elbert knew all about the recent mob activities, and, like others in Brownsville, he was scared. Tip Hunter came in and asked if Elbert Williams lived there. Elbert was wearing nothing but his pajama bottoms and a vest when Hunter escorted him to the parked car and placed him in the backseat beside a terrified Thomas Davis, brother of Elisha. Elbert's mother ran next door to Miss Willie Bell's and explained what happened. She said, "They have taken Elbert, and they wouldn't let him put his shoes on."

The next morning, Annie Williams walked to City Hall. She did not see her husband, but she did see Thomas Davis. When she inquired about her husband, Officer Charles Reid told her that Elbert was not there. Friday morning, Elbert still had not come home. Annie Williams went back to the jail and asked the officer in charge, Hawkins, what had happened to her husband. She explained that they had taken her "husband away without proper clothes on and that he had not come back home." The officer said, "They aren't going to hurt him; they may just ask him a few questions, but they'll let him loose." He told her to come back and let him know "if he doesn't come home in a day or two." She then went to the office of Milmon Mitchell, president of the Jackson branch of the NAACP, where she spoke with Thomas Davis. Davis told her that when they let him go he left Elbert at City Hall. Everyone was sure they would not do anything to Elbert, so Annie went home.[16]

On Saturday, Annie Williams went back to the man she and her husband worked for, Spence Dupree. The night Elbert was taken, her brother-in-law had asked Spence Dupree to find out why Elbert was being held and to help them get him out of jail. Dupree said he did not know anything, but maybe his papa could tell her what to do. He added, "these laws are just wrong, Annie. They're hard-headed. There's just a bunch here, we can't do anything with them." He told her to go back to the post office if she had not heard anything by six o'clock. He would try to find out what happened. Annie Williams didn't go anywhere that evening.[17]

At 7:30 on Sunday morning, June 23, 1940, Al Rawls, the undertaker, sent word that he wanted Annie Williams to come to the Hatchie River. Rawls said the "body of a colored man" had been found in the river. He was clad only in his underwear, with a rope around his neck, still tied to a log. The coroner was at the river when she arrived. He did not want to uncover the body, but she insisted. Annie Williams identified her husband, who "was all beaten and bruised, and there were holes in the chest." They told her the body had to be buried at once.[18]

One Saturday afternoon, while Tonnie was doing the shopping, Opal walked down Jefferson Street to Aunt Cloria's house, across from Haywood County Training School. She was pleased to see Aunt Arizona was visiting too, because it was rare that the three sisters got together. After a while the talk turned to the lynchings. Since Aunt Cloria lived in town and was married to Boy Rawls, she had more news to share than the other two. She learned that on the Thursday night after Tip Hunter picked up Elbert Williams, they went by City Hall, where they dropped off Thomas Davis before they headed out of town. At some point they met up with the rest of the mob. The cars took Highway 76, also known as Somerville Highway, south of town. They wondered what was going through Elbert's mind. They could not have known for sure, but they pictured him sitting in the backseat of the patrol car, probably thinking he would return like the others had. From the car window he could see familiar homes as they sped by. His home on Bradford Street was just a short distance away. The motorcade traveled on for approximately six miles before reaching the Hatchie bottom. There it stopped at the wooded lowland area of the Hatchie River, similar to the swamplands of Mississippi and Louisiana. Scattered patches of water stood just above the land surface, and several narrow dirt roads led down to the river. Arriving at the bottom the mob led Elbert through the pitch-black woods, stumbling across logs and broken twigs that punctured his bare feet, until they came to a spot near the river.

Judging from the accounts of others picked up by the mob, the crowd was large; although, there were not three thousand spectators, like the group in one Tennessee town who responded to an invitation in the newspaper to witness the burning of a "live Negro."[19] Nonetheless, the man mistaken for Clarence said he had never "seen so many cars and white folks in all my life." Both this man and Elisha Davis said they recognized some of Brownsville's prominent citizens in the crowd, which included women and children. Aunt Cloria heard that one father roused his son from sleep to bring him to the lynching, thinking it was an event a young white boy should experience.

Whenever Opal heard anyone talk about the mob lynching Elbert Williams, she remembered the time in grade school when Dick asked her to write a love letter for him. She and the rest of the family had known Elbert "Dick" Williams just about all their lives. Opal became tearful when she thought about the young boy so full of innocence. She said, "it hurt me so bad to hear what they did to someone that I knew. I felt so sorry for Dick."

"When I heard the news that Dick had been lynched, I didn't think I could go on living," Aunt Cloria said. She added, "I just wanted to die myself." Aunt Arizona said when she first heard the news, "It struck me so hard, I just didn't want to believe it was true." Aunt Cloria told them there was a woman in town, "kind of weak," who had actually lost her mind when she learned what happened. They talked about Dick's sister Julie, who married Uncle Tom's second boy, James "Meedie." Opal reminded them how Julie cried in class whenever the teacher moved her away from Opal. Meedie said Julie had taken the news hard. Julie had half-siblings from her mother's other marriage, but Dick was her only brother. Whenever she thought about the lynching, she would call out her brother's name and "just holler and cry." Aunt Cloria cried herself when she repeated this story.

Tonnie had heard that some colored men were setting traps near the river the night Dick was killed, and they reported hearing "all these cars drive up and lots of commotion." They said they moved on down closer to the river, but they were too afraid to leave, so they stayed put and listened. Although they did not see the crowd, they could hear the loud voices of different white men cussing and shouting, and they heard the pounding sounds of all the beating. After a while, they heard a loud piercing scream that echoed through the night and sent chills through their bodies. By then the men had a pretty good idea of what was going on. They heard shotgun blasts, but they were not sure how many. Finally, they heard the sound of water splashing when the white men "threw him in the river." But, they could tell that "Elbert put up a pretty good fight."

Since Boy Rawls sometimes worked with Al, he knew that two or three days in the Tennessee summer heat is all it takes for a body to become a "floater." Bacteria in the water overcome the body and create gas, which causes the body to become bloated. By this time, the body is odorous and the blood vessels have been destroyed. They cannot embalm the body or preserve it, so there is no need to put it in a casket. Elbert Williams was put in a pine box and buried. Al Rawls used sheets to handle the body after pulling it out of the river with ropes. They placed the body in the back of Al's Ford pickup and brought it back to the funeral home, where it stayed in the back of the truck until workers could dig the grave. Then they took the body out to Taylor's Chapel Cemetery.[20]

When Annie first saw Dick's body at the river, she started to cry; then one of the white men said, "We ain't gonna have no hollering here." Neither Annie Williams nor any of her family attended the burial. The next day, she left Brownsville. She had been advised not to spend the night at home. Her destination was New York.[21] Opal said she could understand why Annie would want to get as far away as she could from a place where "the law could just come into a man's home, take him out and kill him like they would an animal."

Dick had been "tortured something terrible." The mob had beaten him. They hanged him from a tree. They shot him. Sometime during the course of deriving pleasure from his torture, one or more members of the mob cut out his tongue. Then they cut off his "privates" and shoved them down his throat before dumping his body in the river. Why did the mob kill Dick Williams when they had turned the other men loose? Aunt Arizona said, "You know Dick always did have a temper, so maybe it was something that he said that made some of the mobbers angry." She reminded the others, " He wouldn't ever want to appear afraid of the white men, either, so he probably wouldn't back down." Not finding any answers, the sisters finally concluded that no one in the crowd spoke up to save him because the mob had been thwarted in recent efforts to carry out their plan. Perhaps they were just ready for a lynching and knew Elbert was a proud black man.

They compared what happened to Dick Williams on the night of June 20 with the Arturo Godoy fight that same evening. They had heard about Godoy being interviewed in his dressing room at Yankee Stadium. He was "battered into a terrible condition by Joe Louis' lethal fists" and was in a semiconscious state, said one member of the press. No one had really given him much chance of winning. Still, after the fight was over, Godoy was able to "lift his hamburgered features" and proudly say, "But I can take it, can't I?" He knew he had lost, but he was proud of the fact that he had gone eight rounds. Someone responded, "Yeah Godoy, you can sure take it."[22] They were certain that at some point before his death, Dick knew he was going to be killed. After it had gone so far, there was no chance of him being rescued from the angry mob. Knowing Dick as they did, they speculated that even though he was beaten and bruised, he decided to take everything the "mobbers" did to him.

After learning that Elbert Williams's body had been recovered from the Hatchie River, one woman in town commented, "There's some more of them in there." Just below Brownsville, white men had lynched a seven-year-old boy because they said he kissed a young white girl. The mother was working for either the family of the girl or another white family. She got word that the men were coming after her son. She decided to send the child to his grandmother's for protection. While the child was trying to make the short trip alone, he heard the men coming, and he tried to hide. The men found the child under a bridge. Aunt Arizona said the tree they hanged the little boy from soon died. She also said that not long after the lynching, something happened to the men who were responsible.

Aunt Cloria said Boy told her he found out from talking to Mr. Rothschild that it was true the mob had a "list of colored people" they had targeted. Mr. Rothschild, who was Jewish, ran a grocery store with Mr. Julius Marks, where Tonnie and a lot of other black people shopped. He said the mob had a long list of colored people they wanted to lynch. Boy asked Mr. Rothschild, "Why the white people took Elbert Williams and killed him like they did? Was it because he was trying to register to vote?"

Mr. Rothschild said Elbert was supposedly dating a white woman he worked with at the laundry. He said Elbert's boss, Mr. Dupree, was watching one day when this white woman took a bite of a banana and gave it to Elbert, who then ate from the same banana. Mr. Dupree said he figured what people were saying about "that nigger messing with a white woman was true." Boy said he heard it was a "colored man that drove the Taxi Cab around town" who betrayed Elbert. The taxi driver told Mr. Dupree to watch Elbert and the white woman. According to Mr. Rothschild, that was why they killed Elbert Williams. But he didn't hesitate to add it was not just Elbert the white people were after; they were also targeting those involved with the NAACP, as well as colored business owners. He said they were after Clarence Taylor because Clarence had opened a restaurant in town. Boy Rawls said he didn't believe the white folks' rumors about Elbert, because it was the same thing they said every time they wanted an excuse to kill a colored man.

Opal read an article in the paper that said lynchings go down as cotton prices rise. Sociologist Arthur Raper had spoken on the topic at the Southern Sociological Conference in Knoxville just two months earlier. Raper told the conferees that over a period of decades he found cotton prices to be a barometer of lynchings, with mob rule usually prevailing in periods of economic stress. In recent years, cotton prices had not been high and neither had the number of lynchings. He theorized that the decrease in recent years was probably due to a wide relief program, and he thought the number of lynchings would increase if the relief program was discontinued or sharply curtailed. Citing statistics, he said studies showed that lynch leaders were punished in less than one-half of 1 percent of cases. In the few cases where they were punished, they received sentences of one to two years. More than one-third of lynch victims are not guilty of a crime, and another third are accused only of misdemeanors. As for cotton prices and lynchings, "there is a direct relation between the two."[23] The Brownsville paper had reported a few days ago that "cotton creeps higher," with a gain of three to six points. Opal figured the local mob apparently never heard the sociologist's theory.

The tension among the townspeople was so high you could almost feel it. The names of some of the white "mobbers" had spread throughout the black community. There were other members of the mob whose names they did not know. They could not be sure whether or not these were the men they did business with every day. Were they the men who sold them their groceries and dry goods, extended them credit, bought their cotton, and smiled in their face when inquiring about their family? Whenever some of the blacks got together, the talk turned to the mob. They talked in whispers even in their own homes, afraid to talk too much, afraid to accuse the white man of something out loud. There was hardly anyone who had not heard some story of mob activities, either in town or somewhere else. Despite everything that was going on, Opal was not afraid for her family, because she did not think there was any reason for the mob to bother them. Still, she hoped with the papers running stories about what happened in Brownsville, it would put an end to all the lynchings.

Elbert Williams's face stared back for the whole world to see. Above his head was one word: "Lynched."[24] The National Edition of the *Chicago Defender*, bound in a neat stack, had just been delivered to the Brownsville post office. Right beneath an article about Al Capone appeared the face identified as "Elbert Williams." The account read, "whose body was found in the Loosahatchie River on June 23 at Brownsville, Tenn., after he had been threatened for heading a campaign seeking voting rights for Negroes in that town." It continued with, "Numerous other residents, many businessmen, were subsequently driven out of town by mob threats because they had sought to register as voters." The article concluded by noting that "Williams was a local official of the National Association for the Advancement of Colored People."[25]

"Reign of Terror Follows Tennessee Lynchings," the large headline read. The second front-page article, with a Memphis byline, said, "The little rural community of Brownsville, north of here, ordinarily quiet and peaceful in its plodding way, is today in the grip of abject terror spread by mobbists who on June 16 lynched three Negro residents because they had demanded the right to vote in the coming election." It stated, "Nearly three weeks after the triple lynching, the stranglehold of hoodlums here and in several adjoining communities is so thorough that identities of only one of the victims, Elbert Williams, 33, had been determined, this despite a pending probe by the Federal Bureau of Investigation." The article had misstated the date of Williams's lynching, but the date given was apparently correct for the other two victims, who had both been "riddled with bullets." One was found in a field two miles south of Brownsville, while the other was discovered in the woods near the spot where Williams was thrown in the river. Efforts of local authorities had not produced a "semblance of a clue" as to the persons guilty of the murders. It pointed out that "T. J. Hunter, sheriff-elect of Haywood County and who is in charge of the investigation, was identified as leader of the mob." A grand jury investigation had been promised, and the NAACP chief was flying from New York to investigate the mob assaults.[26]

Eldred Taylor, Uncle Tom's youngest boy, picked up the copies of the *Chicago Defender* every week. He came to the post office as usual, this time to pick up the July 6 edition. From where he was standing, he could see Elbert Williams's picture, and he did not want to believe his eyes. After he received the news about Williams's lynching, he decided he would write a letter telling what happened and send it to the newspaper. He had no idea the newspaper would write about the lynching on the front page. The white man at the post office had seen the picture, too, and he was visibly angry. He refused to give Eldred the newspapers.

The next thing Uncle Tom and Aunt Prissy knew, white men were following Eldred and Vernal home. This was not the first time they had encountered problems with the local whites. There was the time when Lewis was visiting from school. He was attending Lane College at the time, and he hit a white boy while walking home. During the night, the Klan came to the house and went into the boys' room while they were sleeping. The men shook each of the boys, saying "Lewis, Lewis, Lewis." The men did not know that Aunt Prissy had already sent Lewis back to school because she was afraid he would be lynched. Then she heard about the white men picking up Clarence. A black woman who cooked for a white man in town heard him talking, and she told Aunt Nancy to tell Clarence that he should get out of town. Aunt Prissy pleaded with him to leave, and at her urging Clarence left Brownsville before the lynchings started. Since Leonard and Meedie had already left, Eldred and Vernal were the only two remaining at home.

When Leonard left home, Eldred and Vernal, who were quite young at the time, packed two little boxes because they wanted to follow their older brother. They walked as far as the front gate, but they did not know which way Leonard had gone. So they stood there and looked up and down the road. Now they were being sent away to be kept alive. Aunt Prissy packed up the two youngest boys and sent them to Michigan to stay with their Uncle Dempsy. Like other blacks, she knew that whites who lynched liked to do their dirty work and then pretend it never happened. National attention focused on lynchings usually made a lot of whites angry. Many had heard about the race riot that broke out in Texas in July 1919 after a Negro school teacher sent a release to the *Chicago Defender* saying a colored person was lynched the previous month. Most local people were unaware of all the NAACP efforts. But the attention on Brownsville was just beginning.

On June 24, 1940, representatives from the NAACP held a conference with Buster Walker, O. John Rogge, and Schweinhaut of the Department of Justice concerning "Rev. Walker's being run out of Brownsville by a mob."[27] A few days later, Walter White, secretary for the NAACP, traveled to Memphis to confer with William McClanahan, U.S. attorney for the western district of Tennessee, about the case. McClanahan promised an FBI investigation and said the FBI report would be forwarded to Mr. Rogge.[28] On July 1, Walter White wrote Rogge, providing information he had personally gathered and which he suggested should be considered along with the FBI report. White stated that it appeared "there is no doubt of violation by Tip Hunter and others," who he named in a letter sent to McClanahan. He urged the Department of Justice to "act with promptness and vigor," not only to "protect innocent people and punish" those responsible for the lynchings, "but also because failure of the Department to act may encourage similar disorder in other places."[29]

On July 1, Walter White wrote to Franklin Roosevelt about the lynching of Elbert Williams at Brownsville, Tennessee. The NAACP had obviously decided to use this case to assist in the passage of the antilynching bill. White told the president that "at least seven other reputable Negro citizens" had been driven from their homes "by a lynching mob" because they sought to exercise their "constitutional right to qualify and register to vote in the presidential election of next November." He said that on return from investigating this lynching, he found a letter from the majority leader of the Senate stating he would not make any effort to get a vote on the bill. White suggested to the president that he "specifically request" the majority leader to bring the bill to a vote. Reminding the president of the mob violence that "disgraced America" following the last war, he said no measure pending before Congress was more important, and he appealed to him to "publicly and uncompromisingly insist on action by the Senate on the Anti-Lynching Bill."[30]

July 15, 1940, Walter White sent John Rogge a letter that he received from Irma Newbern, secretary of the Brownsville branch of the NAACP. In her letter, Mrs. Newbern asked that no mail be sent to her pertaining to the NAACP "due to this terrible uproar we're undergoing," and because she had been told the mail was being opened. She advised that all the officers "of this Branch have gone. Some were forced to leave and others fled due to fear of bodily harm. I being a lady is the reason why I guess they didn't get me." She explained that she was "on the spot and afraid to stay at my home at night" and was "almost scared to death." Mrs. Newbern and her husband were "on the verge of moving" because her family was in danger and they were being "threatened and watched" constantly. She asked that the organization "leave no stone unturned in their investigation."[31]

On July 19, Roy Wilkins, assistant secretary of the NAACP, telegraphed President Roosevelt asking him to "safeguard the citizenship rights of American Negroes in Brownsville." Wilkins advised that "the entire population of Brownsville has been terrorized by mobs which have extended their threats to neighboring communities believed to be sheltering exiles from Brownsville." He "urged that the issue is much greater" than the lynching of Elbert Williams. He mentioned Elisha Davis, the father of seven children, who did not dare return home or accept employment in neighboring cities because of threats from local whites. "Because this Brownsville situation involves lynching and the right to vote for president of the United States," the NAACP found it "imperative that every effort be exerted to wipe out this lawlessness at once."[32]

On August 16, John Rogge acknowledged receipt of the telegram, which the president had referred to him. He asserted that the FBI and the U.S. attorney at Memphis had been requested to act as promptly as possible in obtaining evidence of violations of federal law.[33] By this time, the deadline was approaching in Brownsville for the payment of the poll tax to vote in the November election. As a matter of caution, Walter White wired Rogge on September 3, informing him that several of Brownsville Negro citizens would attempt to pay poll taxes and register to vote on September 4 and 5. He urged that FBI agents be instructed to take all necessary steps to prevent a violation of the federal constitution.[34] One week later, Rogge informed White that, based on his communication with U.S. Attorney McClanahan of Memphis, all Negroes who attempted to register were allowed to do so in a lawful manner, and that there were no violations.[35]

The people in Haywood County knew the information received by the Justice Department was incorrect. The truth was Negroes had not been allowed to register at Brownsville. They advised the NAACP that only one Negro had even showed up and attempted to vote. Other Negroes did not go and vote because they were threatened. Local people took the threats seriously. There was nothing to deter whites from making good on their threats when they were not punished for carrying them out. They knew the grand jury investigation into the recent lynchings had been a travesty of justice. The grand jury foreman reported to Judge Bond that "the jury has made a careful and earnest investigation, examining people from all walks of life, including relatives of Williams, and no evidence has been brought out that might place suspicion on anyone as having a part in the case."[36] They reached this finding despite affidavits from Elisha Davis and Annie Williams identifying several members of the mob. Since all the black men picked up and released by the mob identified the same people, everyone was certain that the men who picked up Elisha were the same ones that had done the lynchings.

The campaign for justice in the case of Elbert Williams and the others continued. Local people were aware that some former members of the Brownsville branch of the NAACP, such as Buster Walker and Elisha Davis, kept in contact with the New York office, almost pleading that some action be taken against the mob. News trickled down about efforts of the national organization: On October 29, 1940, the NAACP sent another letter to John Rogge, which said we "once again strongly urge the Department of Justice to act effectively in this particular case." It said the failure of the department and the state of Tennessee to act "permits the members of the mob to circulate in the community and this in itself is a determent to Negro citizens in Brownsville who wish to exercise their Constitutional right to vote on next Tuesday in the Presidential election." It further charged that the failure to act "deprives Negro citizens of Brownsville" of the "right of protection in the exercise of the rights guaranteed them by the United States Constitution."[37] The letter was signed by the NAACP special counsel, Thurgood Marshall.

As lifelong residents of the county, Tonnie and Opal had little reason to have faith in the system. It was much easier to believe the minister who preached on Sunday that "vengeance is mine, said the Lord." He told them they need not worry about the law doing something for what the white man did to Dick Williams. The Lord had something in store for the mob, and He would administer justice in His own time. The people believed the message, and nothing much changed. Everyday life was still the same routine. Sunday morning they went to church; during the week they worked in the fields; and on Saturday they went uptown to do their trading.

One Saturday, Tonnie was in Tamm's Store when the subject of Dick Williams came up. Over the years, Tonnie had developed the habit of striking up a conversation with the local merchants with whom he did business. Brownsville had a large Jewish population, and they usually talked openly about what was going on around town. It had been five months since the lynching, and people were still talking. Tonnie had heard all the different rumors throughout the community, but he wanted to see if he could learn what others were saying about why Dick Williams was killed. Since he had been doing business with the Tamms for so long, he did not think twice about asking Mr. Nathan Tamm what had happened. Nathan Tamm was the oldest of the Tamm brothers in town. He was straight and tall, and Opal always said he "carried himself like he thought he was important." Responding to Tonnie's question, Mr. Tamm commented, "Ah, we told them just to shake 'em up and scare 'em a little. We didn't tell 'em to kill anybody. We didn't mean for them to kill anybody." Tonnie thought it was an interesting comment coming from a Jew, since the Klan hated them as much as they did black people.

Most blacks knew the town's rich had a practice of having poor whites do their dirty work. They also knew that the rich white folks always wanted to know what was going on with black people. They had heard talk of when whites use to hold "Murphy Meetings" to "keep informed of the activities of colored people." Tonnie figured out that the rich whites thought that as long as they could keep their hands clean, they were different from the mob. And the poor whites, by using violence to keep Negroes in their place, exercised a power that society otherwise denied them. Tonnie thought of the mob as he did the pack of dogs rich white folks turn loose at fox hunts. Once the dogs get the scent of their prey and the chase is in full throttle, they can't be stopped. In the end, when the hunted is captured, is it the pack of dogs that is responsible for the kill?

It was after five o'clock by the time Tonnie finished his shopping for the week and pulled out of the "hitch yard." Tonnie had picked up Grandpa Jim before coming to town, so the two of them sat on the plank seat while Jim Howell, Aaron, and Lawrence were squatting down playing in the back of the wagon. In the wagon following behind Tonnie was Mr. Judge Walker and his wife, "Miss" Anna, who was one of Willow Grove Church members. They made their way slowly around the square, filled with wagonloads of people like it was every Saturday. This was the one day of the week that all the black people came to town. They then turned on East Main Street, which a short distance out of town becomes Jackson Highway. The days had already gotten short and night was falling before they were out of the city limits. Tonnie had not meant to stay in town this late.

Mr. Jimmie Joe Morris lived east of town, just beyond Springfield Road. As night fell he stood with his two hands admiring his new car. Mr. Jimmie Joe was foreman of the road hands in Brownsville. He had a reputation for being one of the meanest and the "most cussin' man" some blacks said they had ever seen. He was a brother-in-law of Mr. Guy Harrell, who was in charge of the County Farm, and whose reputation was equally as bad or worse. Mr. Guy Harrell was said to have shot and killed a black man at the County Farm, telling other workers to bury him. He said, "Y'all go on, get him to hell while he's still hot." While Mr. Jimmie Joe was known to have beaten some blacks, everybody talked more about how he was always cursing them. This evening he had his two hired hands, Booker Duckworth and Totty Mathes, with him when he left to test drive his new car. As he turned on Jackson Highway, heading toward town, he said, "Let's see what this damn sister can do."

Tonnie and the others had been riding for about five miles, and they only had another mile to go before reaching their turn when they saw the headlights coming. Almost simultaneously, they heard the roar of a car motor approaching from behind. It happened so suddenly no one had a chance to do anything. The cars met head on, right beside both wagons. Tonnie was frantically beating his mules and yelling for them to "get up, get up." He tried to turn so he could get his wagon off the road. In the wagon behind him, Miss Anna had commenced to praying and screaming. She was yelling, "Oh, Mr. Jim, Mr. Jim, don't y'all leave us, Mr. Jim." The whole time Grandpa Jim was saying, "Go on, Tinnie. Go on Tinnie." Miss Anna called on the Lord a few more times, then went back to calling Grandpa Jim, screaming, "Wait, Mr. Jim. Wait, Mr. Jim." Tonnie had his mules going as fast as two mules could go while pulling a wagonload of people. He did not make it to his turn, but he found a little narrow dirt road and pulled off.

Tonnie and Mr. Judge Walker had not tied a lantern to the back of their wagons like they were supposed to do. The driver of the car coming up behind them did not see the wagons until it was too late. The car hit the back end of the Walker wagon before it veered into the other lane and struck the oncoming vehicle. The force of the impact was so great, Tonnie later told Opal, that when they hit, "the two cars reared up in the air like two horses." Tonnie said he heard Miss Anna pleading, but he was thinking of the possible repercussions for not having a taillight. He could see both drivers were white, and he did not want his wagon to be anywhere around when the law came to investigate the accident.

Tonnie and Grandpa Jim walked back to the site and found the left rear wheel of the other wagon lying in the road, but no one in the wagon was hurt. The people trapped in the wreckage were not as fortunate. The two cars, now one pile of crumpled metal and steel, held the mangled bodies. Steam, spewing from the engines, made a hissing sound as it escaped into the night. They recognized Mr. Jimmie and the black men in the car with him. Totty Mathes was a faithful member of Willow Grove Church. Booker Duckworth had family that attended the church, although he did not come much himself. Booker was dead and the other two men were in bad shape. The man driving the other car, who they did not know, appeared to be seriously injured, but he was still alive.

The first ambulance finally arrive on the scene, and the workers immediately got busy taking care of Mr. Jimmie Joe and the other white man. Totty Mathes was "all broken up" and was in terrible pain. He pleaded with the ambulance driver not to leave him. The driver left Mathes there and took the white men to the hospital first. As they were loading Mr. Jimmy Joe into the ambulance, he said, "My breath is leaving me." Grandpa Jim overheard him and muttered to Tonnie, "I reckon he won't be cussin' no more." Mr. Jimmy Joe died before the ambulance could reach town.

In the November 8, 1940, edition of the *States-Graphic*, there was a large picture of the president with the headline "Democratic Standard Bearers Carries 38 of 48 States." Roosevelt was "swept into office for another four years." He had received 449 electoral votes, while his opponent, Wendell Wilkie, received only 82. Tennessee added its eleven electoral votes to the "Solid South" vote for the Democrats.[38] There was, of course, no mention of the fact that despite the efforts of blacks to register and vote in Haywood County, they were not allowed to vote in the presidential election. As usual, by the time the local newspaper came out, everyone had already heard the election results. But along with the election news, there was one long front-page article that Opal thought made for interesting reading.

The report on the death of Jimmie Joe Morris said, "On November 2 this great tragedy shocked the entire county and took the life of one of Haywood county's most beloved citizens. We cannot understand, we only wonder why he met with such cruel fate." It continued by saying, "Jimmie Joe's religion was the kind that God said 'was the greatest' and upon which all the laws of the prophets hang—love." The article went on to talk about him always having a smile and a word for "every creed and every race," and said "they were his friends." It added that probably "no man in

Haywood county will be more missed." Jimmie Joe was "perfect in love," it read, and also mentioned that he had lost his life in a car crash. Appended, as if an afterthought, it said, "An occupant of the car with Mr. Morris died of injuries." As for the cause of the accident, the writer said the driver of the other car, en route to Jackson, "was attempting to pass a wagon" when the cars collided head on.³⁹

Opal did not know for sure if Mr. Jimmie Joe was part of the mob, but she had heard from others that he had mistreated his share of black people. Some of the Negroes in town were beginning to wonder if a higher justice had been ordered. People were reporting different things that had happened to some of the mob members and their families. Someone said the young son of Spence Dupree was paralyzed and in a wheelchair, and that something had happened to the children of some of the others. Tonnie told Opal about an accident that involved a white man who was known to be one of the mob. The man was driving his tractor up Bells Highway, pulling a trailer loaded with a bale of cotton. He said a car traveling in the same direction came up behind the man at a high rate of speed, hit the trailer, knocked it over on the tractor, decapitating the man. When the man's wife was told about the accident, she went running through the house crying and screaming, "I done told him not to be messing with them niggers. I told him not to be messing with them niggers."

On Sunday, December 7, 1941, Opal was listening to gospel singing on the radio when regular programming was interrupted with the announcement that Japan had bombed Pearl Harbor. The Japanese sank eighteen ships and killed or wounded close to four thousand people. The next day, President Roosevelt signed the Joint Resolution of Congress declaring that a state of war existed between the imperial government of Japan and the government and the people of the United States. As the United States was plunged into the midst of World War II, a different fight continued to be waged on behalf of the black people of Haywood County.

On December 8, before the declaration of war was signed, Thurgood Marshall traveled to Brownsville with Milmon Mitchell. Talk quickly spread about his encounter at the courthouse with Tip Hunter, sheriff of Haywood County. They said Marshall wanted an opportunity to see the sheriff. After this first stop, Marshall continued his investigation into the mob activities by going to the Haywood County Training School for Negroes, where he spoke with one of the teachers, Mr. John Outlaw. He discovered that it was Outlaw who had picked up Buster Walker and carried him to a neighboring town. Outlaw said he knew nothing about the mob except for hearsay. Marshall was looking to interview Jack Adams, who was released by the mob, but learned that Adams had left for Chicago. People told Marshall that the reason FBI agents did not gather more information was because they traveled around with Tip Hunter, who the Negroes knew to be the leader of the mob. No one provided any specific information concerning the case of Elisha Davis or the death of Elbert Williams. The next day, Marshall traveled to Chicago to meet with Jack Adams to pursue his investigation into the lynchings.[40]

Assistant Atty. Gen. Wendell Berge wrote Thurgood Marshall the following month to confirm their recent office conference concerning the Brownsville case. He stated that the Department of Justice "had decided to close its files in relation to this matter in view of the fact there did not appear to be sufficient evidence to warrant prosecution."[41] At the conference, Marshall objected to dropping the case, and he wrote back on January 30, 1942, "to again express our extreme dissatisfaction at the decision."[42]

"The reason there is no more evidence is because of the type of investigation made by the Federal Bureau of Investigation," Marshall charged. "The FBI agents sent to investigate the charges against Tip Hunter talked to Tip Hunter as soon as they reached Brownsville and took him with them on their rounds to question witnesses," he said. He pointed out, "Quite naturally, the Negroes would not 'talk' in front of Tip Hunter, who had already killed at least one Negro and run several others out of town." Berge was reminded that the "charges against Tip Hunter involved the use of force and intimidation to prevent the Negroes of Brownsville, Tennessee from exercising their right to register and vote." Marshall stated, "If no action is taken against him by the Department, the intimidation of other Negroes who want to vote will be complete." He urged that the matter be reconsidered and that it be presented to the grand jury.[43]

"Brother Thurgood," Milmon Mitchell began his February 17, 1942, letter, "I was shocked to learn that the case was closed due to lack of sufficient evidence." He added, "I don't think we shall ever have a case anymore clear-cut than this one. We shall never have a case with eight or ten eye witnesses to a lynching." Mitchell said, "I suppose we will have to dig up Elbert Williams to prove that he is dead." He concluded, "Well, I am hoping that we won't give up the fight."[44]

On March 17, Thurgood Marshall wrote Mitchell advising that although the fight continued in the Brownsville case, things were "just about at a standstill." He stated, "I have already appealed the decision of the Assistant Attorney General to the Attorney General and have received the same ruling. I still believe we are right, but they do not." Marshall concluded, "the best we can do is to keep after it with the barest possibility of getting action." He noted, "as matters stand, things look bad for this particular case."[45]

In July, still not quite ready to throw in the towel, Marshall wrote Victor Rotnem at the Department of Justice, providing information he had received from an NAACP representative in the case. He advised that the "same gang at Brownsville has killed at least two other Negroes in recent months. One Negro was found on the highway out from Brownsville where he had been beaten to death. However, this man was last seen in jail where he was serving a sentence on a drunkenness charge." The man had tried to stand up for his rights. He argued with Tip Hunter when the sheriff tried to extend his sentence after he had already served his time. Tip Hunter released the prisoner at two or three o'clock in the morning, and he was found dead on the highway the next day. The second victim, an insane patient in jail waiting for transfer to the insane asylum, "was beaten over the head with some type of blunt instrument." He died as a result of the beating. Marshall closed by quoting his source: "Well, I suppose we Negroes in this section have only our God to look to for our salvation."[46]

On September 8, 1942, Elisha Davis wrote to Thurgood Marshall saying that he was "very sorry" the attorney general did not prosecute "Tip Hunters and His Mobers." He also gave additional information, apparently thinking it would help his case. "Mr. Marshall, don't you think that we might be able to have some of these men in Brownsville prosecuted?" he asked. He then offered his assistance, saying, "I will do everything in the world I can against those Southern Pecks."[47] "I have done everything in my power to get them to reopen the case, but I regret that they will not do so," Thurgood Marshall responded. He explained, "The only thing we can do is to watch carefully in the hope that one of these days Tip Hunter will be caught in such a situation that the Department of Justice will see fit to take him out of circulation."[48]

It had been a while since Elbert Williams was lynched when Miss Willie Bell Rawls confided in Aunt Cloria that she felt guilty for a long time after hearing about the lynching. She said that she thought their celebration of Joe Louis's victory at the colored drugstore that night had made the white men across the street angry enough to go pick up Elbert. From what people had since learned, she need not have worried. The "fear campaign" was apparently much more systematic. It seem that even voting may not have been the real reason for lynching Elbert Williams and running the others out of town. Aunt Cloria was convinced that what the old Jewish man said to Boy Rawls was true: the mob had "a list of colored people who had started their own businesses." Elisha Davis and the others who were run out of town left behind land and personal property, of which whites assumed ownership. The day before he was killed, Elbert Williams had gone to Jackson and spoken with Davis about taking over the operation of his service station.[49] With Davis gone and Williams dead, whites took possession of the personal items and the land. Word spread that they did the same thing to countless others. Black people said it was a shame that Elbert Williams and the other murder victims had their lives taken and the local, state, and federal government never ordered anyone to pay.

Some kept pushing for some semblance of justice for the things that were taken from the people of Brownsville. Several were relentless in their campaign, not realizing it was a system designed for them to lose. They never understood the futility of trying to effect justice for the injustices done to black people when the scales of justice were not balanced. As Langston Hughes said:

> That justice is a blind goddess
> Is a thing to which we blacks are wise.
> Her bandage hides two festering sores
> That once perhaps were eyes.[50]

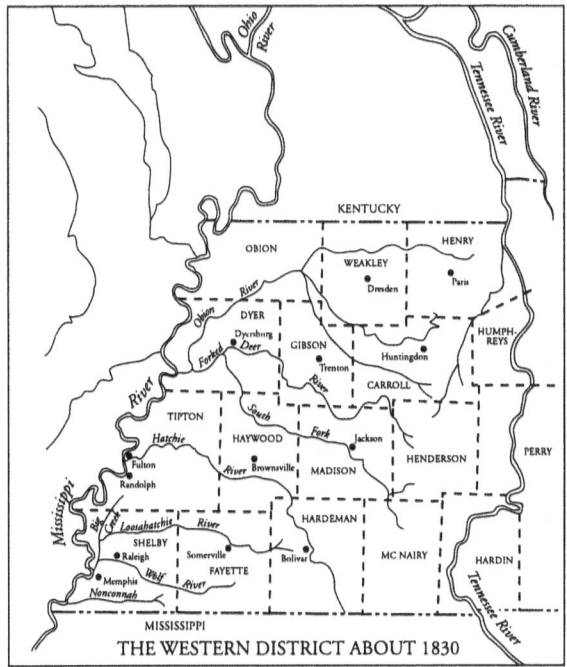

The Western District of Tennessee.

Taylor's Chapel Methodist Church, taken shortly before the church discontinued its services in 1998.

The cornerstone of Taylor's Chapel Methodist Church.

Willow Grove Baptist Church. A brick building replaced the wooden structure that burned in the 1970s.

The Kinfolks campgrounds at Tabernacle Methodist Church.

Dempsy Taylor Sr.

Jim Springfield, ca. 1945.

Ada Springfield, ca. 1945.

Jim Springfield, taken at Tonnie and Opal's home on Winfield Lane, ca. 1945.

Tonnie Springfield, ca. 1940s.

Opal Springfield, 1969.

Arizona Johnson, ca. 1940s.

Cloria and husband Reverend Baskerville, ca. 1954.

Brown and Crettie Mae Springfield, ca. 1940s.

6.

Winfield Lane

On Saturday, December 20, 1941, the country was just under two weeks into the war and Tonnie had killed two of his biggest hogs that morning. He spent the rest of the day cleaning and preparing the meat. He worked on every part of the hog, except for the one job that fell to Opal. The short winter day had grown dark. There was snow on the ground, and the air was frigid by the time Opal stepped outside and began to haul water from the well. She and the boys drew buckets of water until the two big kettles in the backyard were full. Opal cleared the snow from around the kettles and made a fire underneath to heat the water. Standing in the only snow-free spot in the yard, all bundled up from her head to her feet, Opal started the job that she considered the worst part of killing hogs. Jim Howell and Aaron each held a lantern so Opal could see to remove every little piece of straw and every dark particle from the long intestines. The children had not yet learned how to clean chitlins, so Opal worked for over two hours doing the slow, tedious job by herself.

The next morning, Tonnie was up early and getting dressed. When the boys thought it time for them to get up, too, he sent them back to bed. Then he headed out to summon the doctor because Opal was "sick." Within the hour, Dr. Thornton arrived and parked his black Ford in the front yard. A short time later, the children heard crying coming from the other room. Opal finally had another boy after four girls. The last girl, Lois, had been born the previous year on May 31. The new baby was her first child delivered by the doctor. She named the baby Clarence Allen, for her cousin Clarence Taylor.

Three days later, on Christmas Eve, Tonnie went into town to do the usual Christmas shopping. Opal stayed at home, still in bed after the birth of Clarence. All the children waited eagerly for their papa to return home, anticipating the bags of candy and big juicy oranges he always bought at Christmastime. They had been counting down the days before Christmas and talking about nothing but what Santa Claus was going to bring them. Now only one more day remained before they would have their new toys. Opal found it difficult to restrain the children because of their excitement.

Louise came over earlier in the day and cooked Christmas dinner for Opal. First Tonnie killed two chickens from the chicken coop. He grabbed the large birds by the head and swung the bodies around in a circular motion. Soon the headless chickens were jumping all over the yard until their bodies were limp. Tonnie put the hens in a foot tub of boiling water, then Jim Howell and Aaron plucked off all the feathers. Louise baked the chickens and made dressing. She also prepared the rest of the dinner for the next day. Opal was not sure how she would have managed if Louise had not been there to help.

The children heard the wagon coming down the road before it turned up the driveway. They jumped up from their seats around the fireplace in Tonnie and Opal's bedroom and ran to the front door, where they were waiting when Tonnie entered the house. Tonnie sat the sacks of groceries on the kitchen table, then he walked into the bedroom, where Opal was sitting in bed. He carried a little white stove that he had not taken the time to wrap. As he dropped the play stove on the floor, he announced to the children: "This is what Santa Claus sent you." He added, "Santa Claus said he ain't coming." The older boys, Jim Howell, Aaron, Bubba, and Salathiel did not show any emotion, and the youngest children did not understand the significance of what had happened. Lee Arthur made every effort to be brave and control the tears that began to form. But at five years, Cloria Vean could not mask her disappointment. The young child started to cry. Seeing the children so disappointed over not having a Christmas, Opal had to cry herself. Still, she said, "Tinnie is not mean spirited." She knew that he would not intentionally hurt the children. He just did not have the patience to play Santa. She also thought that he may have been concerned about spending money on toys when they were at war.

January 1942 found the country in the midst of war, and the excitement around town had been elevated a level or two. Some of the men in town got together and hung a Japanese man in effigy at the courthouse. They left it hanging there on the front courthouse lawn as a display of their hatred for

Japan. Several days later, Tonnie was in town when an airplane flew low and circled the courthouse a few times. The people suddenly scattered and started running around all over the place in a panic. Tonnie could not believe how scared some of the people got, or how quickly they hoisted a man to cut the rope to get the crudely made little creature down from the pole. The people had feared it was a Japanese plane flying over Brownsville.

The previous month, the president had cautioned citizens to be calm and not be "stampeded by rumors and gossip." He said the "way would be long and hard" and that they must be prepared for "bad news as well as good."[1] Despite the caution, reports of fierce fighting overseas frightened many of the local people. They whispered about the war and warned others to keep their lamps out, apparently thinking they could be attacked. There was a lot of talk about who would be called to fight for their country. Tonnie heard that people with children were exempt from service. He figured with his house full of children, at least he would not have to worry about going to war.

One cold February night, about a month later, Opal was trying to keep the flames from going out in the fireplace. She had awakened that morning to find snow again. There had already been four snows this season. Although it had snowed intermittently all day, there was no accumulation. She was becoming concerned that Tonnie had not returned. He did not given a reason for going out, but Opal knew it had something to do with business. She never knew what was going on with Tonnie when it came to business, because he did not talk to her about those matters. She had just jumped back under the covers when Tonnie came home with an announcement. Catching Opal completely by surprise, he said, "We're moving tomorrow."

Tonnie said Mr. Harbert Thornton owned all the land surrounding their place and he wanted their land too. Tonnie explained that if Mr. Harbert wanted, he could deny them road access. Then they would have to buy land for a road to the highway, and he did not know how much that would cost. He said he thought it was best for them to go ahead and move. Mr. Harbert had a house on fifty acres of land, and he said they could make an even swap. Tonnie told Opal that the land was located on the other side of town, and they had already agreed to trade places.

Opal understood what Tonnie was saying about the road situation, but she tried to convince him to put off moving for at least a couple of days. She needed time to pack all their things. There were all the dirty clothes and dirty diapers. She would also have to cook food to feed the men who helped them move. Tonnie had stopped by Grandpa Jim's on the way home and picked up Louise so she could help Opal get all the things together. He said the people had already moved out of the other house, and Mr. Harbert did not think it should stay vacant for too long. All he said to Opal's further pleas for him to change his mind was, "I promised Mr. Harbert we'll be out by tomorrow."

Since it looked like no amount of talking would change anything, Opal climbed out of bed and got dressed. She had the boys heat water in the kettles outside, then she carried them inside to the number three tub. While Louise was in the kitchen cooking, Opal washed one load of clothes after another: work clothes, children's clothes, and dirty diapers. Although it was the middle of the week, Opal said there was no way she was going to let the moving men see all her dirty clothes. She worked into the night washing clothes and hanging them by the fireplace to dry.

Around noon the next day, they had packed everything, rounded up all the animals, loaded the wagons and truck, and were ready to pull out of the driveway. Opal sat in the cab of Mr. Harbert's red truck, holding Clarence. The four girls squeezed between them, and they led the small caravan. Lee Arthur stood in the back of the truck watching Opal and the children through the window, while Salathiel and Bubba squatted down between boxes to shield themselves from the cold. Tonnie drove his loaded wagon behind Mr. Harbert's truck. He carried Jim Howell and Aaron with him. The rest of the movers followed them.

The wagons and the truck carried everything that Tonnie and Opal owned in the world—their furniture, clothing, dishes, and food. Opal had packed all of her Mason jars of canned fruits and vegetables, and Tonnie had cleaned out the smokehouse of the meat. They loaded one wagon with bushels of Irish potatoes, sweet potatoes, and onions. All the bales of hay and feed corn from the barn were stacked on one wagon, and another wagon carried all of Tonnie's farm tools. The hogs were loaded on a wagon that pulled the milk cow and the other cows, the baby calves, and one bull. All the chickens had been placed in two large chicken coops that were on Grandpa Jim's wagon at the end of the line.

The little two-bedroom house, with the barn that still looked almost new, stood empty. Opal thought it odd how deserted the place already looked, with almost no sign that life had been present there just minutes earlier. She was not happy about leaving her community, her church, and all her kin behind. This time they were not just moving a short distance, they were going to a completely different part of the county. No one had asked whether or not the new place was suitable to her. They rode along in silence. Opal had known Mr. Harbert since she was a child. He came to the camp meetings every year. She also knew all his brothers. Mr. Macon had died, but Dr. John Thornton and several others still lived around town. She did not really have anything to talk about with Mr. Harbert. He told her the same thing he said almost every time he saw her, that he remembered her papa and said, " You know, Howell Taylor was a real smart man." Then they fell silent again.

Opal's first thought upon arriving at the new place was that she did not like the house. It was painted a dull red and had a shiny tin roof. There were no flowers in the yard and no orchard like they had at the other house. Since they built the other house themselves, she had worked real hard to make the place look nice. She knew it would not do any good for her to complain, so she did not plan to say anything about how she felt. Opal walked slowly up the front steps and onto the big porch of her new home. The front door opened into a large hallway that ran the length of the house, separating the two bedrooms. It was big enough for a sitting area. She decided the boys should have the north bedroom, and she and Tonnie would take the large middle room that had a fireplace and adjoined the kitchen. The room was large enough to hold a second bed for the girls.

Mr. Harbert's truck arrived long before the wagons. While Opal was waiting for the movers, she decided where all the furniture would go in each room. When Tonnie and the others finally pulled in the front yard, they immediately got busy unloading the furniture and boxes and started putting everything in place. After the men finished on the inside, they all gathered around the kitchen table and Opal served them the meal Louise had prepared the night before. Once the men returned to work, Opal fed the children.

Opal thought the one good thing about the house was its location on the main road. There was a big elm tree in the front yard near the road and a hickory tree next to the front porch. They would get water from the big well behind the house, which was built with brick from the ground to about waist high. A wood crossing over the opening held a bucket with a rope. They would draw water using the handle on the side. Back beyond the well was the smokehouse, hen house, the outhouse. Still farther behind the house stood the barn in the middle of the pasture, just behind the hog pen.

On both the north and south sides of the house there was plenty of space, which Tonnie planned to use for planting his garden and crops. He decided to put his garden on the north side of the house. Down from the garden he would plant an orchard of peach and apple trees. That still left plenty of room beyond the orchard and on the south side of the house to plant fields of cotton. After they were settled in, he figured they would get used to the new place at Route 1, Box 150, Winfield Lane. Tonnie gave Opal her new address, which she wrote on a piece of paper.

One morning after they had been in the new house for a few days, Tonnie came into the kitchen, where Opal was putting on dinner, and told her that they had company. Opal found the couple standing in the hallway. He was a tall, brown-skinned, somewhat handsome man who appeared to be a little older than Tonnie. She was short, kind of chunky, and was about the same age as Opal. They introduced themselves as Ike and Mozella Rutherford. They were the first people to visit since the move, and Opal was glad to meet some of her new neighbors. She invited them into her bedroom, where they sat around the fireplace. Ike seemed like a quiet person, while Mozella did most of the talking.

Mozella said they lived about a mile up the road in the direction of town. Their house was the one way back off the road with the field in front, located right across from the turn leading to Ripley Highway. She said her brother Lonnie, who everyone called Shorty, lived with them. In the little house up on the hill across the road from them, Miss Pearl Taylor lived with her husband, Mr. Gene. On the other side of Miss Pearl's house was Miss Susie Taylor and her husband, Mr. Johnnie. Mr. Steve Jarrett lived a short distance farther up the road from Ike and Mozella. Mr. Aleck Mann and his wife, Miss Aggie, lived in the house on the right about halfway between their house and Tonnie and Opal's. She said that Mr. Aleck was quite a bit older than his wife. Charlie and Eva Fuller lived across the field to the southeast, and they had children that appeared to be the same age as Opal's. She also told them about the other neighbors who lived in the opposite direction, down below Tonnie and Opal.

Miss Irene Bond and Mr. Dorch lived down the road just before the school and the church. The school, called Oakview Elementary School, was next door to Oakview Church. Across the road from the church and up the road a short distance was Mr. Tom Bond and Miss Suzanna's house. The road behind the school led through the woods to the homes of Mr. Ed and Miss Bessie Bond and Miss Nola and Mr. Lawrence Bond. By the time Mozella and Ike left, Opal had heard about almost everyone who lived in the Oakview community. She thought Mozella was nice, and since they did not have a car, she appreciated Ike offering to take them anyplace they wanted to go in his car.

On the next Monday morning, Tonnie loaded the children in the wagon, except for Wallis, Lois, and Clarence, who were too young, and took them to register at Oakview Elementary School. About a mile down the road, they came to the little two-room schoolhouse. The children were separated depending on their grade. In one room, Miss Shelton taught the first through third grades, and in the other class room Miss Nola Bond taught the fourth through eighth grades.

Farming the new place meant lots of work for everyone. During the months when the children were not in school, the four older boys helped Tonnie in the fields. Often, even when school was in session, Jim Howell stayed home and helped around the farm. One of the first things Tonnie and his oldest boy did was put a barbwire fence around the fifty-five-acre farm. It took days to dig holes to set the posts, unroll the barbwire, and run the three-string barbwire fence around all the fields, the pasture, behind the woods, and around little creek way back behind the house.

From early spring, Tonnie and the boys busily planted cotton, corn, hay, sorghum, and all kinds of vegetables. The vegetable garden had to provide enough food to feed the family and to sell for cash. They worked in the fields all day long, beginning right after breakfast. By noontime, Opal would have dinner ready and everyone would eat and then go back to work until almost sundown. At quitting time, Opal would have supper waiting on the table. On Saturdays, Tonnie and the boys worked in the field until noon before quitting for the day. After eating dinner, Tonnie and some of the boys would go to the woods and chop down a tree. They loaded the log onto the wagon and hauled it to the house for firewood.

Jim Howell and Aaron spent most Saturday afternoons in the backyard sawing and chopping wood. They had a two-handed saw and stood on opposite sides of the raised log. Holding the wood handles tightly, they pulled the jagged blade through the log. The boys took turns pulling the blade, back and forth, back and forth, until the cut piece fell to the ground. They sawed the log into several pieces and used an ax to cut some of the pieces into small sticks. Next, they stacked the pile of sticks for the kitchen stove and the other pile of larger logs for the fireplace. The chips that flew over the yard as they chopped the wood were later gathered and used as kindling. When fall came, the boys had piled both stacks of wood almost as high as the roof of the house. During the winter months the large logs went fast. Every time one of the stacks was reduced to about half its size, Jim Howell and Aaron started sawing and chopping wood again.

By early 1943, everyone was anxious to see who would be included in the next group of young men sent off to war. No longer was the war just the fighting in Europe, Africa, and the Pacific. It had taken on a more human face. The *States-Graphic* printed the names of the Haywood County men in the war zone. The paper also ran a list of the local boys that had been inducted and those from surrounding towns, such as Stanton, Bells, Ripley, Gates, and Somerville. There was one list of "white men up for induction" and another list of "Negroes certified for military service." Jim Howell, their oldest boy, was not yet sixteen, so Opal was glad he was still too young to send to war. When she went uptown on Saturday evenings, she saw soldiers stationed at the nearby camps of Dyersburg and Paris walking the streets of Brownsville, dressed in uniform. There were prisoner of war camps and military bases now located not far from town. Busloads of black soldiers came to town for the weekend. Sometimes they helped with one of the war bond drives, but more often they came to socialize and be entertained by the locals.[2] Opal dreaded the day that one of her boys would be called to join them. She had heard that some of the boys were almost too afraid to report when they were called.

Miss Nannie Bell Leigh, the mother of Miss Willie Bell Rawls, provided lodging for the soldiers and draftees. The Haywood County Selective Service Board required the draftees to spend the night in town before their departure. These black boys, many from rural areas, traveled into town the night before they were scheduled to leave because they had to report for roll call first thing in the morning. The Selective Service Board paid Miss Nannie Bell for keeping the soldiers and the young draftees, who spent the night sleeping on cots she set up for them. Some weeks she had as many as fifteen or twenty draftees per night, making it difficult to find the space for all of them to sleep.

Most new inductees were just young boys who had never been away from home before. They were nervous, scared, and not at all eager about going off to war. By the time they were dropped off at Miss Nannie Bell's house, many were quite inebriated. They had somehow found the means of getting their hands on bootleg liquor, which they downed to calm nerves and erase fears. In the morning, their presence of mind had returned to the extent that they were able to gather what little belongings they brought with them and answer roll call. They then loaded the bus or the train leaving town.

Although they would fight the same war, the black boys and the white boys did not leave town together. Riding on segregated transportation, they left Brownsville for Tullahoma, Tennessee. Once there, they were given a physical examination and the determination was made whether they qualified for service and which branch of service they would enter. Most of the young black boys from Brownsville, like those from other parts of the country, were inducted into the Army. A much smaller number saw service in the Navy, Air Force, and Marines. Still, a large number of boys from Haywood County did not qualify to serve, and, to their relief, they were sent back home. But even those who returned to the farms contributed to the war effort by working to provide food.

In February of 1943, the message to Tonnie and all the other people on Tennessee farms was, "It will take bullets and 'pullets' to end the war." Farmers were asked to increase their poultry and egg production 15 percent over what they had produced the previous year in order for the state to shoulder its portion of the war burden. The county home demonstration agent offered a clinic at the high school to assist local farmers in building their own electric brooders to brood more chickens.[3] Since Opal always raised lots of chickens, she did not find it necessary to increase her numbers. But, she did have to order her baby chicks in advance, because they were selling before they arrived at the feed store.

The Office of Price Administration announced that on March 1 point rationing would begin. Each holder of a ration book had forty-eight points to spend on the more than two hundred food items covered under the program. Point values differed according to the scarcity of the food and the size of the can, jar, bottle, or package. Retail sales were suspended for all commercially canned, bottled, and frozen fruits and vegetables, including juices, soups, and dried fruits under the point ration system. Thereafter, Tonnie and everyone else had to use coupons to buy the rationed foods. But, they had to first complete a consumer declaration form certifying that they were authorized to receive the ration book. They were also required to disclose the number of cans of rationed food and pounds of coffee the family already owned. The notice in the bottom left corner of the form advised that users could be fined $10,000 and imprisoned for ten years if they provided false statements. The information, like most reports about rationing, appealed to housewives. However, Opal just wrote her "memorandum" for groceries and dry goods and tore out the appropriate coupon, while Tonnie did all the family shopping.

At the end of February, Tonnie took his completed form to the ration board site in town, turned in his old book, and registered for War Ration Book 2. The new book contained numbered rationing stamps for buying such items as sugar, coffee, gasoline, and an extended ration to cover shoes. Wartime demands for leather and manpower had slowed down the production of civilian shoes, plus more shoes were needed for the armed forces. Under the program, each man, woman, and child was limited to the purchase of three pairs of shoes per year. The public was cautioned to take the ration book with them when they bought shoes, and they were warned to consider carefully the kind of shoes they needed before parting with their No. 17 coupon. Tonnie bought the children just one pair of good work shoes and one pair of dress shoes for Sunday, so he never had to worry about exceeding the limit.

Tonnie did not need his gasoline stamp, since he had yet to buy his first car, but he sometimes accompanied Ike Rutherford to the Esso service station in town. While Ike filled his tank, Tonnie filled his big ten-gallon can with kerosene to use in the coal oil lamps. The station had put up a big sign that read: "We are absolutely prohibited from extending credit on any petroleum products from our retail stores. All sales must be in cash." Below the notice, it included the provisions of the Petroleum Coordinator's Order Number 4, which said: "You cannot participate either directly or indirectly in granting or accepting of credit in connection with the sale of any petroleum product through retail outlet." Tonnie made a point of always having cash when he went to buy his kerosene.

Tonnie was with Ike on one trip into town when Ike bought a tire for his car. The service station operator said he could not sell them a new tire. Tonnie didn't know what to think until the man explained that he could issue new tires only to those doing something related to the war. Due to the shortage of rubber, most of the tires that the station carried were retreads. Since rubber was no longer an available commodity, the purchase of new tires was restricted to essential drivers who in some way were involved in the maintenance, production, and distribution of the war effort. Both men listened to the service station manager talk about the shortage situation, then Tonnie helped Ike select the best retread he could find.

By summertime, people in the Oakview community were feeling the effect of the point rationing. Most were affected more by the ration of sugar than they were the limit on canned goods. Opal was glad that having a large family worked to their advantage when it came to sugar and coffee rations. They always had more than enough sugar because they had so many children. She also received extra sugar for doing home canning. They were allowed one pound of sugar for each four quarts of fruit that she canned, without surrendering stamps or points from their ration book. Opal canned a lot of fruit and made preserves and jams, for which she used the extra sugar. Starting in the spring and continuing through the summer, she put up peaches, plums, apples, boysenberries, strawberries, blackberries, and pears.

Miss Irene Bond dropped by one morning for a visit, as she often did, and she and Opal sat around and talked about the war and all the shortages. Miss Irene complained of having a headache because she had not had her coffee that morning. She said that she could not drink her coffee without sugar, and she did not have enough sugar to sweeten her coffee. She and her husband only had one son, and he was about grown, and she did not do enough canning to allow for much extra sugar. They talked about why there was a sugar shortage. Opal said she read that sugar was being used to manufacture alcohol, which was used to power the soldiers' guns. However, neither woman had the inclination nor the time to try to figure out the process.

Their talk turned to what they considered a strange request by the government. Opal said she did not understand why they were asking housewives to save waste fats. But Haywood County had a quota to reach and urged every household to save at least one tablespoon of waste fat per day. The county said the purpose of the fat salvage campaign was to provide glycerin to make anti-aircraft shells. Miss Irene said she heard stores in town had collected thousands of pounds of used fat from the people. Opal admitted that she hadn't taken time to save any grease. They talked of people using oatmeal to add to ground beef and pork, which the government suggested to stretch meat rations, but Opal did not need to; they raised their own meat. The two woman could not help with the latest request to salvage silk and nylon stockings. Since they cost about one dollar, both Miss Irene and Opal wore cotton stockings that they rolled and twisted into a knot above their kneecaps.

Miss Irene's visit gave Opal a chance to catch up on community happenings, since she did not get out the house to do much visiting herself. Every few minutes, the conversation alternated between talk about the community to discussions about the war. Opal had read that, because of the war, people were being asked not to make long-distance telephone calls. The article said a big part of the job done by Uncle Sam in this global war involved use of the telephone, so the public was asked to keep long-distance lines clear. This reminded them that the telephone company had not yet extended telephone lines to the Oakview Community, and they wondered when their area would finally get service. They speculated about when the war would end and told each other to listen for any announcement the next time the president addressed the nation. Opal did not realize until after Miss Irene left that she had not thought to offer her neighbor some sugar.

It was the last week of June and Bubba and Aaron were busy stacking their findings in a pile near the road. Jim Howell was not concerned with the search; he chose to rest instead. But for almost two hours, Bubba and Aaron walked across the fields and up and down the road collecting broken plow blades, old potbelly stoves, metal from wagon wheels, broken wash kettles, and any other pieces of cast iron they could find. This was their last opportunity to make money from the scrap pieces, since it was announced on the radio that this was the final week for the "get in the scrap iron" campaign. The announcement said "the steel mills of the nation were hungry for more scrap" to use for making battleships, airplanes, submarine chasers, locomotive engines, and all the other machines of war. Thousands of farmers across the state piled their scrap iron by the side of the road for someone to pick up. A few people ended up taking their scraps to town, but a white man in a big truck always drove up and down Winfield Lane picking up scrap iron. Bubba and Aaron figured this time their efforts should at least bring them twenty or twenty-five cents a piece, which they planned to spend at Mr. Bubber Marks' store.

Some of the other young boys in the community picked up tin cans as part of a separate wartime campaign. They walked up the dusty dirt road with their crocus sack looking for any old cans, or they collected the neighbors' discarded cans. Once they were satisfied they had found all the cans they could find for one day, they emptied the cans on the ground beside a bucket of water. Examining each can, they washed it by dipping it in the water then scraping off the labels. The boys used a pocket knife to cut a jagged circle around one end of the can. Next, placing the smaller section of the can inside the other, they stomped the can until it was almost flat. Finally, they inspected the can to make sure it was not completely flattened. This helped the detinning fluid pass through the cans at the factory. They took their cans uptown to a collection point and were paid for their labor.

Since Tonnie did not buy canned goods, his boys never collected tin cans. Although other boys, with their sack of cans, sometimes rode to town in the wagon with Tonnie on Saturday. He dropped them off at the Coca

Cola Bottling Company or Thornton Gin before taking Jim Howell, Aaron, and Bubba to Mr. Bubber Marks' store. They had strict instructions to remain there until Tonnie finished the weekly shopping and returned. Aaron and Bubba took advantage of this opportunity to spend their earnings, while Jim Howell spent the money that he got from his papa. They each bought a nickel package of Saltine crackers, several slices of hoop cheese, and spent another nickel on a big cold bottle of soda water. When their funds permitted it, they topped it off with a chocolate Moon Pie. After a week of hard work, this was a time to enjoy themselves, which they did as they watched all the black people who came to town for their weekly visit. The boys ate their snack in the back of the store, along with a lot of other men and boys, as other people filed in and out of the store. They did not dare be anywhere else when Tonnie was ready to leave.

During the last days of June, news about the war continued to come in. It was reported that U.S. casualties for the war now totaled over 87,000; of this number, some 15,000 had been killed in action or died of wounds received in battle.[4] The defensive campaign in the Philippines remained the most costly in casualties. However, everyone expected the losses for the enemy were much greater. The *States-Graphic* printed a front-page picture and brief biographical sketch for each local boy who lost his life in the war. Many were only eighteen years of age. The names of other men appeared on the list of new inductees. Though most citizens of Haywood County supported the United States' involvement in the war, they were concerned by some wartime conditions affecting their lives.

On Wednesday night, July 28, 1943, President Roosevelt delivered a major address to the American people that Opal and others were anxious to hear. He said the war against Italy would be pressed until Italy agreed to unconditional surrender. He assured the country that Mussolini and "his gang" and all the other Axis warlords would be brought to justice and punished for their "crimes against humanity." Just two days earlier, the president had signed a proclamation to the people of the United States. "Recognizing the fact that in carrying the war into enemy territory, we shall need greater amounts of money than any nation has ever asked from its citizens in history," said Roosevelt as he officially proclaimed the Third War Loan, which would be launched September 9, 1943. He urged all citizens to give their support in order to "encourage and inspire those of our husbands and fathers and sons who are under fire on a dozen fronts all over the world." Buying war bonds was an opportunity to express the extent to which all would "back the attack."⁵ Those listening for a word about when it would all be over were disappointed.

About two weeks later, on August 16, the children were running up the dusty road, hurrying home from school. When they had almost reached the house, the older ones were the first to notice the black car in the driveway near the road. They soon realized that it belonged to Dr. Thornton, because he always left his car over to the side of the driveway near the road, and he never drove close to the house. Tonnie came out of the house just as they all were rushing into the yard. Tonnie instructed Jim Howell and Aaron to take all the other children to Miss Aggie Mann's house. The younger children may have been puzzled, but the older one had figured out what was going on. Gathering up the younger children, they continued on up the road to Miss Aggie's house.

When they returned home several hours later, the children noticed the doctor's car was gone. They found Opal in bed with a new baby girl. Clarence climbed up on a chair to get a good look. The older children were not very interested in knowing there was another baby in the house, but the younger ones wanted to know her name. Opal said that she named the child Shirley Mae, after the movie star Shirley Temple. Lee Arthur, who was quite surprised to see the new addition, said he didn't even know "Mama was going to have another baby."

With the final days of 1943 coming to a close, there did not seem to be an end in sight to the war. Instead, it appeared the fighting had escalated. The local draft boards were instructed to start calling up married men and even married men with dependent children, although they were further down on the list. Young men from Haywood County continued to answer the call for service. The nation's cry of "let's all back the attack" had made the local war bond drive a success, and the point ration system was still in effect. By now, Tonnie had picked up Ration Book 4.⁶

In April 1944, the announcement came that an invasion may be near. It was beginning to look as though the course of the war might change. The reports of bombs falling on Germany said it was the greatest air blitz in history. Hitler's coastal strongholds and other installations in Germany itself underwent an onslaught of relentless bombings.⁷ However, the war was not over, and reports of bombings and fighting continued. Later that year, while the people were caught up with the war, the country held the presidential election. The Roosevelt-Truman ticket won, carrying thirty-five states, beating New York Gov. Thomas E. Dewey.

It had been over two years since Opal and her family moved, and Opal still had not adjusted to living in the new community. Over the years, she had begun to feel close to Tonnie's family, and she missed his mother, his sisters, and the rest of the family. As for her own family, Opal seldom saw Aunt Arizona, who was now married to Gilbert Johnson and was living way out in the country. She saw Aunt Cloria on the few occasions she ventured into town on Saturday. Except for the occasional trips into town and Sundays, when they went back to Willow Grove, Opal spent most of her time at home taking care of the children.

Tonnie and Ike Rutherford became friends. Ike took Tonnie to town on some Saturdays, and he and Mozella had taken Tonnie and Opal to Willow Grove a few times. Tonnie liked Ike, mainly because he could relate to his new neighbor; they both worked really hard on the farm and neither man did very much talking. Though there was one big difference between the two men. Tonnie often commented to Opal that Mozella never did any work. Ike worked in the fields and did the housework, too. He said all Mozella did was lay around all day and sleep. Opal knew what Tonnie said was partly true. She was in the backyard the other Saturday washing clothes when Ike came by to see Tonnie. "I done beat you," Ike said. "I done washed and cooked too." Ike then thought an explanation might be necessary, so he added, "You know, Wife stay sickly. Wife ain't able to do no work."

Opal thought Ike was a nice man. She knew there was no way Tonnie would ever do all the work and let her stay at the house and sleep all day. Still, Mozella was friendly whenever she came around, and it seemed she tried to be friends with everyone who lived in the community. Opal decided that she would not hold the woman's laziness against her. Tonnie, on the other hand, didn't have much time for anyone who did not believe in working. He told Opal that, sooner or later, he knew Ike was going to get tired of Mozella and her "contrary ways."

Late in the fall of 1944, Tonnie got out of bed early that morning as he always did. As he opened the back door to go outside, he yelled back to the bedroom, "Kid, come here and look." Opal, who was now used to Tonnie's nickname for her, jumped out of bed and went running to the back door, where Tonnie was standing. There in the yard where the old well had stood was a great big hole in the ground. The entire well—the bricks, the wood structure, and even the bucket—was gone. It had just caved in, leaving a very dangerous hole in the backyard. Tonnie got Jim

Howell and Aaron out of bed to help him fill the hole. It was a cold, overcast morning, so the three of them wrapped up before they began carrying and rolling logs to drop into the well.

Opal was in the kitchen getting ready to fix breakfast when she heard Tonnie's wagon leave. They had only been working for a short time, and she knew they had not finished the job. The boys came back in the house and said Miss Aggie had sent word for Tonnie to come because something had happened to Ike. Tonnie was gone for what seemed like a long time, and Opal was worried until he returned. Tonnie said that Ike had been "knocked in the head" and was lying near death in the clinic in town. He said Miss Aggie told him that Shorty had come to get her and Mr. Aleck sometime during the night to come help Ike. Mozella said some man had knocked on the door, wanting to rob them, and when Ike opened the door, the man knocked Ike in the head. Miss Aggie said Ike was suffering so badly he could hardly talk.

When Tonnie and Opal arrived at the little clinic, they were escorted to the room where Ike lay on a small cot. Ike did not look like the same man who had driven them around town, to church, to the store, and even to Grandpa Jim's house. There was a bandage around his head that was soaked through with blood. He could not speak at all, and he was making strange gurgling sounds as he labored to breathe. Tonnie removed his hat out of respect for his friend, while Opal wiped her eyes with a handkerchief. They both stood looking down at Ike, who never knew they were there. After a few minutes, Tonnie turned and abruptly walked out of the room, putting his hat back on to shield his face. The next day, Tonnie came home and told Opal that Ike had died sometime during the night.

A couple of days later, Tonnie was in Rothschild's when Mozella and Shorty came into the grocery store. Tonnie figured Shorty had brought Mozella uptown to make the funeral arrangements. She was walking up and down the aisles looking pitiful, and everyone in the store ignored her. Since Ike's death, people around town had begun to talk. They thought there was something funny about the story of an attempted robbery when there had been no sign of a robber. They knew the sheriff was also suspicious and had been in the neighborhood asking questions. As Mozella walked around the store, she suddenly collapsed on the floor. Not one person in the store approached her to see if she was all right. Since Tonnie thought she was just trying to get some sympathy, he acted as if he didn't even see her. He had no time for Mozella. He thought if she had got down on the floor by herself, she could get up by herself. After a few minutes, she got up without anyone helping her.

Sheriff Tip Hunter had already questioned Mozella and her brother twice about what happened that night. The people thought if anyone could get to the bottom of this thing, Tip Hunter could. He and his deputy had been out to the scene and searched the premises. There was a rumor spreading that he had found the murder weapon in the weeds behind Mozella and Ike's house. Opal did not want to believe that Mozella could do such a thing, although she knew that Shorty was not quite right in the head and was just like a big child. Whenever they were out together and Tonnie bought something for the children, Mozella always made sure Ike bought something for Shorty. Opal was still surprised when right after the funeral Tonnie came home somewhat excited and said, "You know, the sheriff done picked up Mozella and Shorty for killing Ike."

On January 22, 1945, about a month after their arrest, the Haywood County grand jury was convened in the case of the *State of Tennessee* v. *Mozella Rutherford and Lonnie Searcy.* The grand jurors were sworn and charged to inquire whether the two parties "unlawfully, willfully, maliciously, deliberately, premeditatedly, and feloniously did with a deadly weapon hit, strike, wound, murder, and kill in the first degree, Ike Rutherford, against the peace and dignity of the State."[8] Most of the people who lived near Mozella on Winfield Lane had been summoned as witnesses. The state called Mr. Aleck and Miss Aggie Mann, Miss Pearl and Mr. James Taylor, Miss Susie and Mr. John Taylor, Mr. Julius Tucker, Mr. Steve Jarrett, Tonnie, and a number of other people, including the funeral director, Al Rawls, and his assistant, George Lyle.

Mr. Aleck Mann testified that he and his wife were the first to arrive at Ike and Mozella's house that night. Ike was stretched out on the floor and Mozella had a cloth and was leaning over him wiping blood from his face. Mozella seemed real upset and she was "crying and carrying on," saying some man had "knocked Ike in the head." Ike kept trying to say something, and although he could barely talk, it sounded like he said, "You know you hit me." Both Mr. Aleck and Miss Aggie testified that Mozella was burning some type of rags or cloths in the heater when they arrived.

Tonnie testified and admitted that he knew Ike was seeing another woman. Not long before Ike's death, Tonnie had seen him driving his old car into town. A short distance behind Ike, he passed Mozella walking to town. Mozella appeared to be very angry and hardly acknowledged him.

He did not mention that everybody thought Mozella had gotten jealous and hit Ike on the head while he was asleep in bed. Tonnie just said he knew there was friction between them because Ike had finally gotten tired of Mozella never wanting to work.

Sheriff Tip Hunter brought out the "pea" that he said was found in the grass behind Ike's house. It was the same type of weight that Tonnie and other farmers used to weigh cotton. The sheriff said it was covered with what appeared to be dried blood when he found it, and it was believed to be the weapon used in the case. When he set the big iron ball down on the table in front of Mozella and Shorty, everyone in the courthouse watched the two for a reaction. Tonnie later told Opal that Mozella recoiled in her seat, but Shorty looked at her, then smiled and winked his eye.

"They indicted both of 'em for first degree murder," Tonnie said. By the time he got home, Tonnie felt as tired as if he had worked all day. Although he usually did not talk very much, he told Opal everything that had gone on in court. She could tell he was having a difficult time accepting what had happened to Ike. Tonnie said that one day when he drove pass Ike's house coming home, all of Ike's big killing hogs, his geese, and his chickens had gotten out and were running all over the place. Some of the hogs had even run out into the road. Ike was planning to kill the hogs about the time of his death. Tonnie said Ike had always kept his place in such good condition; it sure was a shame to see it now. Opal thought it was terrible how the family had been destroyed in such a short time.

February 1, 1945, was the trial date for Mozella and Shorty. Tonnie arrived at the courthouse early, but the courtroom was already packed. Many in the crowd were the same people who testified before the grand jury, while others were curious and wanted to see if Mozella looked guilty. The jury was sworn in and the indictment was read, charging Mozella and Shorty with first degree murder. Before the district attorney general called the first witness for the state, he announced to the court that both defendants would plead guilty to involuntary manslaughter. The jury fixed the sentences that were pronounced by the court. They sentenced Shorty to six months in the county workhouse and Mozella to one to five years in the state penitentiary, which the judge said she was to serve at the county workhouse.[9] While the whole community was left in shock, Tonnie, in his own way, mourned the loss of his friend.

On April 12, 1945, regular station programming was interrupted with a special announcement. Since the war, news bulletins had become almost common. This time the news was not about the war. At 4:35 in the afternoon, President Franklin Delano Roosevelt had died in Warm Springs, Georgia.[10] His death came less than three months after he took the oath of office for a fourth term. Only a few weeks earlier, Roosevelt had returned from the Yalta conference. He died just when many thought victory was about to be achieved. A later report said Roosevelt suffered a cerebral hemorrhage. As the news spread about Roosevelt's death, many called him one of the latest casualties of the long war. Opal and her neighbors had never heard of another time in history when an American president had died in wartime. Like most others in the country, they had come to consider FDR a good president. They joined the entire nation in mourning the death of the man who had led the nation for just over twelve years.

Approximately four months later, on Tuesday evening, August 14, 1945, the word came from the White House that everyone had been waiting to hear. President Truman announced that Japan had surrendered unconditionally to the Allies. It was a little over one week since the United States had dropped atomic bombs on Hiroshima and Nagasaki. Subsequent reporting led to many rumors and days of anxiety. Haywood County would now prepare for its boys to return home. World War II had finally come to an end.

The whistles in Brownsville were turned loose. Cotton gins in town let off steam, and whistles that normally signaled noontime to fieldworkers blew steadily. The joyous mood was contagious. People drove around the square with their horns blasting, and people paraded round and round the square yelling and cheering excitedly. All the stores in town were closed for the day. Although it was the middle of the week, people came from all over the county to celebrate world peace. The entire town was caught up in the furor.[11]

The celebration began on Tuesday with the anticipated presidential announcement. The truck announcing the Wednesday program took to the streets with a loudspeaker. People stopped what they were doing and came outside to listen. The announcer said the mayor had issued a proclamation that all churches of the city be open at 9:30 in the morning so that worshipers might gather to praise God for the defeat of the Japanese and the restoration of world peace. After the church meetings, the people were invited to gather at the courthouse for a program where there would be prayer and the mayor and soldiers would speak. Everyone was urged to come out and participate.[12] On Wednesday, August 15, 1945, the people of Haywood County joined together in celebrating the end of the war just as hundreds of thousands of others did all across the country.

Opal saw all the pictures of the celebration in the magazines. There were pictures of soldiers coming home, parades and crowds, dancing and singing in the streets, sailors in uniform carrying girls on their shoulders, and men kissing their loved ones or complete strangers. She especially liked the pictures of the celebration in Times Square. It was exciting just to see all the happy faces of the people, but it did not take long for everything to return to normal.

On Friday, the next week after the war ended, Tonnie rushed out of the house in the middle of the night to get Dr. Thornton. Upon his return the doctor immediately got busy, working by the light of the coal oil lamps. Around midnight the doctor congratulated Tonnie on having another baby. Doctor Thornton suggested they name the baby Opal, and Tonnie added the middle name. Opal Ree was born on August 24.

In early 1946, news came from the doctors that was distressing for all the family. Grandma Ada had taken ill with "rabbit fever." She became sick right after cleaning a rabbit that apparently had rabies. At first, she broke out with sores between her fingers, and they swelled badly, and she felt ill. When she did not improve, Grandpa Jim put her in the hospital down in Memphis. She was in the hospital for some time, and her condition worsened. She suffered one stroke and then another. The second stroke caused her mouth to become twisted and left her in a terrible condition. On June 7, 1946, Ada Shaw Springfield died at John Gaston Hospital in Memphis. She was fifty-nine years old.

Rawls Funeral Home brought Grandma Ada's body back to Brownsville for the funeral. The procession traveled from the funeral home on Jackson Street to East Main, then kept straight on Jackson Highway for about seven miles east of town until it reached Willow Grove Church. The church was crowded. All of Tonnie's sisters and brothers had come home for the funeral, and the people from Willow Grove community came too. The sisters, who had all grown up and married, took their mother's death hard. They spent most of the service screaming and crying. Tonnie, who had always been so close to his mother, had difficulty believing that she was gone. Grandpa Jim remained stoic through most of the service and the burial at Rosenwald Cemetery.

A few days later, Grandpa Jim was out in the field near the house chopping cotton. Ever since the funeral he had been going about his usual routine. As he worked, he thought about Grandma Ada and all their years together. This year made forty-four years that they had been married. They had started out in the little two-room log house on Willow Grove Road, which was where the older children were born. Due partly to Grandma Ada, he was able to buy their current house and land. Her father had died while working for the railroad, and she contributed part of her inheritance as a down payment on the farm. She had always been a good wife and mother, and she had always allowed him to be in charge, never wanting to disagree with him. Grandpa Jim worked on for a little while longer, then he threw his hoe down on the ground. He walked back to the house, flinging his arms and crying. His children could not recall any other time when they had witnessed Grandpa Jim show such emotion. Seems no one in the family realized until then how much he must have appreciated Grandma Ada.

Only later did anyone stop to think about the irony of the timing of Grandma Ada's death. At the funeral, four of her daughters, Meg, Vernise, Louise, and Ada, were expecting babies. The older folks in the community had a saying that whenever a person died there was always someone else born to take their place. This way life goes on.

7.

Forced Dancing

"I pushed a button and it was the proudest moment of my life," said the model in the magazine advertisement. The woman had obviously been chosen to represent the average American housewife. She smiled as she stood in the kitchen, wearing a brightly colored gingham dress with a ruffled apron tied around her waist, and described how good it felt to have the convenience of electricity in her home. Although the woman in the magazine ad was white, Opal felt she could relate to what she was saying. Opal did not exactly think of herself as being overwhelmed, but she felt mighty proud of her new lights.

Sometime close to the fall the men had started working in the community, and they continued for days. Trucks carrying men and equipment were driving up and down the road, each time leaving a long trail of dust. They had slowly worked their way down the road, setting tall poles, stringing long wires, and hammering nails. Everyone in the community had been watching the men work and waiting for them to finish each new job. In the meantime, neighbors eagerly discussed the progress. They all knew as soon as the work at one house was completed, the men would move on to the next one in line. After Miss Pearl Taylor, they went across the road to Ike and Mozella's old house, where a white family, the Forsytes, had moved in. Then it was on to the Manns and the Fullers. Finally, the day came when two men in a truck pulled into Tonnie and Opal's front yard. One of the men explained what Opal already knew. They were there to wire the house for electricity.

The younger children watched as the men ran wire from a pole to the house. The men traveled back and forth between the outdoors and inside the house all morning, banging the screen door behind them each time.

Forced Dancing

After bringing their equipment in, they climbed up the ladder to reach the ceiling. They cut holes in the wall-papered ceiling and walls and ran wire down to the floor. They moved from room to room, running wire throughout the house. Then, one man screwed a sixty-watt lightbulb into the ceiling socket in the hallway. The men had completed their work, and they moved on down the road.

Opal had been using coal oil lamps all her life. She studied by the lamps when she was a girl, and her children did the same. At night, the children took the lamps into their rooms and studied by the dim light. The glass would become smoke covered after the wick had burned for a long time, and Opal constantly rubbed and shined the chimney to get better light for the children to see to do their homework. She was constantly adding kerosene to one or more of the many lamps in every room of the house. She tried not to think of the potential danger the lamps posed. Now, after all those years of not having electricity, with just the flip of a switch, her family had bright lights. The younger children were giddy with excitement, and Opal thought the electric lights were quite remarkable. She assumed this was one of those postwar changes that she had read was the result of the New Deal and the TVA.

With the war over, there had been lots of talk about making the country better for the soldiers returning home. As a result of the war, the country's industrial growth had reached a new level. Several black boys from the Oakview community and other parts of Haywood County had fought for the freedom of all Americans. They returned home to reap the benefits of their valiant efforts. They found new technology, and the people held greater expectations for the future and hope that things would get better. They recognized, as some folks said, that progress was slow. So Tonnie, like others in Haywood County and across the country, accepted the few things that had changed.

The sound echoed across the fields as the motor kept starting and stopping. It revved up and ran for a few minutes, then the engine would abruptly die. It started and stopped. Over and over again the engine would start and run for a short period of time then stop. The men talked loudly, and their voices combined with the engine noises. A small crowd gathered. Mr. Aleck Mann, Mr. Charlie Fuller, and a few other men who had stopped by to see what was going on, had joined Tonnie down in the pasture. Jim Howell, Aaron, Bubba, Salathiel, and Lee Arthur stood a few yards back, but close enough to have a good vantage point. Even the cows stopped and stared for periods of time before they resumed chewing grass. The object of the everyone's attention was a 1946 Ford. And Tonnie was in the middle of receiving his driving lesson.

Tonnie's first car, although the previous year's model, looked almost new. He did not need much persuading to convince him to buy the car. More and more blacks who lived on the farm were driving now. He thought it was about time he had a better source of transportation for the family. The new purchase was a sleek, black two-door sedan. Everything about the car looked and felt good. But since all the cars had a standard shift, Tonnie did not know how to drive the car. Mr. Charlie Fuller had driven it home for him. Then, they drove around behind the house to the pasture, where Tonnie thought he could safely practice driving for the first time. He had some difficulty trying to maneuver his foot between the brake, the clutch, and the gas peddle. No matter how slowly he tried to raise his foot from the clutch, the car cut off every time. Tonnie continued practicing into the afternoon, but he had only been able to advance the car a few feet.

Once he finally mastered the mechanics of driving a stick shift, Tonnie's trips into town became much more frequent. Tonnie had been on the go ever since that morning in the pasture. He did not need an excuse to make trips. Even when he was not around, Tonnie made sure work got done. The boys handled almost all of the farmwork now that they were older. Tonnie stayed on the move and left the boys to work by themselves. He slowed down a little when the crops were ready for harvest.

Local people considered picking the season's first bale of cotton a major newsworthy event. The *States-Graphic* ran a front-page article giving details about the event, as it did every year. The paper told the farmer's name who picked the cotton. If he lived on someone else's land, it mentioned the owner of the farm where the bale was picked. The article named the cotton gin in town that processed the bale, including how much the bale weighed. The paper also informed readers of the condition of the years' cotton crop. Farmers knew that boll weevil and drought affected their cotton production. Still, each year they waited for an official prediction of how Haywood County farmers expected to fare with their cotton crops that fall. But other locals paid attention, too, because the amount of cotton produced for the year affected not just the farmers but also every merchant in town. By the time fall arrived, farmers all across the county were busy with the crop harvest. This was the one time of year, more than any other, when farmers realized the benefit of their labor. Tonnie and the boys picked their first bale of cotton for the year sometime in late August.

Before sunrise, Tonnie brought an armload of wood into the kitchen. A while back, he had built a new room for the kitchen, at the end of the hallway. As the family continued to grow, he decided they needed to make another bedroom from the room originally used for the kitchen. Now, all the girls shared the room at one end of the house and the boys occupied the room at the other end. Tonnie had planned where and how the room would be built, and he also added a large back porch off from the kitchen. He was pleased with how it turned out. On this morning, he tended his job of starting a fire in the stove for Opal, then he called out, "Okay Kid, get up. Kid, it's time to get breakfast ready."

Tonnie's daily call to Opal stirred her out of bed, although most of the time she was already lying there wide awake. She was still nursing the baby. Betty Ray had been born last December 15 and was now nine months. Opal had named her after Uncle Dempsy's wife, Betty, and their daughter, Mattie Ray. Laying the sleeping baby in the center of the bed, the very first thing Opal did before she started the day was get down on her knees and pray. Then, every morning, without fail, Opal made biscuits from scratch. She sifted together the flour, salt, and Clabber Girl baking powder, then she added milk and lard. After mixing the ingredients with her hands, she turned the dough onto the counter that had been sprinkled with flour. With the white mixture stuck to her fingers, she kneaded the dough before pressing it flat with her rolling pin. On some mornings, she fried the large piece of dough in a skillet and made hoecake. This time, she used the round tin cutter to cut out the biscuits and placed them on a long black pan, which she slid into the oven. She took fresh eggs from the hen house, beat them in a bowl, and poured them into a skillet. Grease popped over the stove from the sausage frying in another pan. When everything was almost done, one of the children set the table for breakfast. Tonnie called the others to get out of bed, get dressed, and come eat, so they could go to the field. He took his seat at the head of the table, and when they were all seated, he blessed the food. Then Opal and each of the children said their Bible verses.

There was not much conversation during breakfast, although the children were usually the source of any talking that went on at meals. Most of the time, Tonnie just sat and ate and never said much. He had a very strong presence, and the others always respected his position at the table.

Opal made sure she served Tonnie first, and she always chose for him the biggest piece of any meat that she cooked. It was early and everyone was still drowsy. They all ate in virtual silence, except when someone was asked to pass a plate or bowl from one end of the table to the other. Immediately after he finished eating breakfast, Tonnie spoke for the first time since he gave the blessing. He was ready for the field and there was a lot of cotton that had to be picked. The children knew their papa did not believe in playing around when it came to work, so he did not have to repeat himself. "Y'all come on, get your sacks, and let's go," he said.

It was barely daybreak, and the first red and orange streaks were just appearing in the eastern sky. The rooster's crowing had started the chickens cackling and the cows mooing. The hogs had been making noises since the slop was poured in their trough, and the pigs were vying for the best place to suckle the large sow. One of the most pleasant sounds of the morning was the wrens' chirping. Enjoying the sounds required time to stop and listen; but when the children filed out of the house, they were focused on getting to the field, and they ignored the different calls of morning.

"Oh Lord," Jim Howell muttered to himself. "I can't believe I done left this here harness out in the grass again." He could see before he reached it that the harness was completely covered with wet dew. As he walked across the yard, the dew on the grass covered his own shoes and wet the cuffs of his pant legs. Jim Howell knew Tonnie would be upset if he saw his harness lying there in the grass. He knew he had better pick it up before Tonnie came out and saw it, especially since this was not the first time he had left it out. Jim Howell continued to talk under his breath, saying, "I don't feel like having Papa jump all over me this morning."

Jim Howell walked the two mules around in front of the wagon. Aaron helped as they put one mule on each side of the long tongue. With the bridle and harness on the mules, they hitched the animals to the singletree and secured them to the wagon. The tall sideboards that stayed on the wagon in the fall when they were picking cotton swayed slightly from side to side as they drove the mules to the house for everyone to get in the wagon. The other children took a few minutes to find their sacks. Some of them had used wild berries to rub their name or initials at the top of the sacks. Once they had their sacks, they climbed into the wagon and headed to the field. They had already picked the cotton in the fields near the house, so they moved on to the large field across from Oakview School, which Tonnie rented from Miss Lily White.

"All right, y'all. We here," Jim Howell called out, taking charge until Tonnie came. "Y'all grab your sacks and c'mon. Let's go." The cool wind blowing through the cracks of the wagon had finished waking everyone up by the time they traveled the mile and a half to the field. There was little reluctance in getting started for what would be at least a ten-hour day. As the children jumped down from the wagon, they placed the sacks over their heads. The sacks came in short and long versions. The boys used the nine-foot sacks and the girls used the seven-foot sacks. Whoever invented the cotton sack designed it perfectly. A long strap goes around the neck, and the opening on the front, the side away from the body, is about even with where the fingers naturally fall. What look like hundreds of little raised leather beads cover the underside of the sack and drag against the ground. When the sack hangs just right, the user doesn't have to think about the fit while concentrating on the work.

Eight children, five boys and three girls, spread across the field. Each one stood between two rows of cotton and picked from both rows. The long-sleeved shirts protected their arms, but that was little comfort for the girls, whose skirts did not cover their bare legs. The cotton stalks scratched their legs and at times dug deep enough into the skin to draw blood. With their heads down, they pulled the cotton from the bows and stuffed it into their sack, never looking back to see if it fell into the open space. Every so often, the distribution of the load forced the crew to stop and shake their cotton to the bottom of their sacks. If the sacks were almost full, shaking did no good, so the girls put one foot in the sack and pushed against the cotton as hard as they could. They continued packing their sacks until Jim Howell called, "Okay, y'all. Time to go weigh this cotton up."

One by one, the boys weighed each sack. Jim Howell slipped the metal ring on the end of each sack over the hook on the scales. Then, he raised the other end of the sack, folded it up, and wrapped the strap around the hook. Jim Howell, Aaron, Bubba, and Salathiel each picked huge amounts of cotton. However, Aaron could beat all the others. Two boys had to wrestle with his sack to get it on the scale. Once they weighed the sacks, they emptied the cotton into the wagon. Jim Howell hated emptying his sisters' sacks because they were packed tightly. He fussed every time he ended up with their sacks. When they finished the weighing, they walked back to the field with their empty sacks.

At exactly noon, Tonnie brought dinner to the field. Whenever the family worked away from home and there was a lot of cotton to pick, Tonnie did not waste time going back to the house for dinner. Instead, he would buy food from the store. But, this day Opal cooked. Tonnie delivered a big pot of turnip greens with pork, stewed sweet potatoes, a pan of cornbread, sugar pudding, which was cake without frosting, and a big jar of tea. They all gathered around the wagon, where they ate dinner and rested until Tonnie let them know it was time to go back to work. With the midday sun shinning high in the sky, they returned to the field and resumed picking cotton.

Within a few minutes, music filled the surrounding woods. "Oh, rock my soul in the bosom Abraham, bosom of Abraham, bosom of Abraham. Oh, rock my soul in the bosom of Abraham, oh, oh rocka my soul." Salathiel was the only one of the boys who could sing. He had a beautiful voice, and once he got started, he would go on for what seemed like hours. He would stop for brief periods of time only to get started up again. By the middle of the afternoon, he was still going strong. Listening to Salathiel sing helped pass the time and made backbreaking work a little easier to bear.

"All right, y'all, it's quitting time," Jim Howell yelled. "Let's call it a day." Picking up his sack, he let it fall over his shoulder and started for the wagon. The girls pulled theirs along, dragging them all the way to the wagon. The boys threw the sacks of cotton up on the wagon to be emptied the next morning. With Jim Howell holding the reins, the others climbed on top of the soft cushion of cotton and collapsed in utter exhaustion as they made their way home. The sunlight was quickly fading in the west by the time the mules pulled the wagon into the backyard. It was almost the end of another day. And Opal had supper waiting on the table.

For supper Opal cooked her lightest meal of the day. She served a plate of hot biscuits, which she had made from scratch for the second time that day, and cooked apples and fried thick slices of country ham. After they finished eating, the children still had chores to get done before bedtime. The boys went down to the barn and got hay and corn to feed the animals. The younger girls ran the chickens into the hen house, and the older girls heated water in the dishpan and washed and dried the dishes. Finally, everyone was through with work for one day of the cotton picking season.

The farm work did not seem too hard on Saturdays. They began the workday the same as the weekdays, climbing into the wagon for the ride to the field. This time, though, the mood was lighter and they talked on the trip down the road. The boys had plans for the evening. They arrived at the field at first light, as usual, but they all looked forward to quitting early. They lined up and went down the rows at a quicker pace. It did not take long to pack their sacks, weigh up, and head back to the field. Salathiel entertained them again with his singing, and they all watched their shadows to keep up with the time. When the sun was directly overhead and they could not see a shadow, they knew it was noon. Tonnie had already come to the field to oversee taking the bale of cotton to the gin. Shortly past noon, he signaled that it was quitting time for the day, and they all rushed to the wagon.

On the short ride home, the conversation again turned to the plans for the evening. Except for Jim Howell, the boys planned to go to the fair. The Haywood County Negro Fair was a four-day event that came to town in October. The Haywood County Fair for whites had already come and gone. Someone mentioned that the white people always held their fair in late August or early September. Aaron corrected them and pointed out that there were several years when the whites did not have a fair. Aaron was considered the smart one, always reading books and papers and even studying the dictionary. He would challenge the others to ask him a word he did not know. No matter how they tried, they could never stump him. Though he was usually right, some of the others didn't know for sure whether he was or not.

Conversation about the county fair gave Aaron an opportunity to display for his siblings his knowledge on another topic. Aaron knew that the Negro fair in Haywood County had been held continuously for over forty years, even through the Great Depression and both world wars. He also knew that Professor Jeffries, the former principal of the colored high school, and several other prominent Negro citizens in Brownsville were involved with bringing the fair to town. The fair promoted interest in agriculture and livestock, and Aaron thought the local people should be interested in something other than just the entertainment. He failed to convince his brothers, who were going to the fair for the same reasons that most of the other black people were attending. They were especially looking forward to going this year because the fair was advertised as being better than it had been in previous years. The brothers hated that they missed the opening day because of work. The fair opened with a parade that was led by the Booker T. Washington High School band from Memphis. They wanted to know if there were girls marching in the band. They were still talking about the fair when they sat down to dinner.

Opal made dinner earlier than usual so she could get ready. She had been attending the fair since she was a girl, when her teacher took her and the other students for children's day. She remembered when her boys were little and Miss Polk, their teacher at Springfield School, took them to the fair. She always thought of the time Miss Polk had the little children march in the parade dressed like different animals. She could still see Bubba stepping proudly in his pig suit with the little tail curled behind. The whole family enjoyed the fair coming to town. Opal looked forward to Tonnie taking her and the younger children again this year.

It did not take the boys long to do the chores, clean up, and change their clothes. They had finished their work in record time so they could enjoy the fair while there was still daylight left. They rode their mules as far as Miss Emma Tyus's place, on the edge of town, because Tonnie did not want them to ride his mules uptown. Then they walked the rest of the distance, cutting across the field to the fairgrounds.

Tonnie and Opal heard the ringmaster's voice and the other carnival sounds even before reaching the front gate. They paid the sixty-cent adult fee and joined the large crowd that had already gathered. Trying to maneuver their way around the people was like trying to get through a maze. Groups were congregated at every event and food stand on the ground. A man standing on a stage in front of a large tent was calling on a loudspeaker for people to come watch the show. When the music started to play and skimpily clad girls began to dance, a crowd rushed to the front of the stage. The girls danced for a brief time then disappeared back inside the tent. The man on the loudspeaker yelled out the price of admission and urged people to come in and see the show. The gimmick worked for the men standing in the long line waiting to buy a ticket.

Opal kept Tonnie with her as they moved along. Each year the fair had all kind of exhibits, and she always liked to see what was on display. A large sign painted on one booth advertised a "snake woman" and showed a creature with a woman's head and a snake's body. At another booth, a man tried to attract people to see the "two-headed sheep." There were the usual fortune-tellers with their large crystal balls. Opal figured none of it was for real, so they found the merry-go-round for the kids. Then they were on to the train. After the rides, they were ready to stop at one of the many food stands. Most of them sold the same thing: hotdogs, hamburgers, barbecue sandwiches, and cold drinks. Tonnie bought corn dogs and cotton candy for the children, and he and Opal got barbecue. Opal always loved the barbecue sandwiches the vendors sold at the fair. With food in hand, they headed for the grandstand and watched the horse races.

Forced Dancing

Salathiel and Lee Arthur were among the crowd of people gathered in a semicircle to watch the dance contest. The participants were locals, including the tall light-complexioned young man with sandy red hair who danced in the contest every year. "Red," as everyone called him, stood with his partner, a pretty brown-skinned girl with shoulder-length hair. She wore a wide flare skirt that swirled up in the air while she danced. Red had a reputation for being a really good dancer, and every time he got the chance, he demonstrated his talent. A real crowd pleaser, every year he won the contest. Once again, neither Red nor the fair disappointed those who came for a brief respite from farm work.

Jim Howell drove the wagon for a short distance then pulled on the reins for the mules to stop again. In the late fall, the temperature in west Tennessee could get quite cold. This was one of those mornings when the cold wind blew from the north right through the cornstalks. All morning they had been gathering the last of the corn, which by now had become extremely hard on the ears. Aaron, Salathiel, Lee Arthur, and Bubba helped pull the ears off the stalks and onto the wagon. When they had cleaned all the stalks in one spot, Jim Howell moved the wagon a few yards down the row. They continued to pull all the ears in a section and moved on to the next until they had gone across the large field covering acres and acres of corn. By the time they finished, their fingers were stiff and cold.

Back at the house, Jim Howell drove the wagon to the crib, a huge room about three times the size of the smokehouse. The corn stored in the crib and the bales of hay stacked high in the barn loft were used to feed the animals during the winter. As Jim Howell slowly inched the wagon close to the doors of the crib, the other boys found the pitchfork and began throwing the corn on the floor of the crib. The corn steadily piled higher and higher as they pitched more corn inside the barn. By the time all the corn was pulled from the fields, the crib was filled to capacity. On the way back to the house, they stopped at the pigpen and pitched lots of ears of corn inside the pen to feed the hogs.

Tonnie had taken five of his biggest hogs and separated them from the other hogs. He kept these five hogs in a smaller pen and gave them more food than the rest. The boys pitched corn into the smaller pen until the ground was completely covered. The hogs didn't even have to move to eat. After they had been isolated for about a month or more, they were so fat that they no longer bothered to stand up. Instead, the huge animals sat on the ground and ate the corn. Tonnie was with Grandpa Jim one time when they were talking with a white man about buying one of his hogs. The man lived out on Jackson Highway, and Grandpa Jim, referring to the hog, asked the man, "Can he walk from here all the way to my house?" Without a moment of hesitation, the man replied, "Yeah, Yeah. Shucks he can run to your house and back." He thought this was what his potential buyer wanted to hear. Grandpa Jim looked at the man and said matter-of-factly, "Well, I don't want him then." Like his papa, when Tonnie was fattening his hogs for the kill, he preferred a hog that could not do much walking around.

In the middle of December, the ground was all but frozen, and Tonnie and Charlie Fuller were out in the yard wrestling. Both men had laid their coat to the side, and they had been going at it for a few minutes trying to see who could get the best of the other. Mr. Aleck Mann and the boys stood nearby and watched. Tonnie grabbed Charlie and quickly flipped him down on the ground. Tonnie was laughing and having fun with the horseplay, and the onlookers laughed too. The boys knew one thing for sure, there were very few times that they had witnessed their papa laughing and enjoying himself. Tonnie was different from Grandpa Jim in that the two men did not share the same sense of humor. This was one of the rare occasions when he allowed himself not to take life so seriously. After Tonnie and Charlie Fuller quit kidding around, they were ready to carry on with the job for which the neighbors had come to help.

Tonnie hollered for one of the boys to open the gate to the small pen. To his surprise, the first hog that made its way out into the yard could still run. The overweight animal bolted through the gate and past everyone. With the men after him, the hog ran alongside the fence as if he knew by instinct what fate awaited. When they got around to the largest hog of all, the boys bet on how much it weighed. Mr. Aleck said he had no doubt that the hog weighed six hundred pounds. The hog was so fat that when he ran he broke his leg. He started to run again, but every time he tried to run he would break his legs. It was no trouble to capture the animal, and it was almost sad the way he looked at the men. Tonnie held on to his head while Charlie grabbed his legs. Taking the butcher knife, Tonnie cut a long slit across the hog's throat. In the past, he sometimes used his .22 caliber rifle and shot the hog before cutting, but most of the time he bypassed the shooting. The hog lay on the ground until much of the blood drained from his neck, making a trail as it ran down through the grass.

"All right, y'all. Grab that hind leg. Now put the hook through there."

Tonnie was directing the movements and giving the instructions. "Go on, pull. Keep pulling. C'mon, pull it harder." It took all the men pulling on the rope to lift the hog off the ground. They had been boiling water in the wash kettles all morning and then pouring the hot water into a big steel drum. Lee Arthur and Salathiel scooped up hot ashes and coal and dumped it into the boiling water. Now the hind end of the hog was slowly lowered into the water. After a few minutes, the hog was raised out of the water, turned around, and the other end was lowered into the water. At this point, the hind legs of the hog were placed on the metal hooks of the singletree and pulled out of the water. They pulled the rope until the large animal, its hind legs stretched apart, was hanging from the big tree in the yard.

The knives made a scraping sound as Tonnie and Charlie Fuller went over every portion of the hog, removing the fine, dirty white hairs. Dipping the hog in the hot water made the hair removal easy. Once all the hair was removed, it was time to open up the hog. They placed several large buckets nearby and proceeded to remove everything from inside the hog. Tonnie did not throw any part of the hog away, not even the tail, the feet, the brain, or the tongue. They cleaned every part for eating later.

Killing five big hogs at one time meant all-day work for everyone except the youngest children. Tonnie and his helpers carefully cut around the hams and shoulders until they were perfectly shaped, and they laid aside the strips of meat that were cut away to use for grinding sausage. Several of the children took all the fat meat, spread it out on a long makeshift table, then cut the meat into lots of small squares. They cooked the pieces in the kettle to make lard. Opal used the little crisp pieces of fat that were left after the cooking process to make cracklin' bread. She set aside the hog heads until later, when Opal cooked them and added vinegar and spices to make souse. When they finally finished with the hogs, they had shoulders, hams, and middling, and long sacks of sausage hanging all over the smokehouse. Even with a large family, they never ran out of meat before the next year.

In January 1949, after his reelection, President Harry S. Truman took the oath of office for a four-year term. At sixty-four, he astounded the political world by defeating Gov. Thomas Dewey of New York. In what had become a tradition, Opal always listened to the broadcast of the president's inauguration. The announcer said this was one of the most spectacular inaugurals in the nation's history. The address itself, however, contained no surprises and was primarily a reiteration of Truman's campaign's pledges and an appeal for support of his programs.¹ Since the Negro in Haywood County still could not vote in the elections, joining the rest of the nation listening to the inaugural ceremonies on the radio was the closest they came to any form of participation.

Some months later, Aaron made an announcement that caught the entire family by surprise. He decided for some reason that no one was quite sure of, that he was going to enlist in the military. When Tonnie and Opal found out what he was planning, they tried to talk him out of joining. There was no way Tonnie was ever going to agree to his son volunteering for the Army or any other branch of service. He may have to fight and could be killed. Aaron dismissed all the arguments against him going into the service. He had already made up his mind, and regardless of what was said, he was determined to enlist. Aaron said the country was not at war and this was his way out of Brownsville. According to his brothers, when Tonnie refused to agree to Aaron joining the service, Aaron went uptown and convinced one of Brownsville's prominent Negro citizens to sign him into the Air Force. Opal was never quite sure that was actually the way Aaron had come to enlist.

Aaron explained to his mother that some of the teachers at school had encouraged him to join the Army. His teachers recognized Aaron's ability and apparently thought he should consider the armed service as a career. Sometime during his senior year, Aaron took the test for the Army, but his scores were high enough to qualify him for the Air Force. After he expressed an interest in the Air Force, he said an officer told him that he had the option of serving in the States or going to England. Being both smart and ambitious, Aaron was excited about the prospect of traveling abroad. He said he wanted to travel and see the world that he had so far only read about. Shortly after graduating from high school, Aaron joined the Air Force and left for Liverpool, England. His leaving home signaled only the beginning of how things would eventually change.

By the following year, Bubba decided that the time had come for him to leave home as well. Since Jim Howell was a loner, Bubba and Aaron were very close. They could fight, then talk, play, and hang around together. They were as close as any two friends. When Aaron left, Bubba was in a state of depression the rest of the year. For the first time, he considered a future away from Brownsville. After they planted the crops and garden in the spring, he left for Michigan. When Bubba first arrived in Ypsilanti, he stayed with Uncle Dempsy and Aunt Betty. Like many others, his only ticket out of the South was with the help of friends and relatives already living up north.

While the boys were growing up and leaving home, there was an addition to the family. On May 3, Opal had another girl. She named the baby Dorothy Fay. Two school girls in the community who were friends of the older children sent Opal the name to use if the baby was a girl. At the same time things were changing for the family, things were about to change again locally and nationally.

In late June of 1950, America's so-called golden age came to an end when President Truman ordered forces to help defend South Korea.[2] With the beginning of the Korean War, the country was once again focused on conflict. The local paper resumed its listing of all the white and colored boys who were to take physical examinations and those who were accepted for service. Every week, the long list of names appeared in the paper as the local Selective Service Board sent letters to more and more young men. This time the names appearing in the paper were more familiar. Opal knew all her boys, with the exception of Clarence, the youngest, were at the age where they would soon get their notice. They all knew that it was just a matter of time before the letters started to come.

Six months later, Jimmie Lee, son of Tonnie's sister Cherry, got his draft call along with eighty-five other "Haywoodites" who were asked to report on February 14.[3] Opal read the names in the paper of the white men and the Negroes in the call. She did not pay any particular attention to the way the paper phrased the headings, she was more concerned with the boys included on the list. In addition to Jimmie Lee, several boys in the community were named. Charlie Fuller's boy Isaac was called, along with one of the Mann boys and two of the Tyus boys. The next list came out in March and contained the names of eighty-six young men who were drafted. This time Opal already knew one of the names that would be on the list. Salathiel had received his letter in the mail. The paper printed his name next to Brown's boy, James Edward. Salathiel was greatly relieved when, after reporting, he failed to pass the physical examination.

Tonnie breathed a sigh of relief when he learned Salathiel was not leaving. He had come to rely a lot on the boys for planting and harvesting the crops. It was the boys who had actually done most of the work over the past few years. Now he still had three of the older boys to help on the farm, but, even so, they missed the work that Aaron and Bubba had previously done. Some people in the community were buying tractors to use in farming and found the machine made their work a lot easier. Riding the tractor cut down considerably on the time necessary to cover the same number of acres using mules. Tonnie thought about the idea for a while and decided since he was short two hands, buying a tractor made sense.

Jim Howell was the only one of the boys who drove the new Ford tractor. Once Tonnie found out that Jim Howell already knew how to operate it, Tonnie turned all the cultivating, plowing, and planting over to him. Jim Howell had learned to drive a tractor while working for Mr. Coffin, who lived on Ripley Highway. When Jim Howell finished working at home for the day, Tonnie let him go to the white man's house at night to work. Even though Jim Howell had to work at night and drive the tractor with the lights on in order to see, he wanted to make his own money. Mr. Coffin paid him a few dollars at the end of every week. Tonnie also let the boys plant their own cotton crop on a few acres of land. In the fall, he gave them the money from all the bales of cotton they sold.

Cotton production for 1951 turned out better than expected. This was especially true given the grave predictions reported by the newspaper in the summer. During that time, the farmers in Haywood County and others parts of the country were experiencing a serious drought. Things looked bleak with no rain. Not only the cotton fields suffered, but also the corn and other crops and pastures that provided grazing for the animals. When the rains finally came, the prospects for the county's cotton crops made a remarkable change. The rainfalls in June could not have come at a better time. Salathiel and Lee Arthur were quite happy when Tonnie handed them the proceeds from their crop. They each had a couple hundred dollars in their pocket the next time they made the weekly Saturday trip to town.

Uptown Saturday night did not call for having a particular purpose. The event was just being in town with the crowd. By now the blacks had decided that the whites only came to town during the day, because at night they did not see any on the streets. The favorite place to hang out was the "Alley," where almost all the black people ended up sometime during the course of the evening. The Alley was actually Jackson Street, and it was not really that narrow. It was home to Rawls Funeral Home and a pool hall, and not much else. But every Saturday night, the Alley was so packed with people that you could barely navigate your way through the crowd. Most people did not feel as though they had been to town unless they went to the Alley. It was the place where they saw everyone they knew, and when

Forced Dancing

looking for someone this was where to find them. Salathiel quickly spied a young girl he wanted to talk with and disappeared. Lee Arthur was walking around town by himself when a white man passed him in a truck, and he recognized Red on the back of a truck. He figured the only reason the white man had come to town was to pick up one of his workers. Red was snapping his fingers and dancing, like he did at the fair, as the truck drove out of town.

Later, a white officer slowly drove through the streets uptown, blowing his bird whistle. Everyone knew that it meant the crowd was supposed to move along when the policeman started blowing his whistle. The crowd in the Alley quickly began to thin out. No one wanted to cross one of the white officers in Brownsville. Billy Whitten, a big, burley white police officer who was considered as mean as any of them, was known to kick black men who accidentally bumped into him while walking down the street. Blacks from Memphis, especially those with nice cars, knew not to drive through Brownsville because, even if they were driving thirty miles per hour in a forty-mile-per-hour zone, they were stopped and given a ticket for speeding. The city's reputation was immortalized in a blues song by native Sleepy John Estes, who sang: "If you hobo through Brownsville, don't be looking out. 'Cause Billy Whitten will get you and Guy Harrell will wear you out."

On one occasion when Red Hunter, a brother of Tip Hunter, was blowing his whistle for the black people to leave town, Bubba told his friends, "He's blowing it because he can't suck it." Before he could walk away, the big fat man was out of his car and walking through the crowd with his flashlight in hand, trying to get to the person who made the comment. He reached Bubba with the flashlight raised and brought it down with all the force he could, striking Bubba on his hand, which later swelled to twice its size. Bubba thought for the longest time about how he could kill the corpulent officer, but finally decided he did not want to go to jail.

This Saturday it was getting late, and any black person caught on the street after 10:30 would spend the rest of the weekend in jail. As people began leaving town, storekeepers started closing up shop. One shopkeeper got quite a shock when he went to get in his car. He had left the doors unlocked because no one bothered to lock cars in Brownsville. Since it was dark and the windows were foggy, he could not see inside the car. Only after he opened the door did he see the two Negroes in the back seat of his car. The two intruders were just as surprised when the door opened and they saw the white man standing there. Salathiel was scared to death thinking of what the white man might do. His heart was pounding like crazy as he and the girl scrambled out of the car. He thought it was his lucky night when the white man just stared at them with a shocked look and open mouth, unable to say anything. Salathiel was still excited about his close call when he finally located Lee Arthur. They were getting ready to head for home when they saw people hurrying back to the Alley. Word always spread fast when something happened. "Did you hear what happened?" someone asked. "They say Al just picked up a body," one man said. "Do you know who it suppose to be?"

Lee Arthur and Salathiel turned around and followed the crowd. George Lyle had parked the hearse on the street in front of Rawls Funeral Home. The back doors to the long van stood open, and people walked to the back of the hearse and peered in. Lee Arthur looked at the body laying there on the floor. It looked to him as though someone had picked the body up and just tossed it in the hearse. Before he looked in, he heard someone say who it was. He stared at the body with the blood stain on the front of the shirt and realized he had never heard the man's name. Even now, people just said that Red was dead. In the span of little over an hour, someone who seemed so full of life was now a body on the floor of the hearse. People were whispering about what happened, saying the white man that he worked for shot him.

Only later did everyone learn the supposed facts of what happened that night. The people in town already knew that Red worked as a field hand for a white man, Dr. Poston, who had a farm about three miles east of town. Dr. Poston hired a white man to run the place. Black people described the man as an "old po' straw boss." They heard the straw boss came to town and picked up Red that night, telling him that he needed him to do some work for Dr. Poston. He later claimed to the magistrate that Red was drunk, cursed him, and approached him with his hand in his pocket, so he picked up his twelve-gauge shotgun from the truck and shot him just above the heart. He said that it was self-defense, and another white man who was present confirmed his story. The blacks heard a different story of why Red was shot. According to those who said they knew the truth, the white man had killed him "all because of some woman he was suppose to be messing with." Most people figured regardless of which story they believed, Red was dead and nothing was done to the man who shot him. One old black woman's take on the whole thing was, "Next day,

Forced Dancing 133

ever'body act jus like ain't nothin' happen. After all the dancin' that boy use' ta do, now they wanna p'tend like he ain't never live."

"The more things change the more they stay the same," Opal had heard someone say, but she could not remember what the comment was about, although it seemed to apply to just how much things had not changed in the years since the war. Many thought the people of Brownsville had been conditioned to accept things for too long, without ever questioning the "white only" signs. It was a culture where everything was segregated, where black people still bought food at the back door of the restaurant and grown black men and women said "yes ma'am" and "yes sir" to all white people. Whites and blacks lived a separate existence, even down to the "colored news." Every single thing that was done in the town was to leave no doubt who was in charge and who was supposed to be subservient.

Opal had recently seen where both the banks in town were giving money to Carver High School to purchase typewriters for the class that trained students to work as maids. The city had said it was terrible there was a shortage of good maid service, so they wanted the Negro school to educate students to be maids. She could tell the young children were beginning to take notice of the way things were, and she knew that change would have to come with them. She listened to her children come home from school and talk about how black boys fought and died in the war, too, and how they were treated when they came back. Opal always heard the children talk, but they did not ask for her opinion, and she never joined in their conversation. She knew how much Tonnie relied on the children to help on the farm, but she understood why they wanted to leave home in search of something better.

George Lyle, the man who worked with Al Rawls, drove all the way from town to deliver the telegram. Opal could not recall having ever received a Western Union telegram before, and she did not know any reason why someone would send her one now. George Lyle read aloud from the short yellow piece of paper before handing it to her. After he had gone, she read the words again. The Air Force telegram informed her that Aaron was in the hospital. Even though they did not put it in words, she knew they were saying something was wrong with his mind.

One day a short time later, Opal and Tonnie were sitting on the porch when a new car with an official seal on the door drove up in the yard. They parked over to side of the yard, near Opal's rose bushes and forget-me-nots she had planted along the fence enclosing the garden. Two men in uniform got out of the car and walked across the hard dry dirt in the front yard. The children played in the front yard so much, there was no grass anywhere except near the road. Instead of mowing the lawn, the children broke a branch off the tree and swept the yard. The men from the Air Force made their way to the porch and spoke to Tonnie, but Opal listened to the conversation. One man was real friendly and did all the talking, while the other just stood there. She could tell they were telling Tonnie pretty much the same thing that was in the telegram. The officer said Aaron was still in England, but they would soon be bringing him back to the States. He did not explain to either Tonnie or Opal's satisfaction what had happened to Aaron to make him "sick." On behalf of the U.S. government, the men expressed their regrets before they left.

Opal and Tonnie accepted the news about Aaron, because they did not think there was anything else they could do. Still, Opal thought it odd that something like this would happen to Aaron. He was handsome and intelligent and he loved books. Of all the children, he was the one who was determined to make it in life. She had thought he was born to be somebody. When Aaron was just a young boy, an old man came by the house and watched all the children play in the yard. Before he left, the old man ran his hand over the top of Aaron's head and told Opal, "This here boy is gonna grow up to be real smart, you watch my word."

"You know, Kid," Tonnie had recently said to Opal, "they say after all these years that Elisha Davis is trying to have the law do something about that mob killing Dick Williams and taking his land." It had been over a decade, but Davis had written Thurgood Marshall again and sent him additional affidavits about the case, asking that the NAACP try to persuade the Justice Department to prosecute the sheriff and the others involved in the Elbert Williams lynching.[4] "It is now much too late to do anything about Tip Hunter and the other persons involved in this case," they wrote him back. The response continued, "as you know, the incident occurred more than ten years ago and the Statute of Limitations would probably prevent the bringing of an action at this time."[5] The letter was signed by Constance Baker Motley, assistant special counsel. "Surely it's too late for anybody to do something about it now," Opal told Tonnie. It looked to her like no one would pay for the crimes committed against Dick and the others. Elisha just had to decide whether he could accept the fact that nothing was going to be done.

Opal had heard Aaron say one time what he read about the whites bringing slaves to this country. He said the white man would go down into the ship and get an African boy or girl to bring on deck. Then they would make the child sing or dance or anything else to entertain the white people running the ship. It did not matter whether the African wanted to do it or not. The men would sometimes send for a girl whose stomach was ravaged with hunger and who was sick, and there were young girls the men had already violated in terrible ways. They just forced them to dance anyway. Sometimes they danced for hours. Aaron said some of them refused to dance and chose instead to fling themselves over the rail of the ship into the shark-infested water below. She guessed people always had a choice about whether or not to accept something, and just because they accepted it didn't mean it was what they wanted to do.

On June 20, 1952, Opal had a baby boy. Of the last nine children, there had been eight girls. She named the baby Norman. He did not have a middle name. Although he was a pretty baby, he was never healthy. Opal took care of the sick child for almost three months. In September, Norman died. There would be no more children.

# 8.

The Mourning Bench

"When God is busy working, you need to get somewhere and sit down and be still," Opal told the children. Every time it rained or stormed, she said it was God doing His work. He had been extremely busy this afternoon, because for about two hours or more sheets of rain poured down without any sign of letting up. The thunder clapped so loud it sounded as though it would shake the little wood house right off its foundation. Bolts of lightning cut zigzag patterns across the sky that seemed to come right down to the ground. The summer rains mixed with the smell of grass and earth, and the wind blew the fragrance through the screen door. "How long we gotta sit here?" one of the children whispered, having grown tired of sitting. "Until it stops raining," came the somewhat irritated reply of an older sibling. "What if it rains all day?" came another whisper.

The children got a break from fieldwork during the period between chopping cotton and picking cotton. On these days they had plenty of time to go fishing in the creek behind the house. The creek was beyond the large pasture and just before the woods. The children took a cane pole with a long string and a hook attached. The earth behind the smokehouse was rich and dark, and they used Tonnie's shovel to dig down just enough to break the earth and uncover earthworms. With their fishing pole and tin can of bait in hand, they walked through the field, which was to the left of the pasture, and on to the creek. Many times they caught enough catfish and perch for Opal to cook for supper.

Wallis, Lois, and Clarence sat on the creek bank fishing. They tapped the worms to make them stop wiggling, then they pushed the bait onto the hook. Clarence moved his line farther down the creek to get the fish

The Mourning Bench

to bite. They heard Opal's voice calling them from way off in the distance, and they could barely make out what she was saying. She stood on the back porch, looking out toward the pasture and yelling at the top of her voice, "Rain's coming. Y'all c'mon home, now. Rain's coming."

The children had made it to the house just before the rains started. Now they sat shoulder to shoulder on the floor in the hallway. With their backs against the wall and their knees drawn up under their chins, they faced Tonnie and Opal's bedroom. They were not supposed to talk, so most of the time they sat not making a sound, just listening to the rain as it fell on the roof. The tin roof amplified the steady tempo of the rain and made a soothing rhythmic sound. After a while, they were lost in thought, dreaming of faraway places and what they wanted to be when they grew up, who they would marry, how many children they would have, and where they would live. Before they knew it, they had mapped out their futures. They looked out the screen door at the dreary, overcast day with a slight golden yellow glow caused by the sun shining behind the thick gray clouds. The children waited for the rainbow that always showed up after the rain and arched across the sky.

Opal moved the chair away from her bedroom window. She did not like to be near windows when there was lightning. But, she had always liked to listen to the rain, especially at night. The sound of the rain falling on the tin roof always made it easy for her to fall asleep. Looking at the children in the hallway, she was reminded of how much the family had changed over the past three years. Half the children, all five of the older boys and the two oldest girls, had left home. She had been determined to send Sister and Cloria Vean to A & I State in Nashville for an education. Someone told Opal that before her father died, he had said that he planned to send his children to college. Since she married so young, Opal never got the chance to go, but an education for her children had always been important. She thought this was the only way to prepare them for something other than farming.

Opal never worried about her own status. She and her family were just like all their neighbors on Winfield Lane who owned their land and farmed for a living. If she had to categorize their status, she would say they were middle class. She figured that while Tonnie's income was not great, they had their home, land, and livestock; therefore, they were much better off than people who lived on the white man's place. Since the majority of people in the county were farmers, Opal considered her family about the same as almost everyone else. Other than the landowners, the only people she knew that had any status were the teachers and the preachers. Opal was convinced she had done the right thing by sending the girls to college. She wanted her children to be somebody.

Opal could not recall exactly when her strong beliefs about education were first fueled, but she did not think of herself as different from many other blacks. In fact, the value African Americans place on education has always been extraordinarily high.[1] There is deep historical and cultural belief in the efficacy of education.[2] The thirst for learning crossed the Atlantic with the African captives. Even in the dilapidated log cabins of slave quarters the desire for education was nurtured and strengthen as an integral part of the socialization patterns and kinship networks of black men and women.[3] Education has been the traditional opportunity through which black families have found their place in life. Having found it, they replicate their experience again and again through their children.[4] Opal hoped the same for her family.

The telephone in the bedroom rang, breaking the silence. Telephones had finally spread to the rural communities in Haywood County. It was part of the Southern Bell program to extend the convenience of telephone service to farm families. The telephone company had come into the Oakview community and constructed new lines by setting poles and installing cross arms. As soon as that phase was complete, the workmen began stringing wires. Company representatives called on farmers in the community to work out details with those subscribing for service. When someone came by the house to talk to her about having a telephone, Opal was as enthusiastic as all the other people. The representative explained that because it was a party line, their telephone would ring three times whenever someone called their number.

Neither Opal nor the children moved when the phone quit ringing after the second ring. The big, heavy black phone sat on a white crocheted doily on a small table against the wall. The number, 1105-W3, was printed on a round white card on the front of the telephone. Opal could not think of any time that she had needed to use the phone herself. The children were the ones always on the phone. When they were not calling someone, they spent a lot of time playing on the phone, sometimes eavesdropping on the neighbors; other times, they argued about who would get to use the phone. With the party line, they always knew what was going on with everyone else in the community. It was also how they got the news right away when there had been an emergency.

Opal remembered how excited the children were the time they learned that an ambulance was being called for the little boy down the road. Larry and his two older brothers, Charles and James, had lived with their grandmother in Miss Aggie Mann's old house after she and Mr. Aleck moved to Dyersburg, but the children were living near Oakview School when it happened. The three boys always walked down to the house to play with the children. Many times they stood around and watched while the children picked strawberries in the field near the pond, or peaches and apples from the orchard. When the boys asked for peaches, Wallis bribed Charles and James by telling them, "I'll give you some peaches if you play Hambone." Wallis and the other children would laugh as the boys sang, "Hambone, Hambone, have you heard, Papa gonna buy me a mocking bird." Slapping their thighs to a beat, they continued, "If that mocking bird don't sing, Papa gonna buy me a diamond ring. If that diamond ring don't shine, Papa gonna buy me a bottle of wine." When they finished with their performance, Wallis rewarded the boys by giving them a handful of big peaches.

Opal and the children always recalled what Larry did when he was no more than five or six years old. Larry was quiet and cute, with light brown skin, a round face, and curly hair. Some of the children were in the kitchen one day when he came by the house with his dog. Wallis and Lois had been teasing him about making a face while he was sucking on a lemon. He looked passed them, right at Betty, and said very sincerely, "Give me that little girl there. I won't let that big dog get her."

The phone started ringing every few minutes the day after the ambulance was called. The children knew something was going on. They picked up the phone to listen and soon discovered that Larry had died. People said it was locked bowels. All the children went to his funeral, and for a long time they talked about how sad it was.

In July 1956, on the first day of classes at Oakview Elementary School, the last of the children went off to school. This was the first time in almost thirty years that Opal did not have a child at home during the day. Wallis, Lois, Clarence, and Shirley rode the bus to Carver High School in town, while Dorothy followed Betty and Opal Ree as they walked down the road to the elementary school. Dorothy was such a quiet, shy child that she did not want to make friends with the other children in Miss Jeanette Glass's first grade class; instead, she wanted to follow Betty and her classmates around. Since she was in the fourth grade, Betty was now in the adjoining room, where Miss Nola Bond taught fourth through eighth grade. Dorothy did not want to be left in Miss Jeanette's class by herself, and Betty thought she was too old to have her little sister following her around everywhere. She tried to ignore her, but Dorothy would just cry, and that only got on Betty's nerves even more. A few times at recess, though, all the children enjoyed being together.

Each school day always began with the teacher having devotion. The children quickly came to order in the morning, because no one wanted to get caught disobeying the teacher. The teacher prayed, and one child read a scripture from the Bible, then they sang a song. With all the children standing, they sang: "Jesus loves me this I know, 'cause the Bible tells me so. Little ones to Him below, we are weak , but He is strong. Yes, Jesus loves me. Yes, Jesus loves me. Yes, Jesus loves me, 'cause the Bible tells me so."

The little, two-room school had changed little since the older children had attended there and found almost everyone, including the teacher, related except for them. They had to spend a portion of each day fighting just to prove they would not be bullied. The potbelly stove was still in the middle of the floor, and the teachers had arranged long tables, surrounded by chairs, throughout the room to seat the different grades. A large blackboard took up the biggest part of one wall, and Miss Nola frequently called on students to go to the board to spell and do arithmetic. Some days the school served a complete meal at lunch; on others, the children brought their lunch from home. During recess, the children played games such as the bunny hop, the hokey pokey, ticktacktoe on the black board, and board games. Opal played checkers with Mr. Lawrence Bond when he came by to see Miss Nola while the younger children played outside.

The dust flew up in the air as the children squealed with delight. One of the fourth grade boys was pushing the merry-go-round in front of the school, round and round and round. There was also a large slide and a swing set on the playground, but the merry-go-round, which had wood-slab seats with worn red paint, was the favorite of all the children. The young boy held on to the iron bar, his feet digging into the bare earth. He went faster and faster, until he was about to fall, then he jumped on the seat, holding his feet out to keep them from dragging the ground. With the dust still flying, the merry-go-round circled as the children screamed with excitement. Whenever they began to gradually slow down, the other children would take turns pushing the merry-go-round. They kept going until they were dizzy.

The children gathered in a circle on the dusty playground, their eyes closed and their hands covering their eyes. Every now and then, one of them would open an eye and peek between his fingers. Outside the circle, one child held a handkerchief as she skipped around, singing: "A tisket, a tasket, a green and yellow basket. I wrote a letter to my friend and on the way I lost it. I lost it." She skipped and sang until she had gone around the circle at least once; then, she dropped the handkerchief behind one of the unsuspecting children in the circle and took off running, trying to keep that child from tagging her. Next they played Little Sally Walker. The children remained in the circle, this time holding hands. One child squatted in the middle of the circle, and they all sang: "Little Sally Walker sittin' in a saucer; Rise Sally rise; Wipe your weeping eyes; Put your hands on your hips and let your backbone slip." The child slowly stood, placed her hands on her hips, and began to twist her hips from side to side. The other children continued to sing: "Shake it to the east; shake it to the west; shake it to the one that you love the best." The children did not stop playing until they were called back in for the afternoon.

At three o'clock, the children rushed out the door and into the road for the walk home. They started out with a big group of children leaving the school together, and the number got smaller and smaller the farther they went up the road. The first stop for some of the children was on the side of the road right across from the school, where honeysuckle grew on the edge of the field. They pulled the bloom off and sucked the sweet juice. The group would then split up, with some going down the road and most going up the road, in the direction of town. Almost half the children left the group when they got to Mr. Tom and Miss Susanna Bond's house, which was on the right side of the field and diagonal from the school. After passing the homes of the three or four other children, it was just Opal Ree, Betty, and Dorothy hurrying up the road for the rest of the way. When they came around the big curve in the road, they were almost home, and they ran the rest of the way.

Grapevines ran all along the fence row on the side of the small orchard located next to the road. The small and large orchards were adjacent to each other but were separated by a barbwire fence. The trees Tonnie planted when the family first moved there were big and tall and were producing in abundance. The big orchard had several tall apple trees, and the peach trees were loaded with peaches that grew big and yellow with a light shade of rose. The little orchard had smaller trees, and they were covered with big, dark red peaches with red meat. As the children made their last dash for home, they stopped at the fence just long enough to pick a few grapes to eat, then they sprinted across the yard and up the steps to the front porch.

While the children were at school, Opal spent a lot of time sewing clothes for the children. Sometimes the white woman up the road, Miss Kate Forsythe, came down and asked to use her sewing machine, which Opal always allowed her to do. Opal bought few readymade clothes, making all of the children's Sunday clothes and school clothes herself. While she was sewing, she listened to "Just Plain Bill" and "Stella Dallas" on the radio. When the school bus dropped the older children off at the road in front of the house, they came rushing through the screen door to get to the radio and listen to "Search for Tomorrow." They sat gathered around the radio until the soap opera went off. Opal had the meal prepared when the children got in from school, so they never had to wait for dinner. After dinner, there were always chores to do, even on schooldays.

Clarence was the only boy left at home, so chopping wood was his job. Most of the time, Lois would help him saw the logs into smaller pieces. Clarence chopped the wood for the kitchen stove then fed the hogs and gave hay to the mules. As evening approached, the girls put the chickens in the hen house to roost. One of the girls closed the door to the hen house to force the chickens through the little square opening high off the ground and closer to the roof of the building. Opal had constructed a little ladder made of sticks leading up to the opening at the front of the hen house. The chickens made their way up the ladder, through the hole, and onto the long poles running across the hen house. Once they were all on the roost for the night, the girls covered the hole to make sure the chickens could not get out.

"Boy, you better quit doing that while I'm under this here tree," Lois yelled. Apples fell down all over the ground as the children underneath the tree scrambled to get out of the way. Clarence had climbed up in the apple tree and was shaking the branches. They stood back until the apples stopped falling, then resumed filling the bushel baskets. They were gathering apples and peaches for Opal to can. In the little orchard, the younger children found the juicy red peaches to be a real treat. As they bit into the peach, the red juice ran down their dirty little fingers. With their baskets filled, Lois yelled at the younger ones, "Y'all better get outta there, it's almost night." There were lots of thick bushes along the fence in back of the orchard, where blackberries grew in the spring, and they had seen snakes out there before. As they started for the house, someone said, "You know Mama said for y'all to pick some tomatoes." Leaving the orchards, they walked through the garden on the way to the house. "Mama said get some green ones too," the little ones reminded them. This meant the next morning Opal would fix fried green tomatoes for breakfast.

Having the older girls around to help with the younger children meant Opal did not work nearly as hard as she did when she only had the boys at home. Years had passed since she last worked in the fields. Still, there was never a shortage of work to do. Opal was grateful to Tonnie for making one of her jobs a lot easier. "I was a proud soul when I didn't have to bend my back all day scrubbing clothes," Opal said. The days of scrubbing clothes on a washboard all morning, stopping to fix dinner, then going back to washing clothes all afternoon were over. She had heard everyone talking about owning a washing machine. The insurance man came by the house one day when Opal was washing clothes and said, "Why don't you get your husband to buy you a washing machine?" Opal convinced Tonnie that they needed to go shopping at the Economy stores uptown on the square. They had three big floors crowded with all kinds of merchandise. They walked around the store, looking at the different displays under long fluorescent lights. The store had recently installed a new lighting system, and businesses in town were just beginning to get air conditioning. People living in the country usually did not have this convenience, and they felt good being inside the stores, where the temperature was cool. Opal kept looking until she found exactly what she wanted. Tonnie bought her a new wringer washing machine. After that, Saturday was still wash day, but it was no longer the same.

They put the washing machine on the back porch and ran a long extension cord from the machine to the electrical outlet in the kitchen. With the agitator now doing the work, Opal was free to do other chores until the wash cycle was complete. Then she drained the water through the long black hose connected to the machine. After rinsing the clothes, she pressed the lever to set the wringer, which looked like two long rolling pins. As it began turning over and over, Opal ran the clothes through to squeeze out all the water. Although they had had the machine for a while now, the younger children still climbed up on the back porch, high off the ground, to watch the clothes washing. Sometimes they liked to stand behind the washing machine and catch the clothes, pressed flat, as they came through the wringer. They were always careful not to fall off the back porch as they climbed down the steps.

The children ran around the house, yelling, "Chunk the ball, chunk it now." With Opal Ree at the front of the house and Betty and Dorothy at the back, they played a game of "over." The object was to throw the ball over the house without the ball becoming stuck on the roof. They watched for the ball and tried to catch it before it hit the ground; then they ran around the house and tried to tag their sister. Betty and Dorothy waited impatiently, both jumping up and yelling again, "Chunk the ball, chunk the ball." When they saw the little red rubber ball come sailing through the air, they raced to catch it, but it went over their heads. Dorothy grabbed the ball, and they ran around to the front of the house to switch sides. They heard the wagon and forgot all about playing.

"Here come P-A, P-A, P-A. Here come P-A, P-A, P-A," the children sang as they ran to the road. Tonnie was coming back from town, where he had gone to sell watermelons. The children could hear the clopping sound of the mules and the rackety sound of the empty wagon on the gravel road before Tonnie was in sight. They knew their papa did shopping on Saturday, and he always brought back something good. Opal had fixed dinner in the middle of the day; but on Saturday, Tonnie always bought a package of big wieners or ground beef. For supper, Opal would fix hamburger or wiener sandwiches, with thick slices of Wonder Bread and French's mustard. The children stood waiting at the road. Tonnie did not disappoint them. After he brought in the sacks and showed Opal everything that he bought to get her approval, he took out a Baby Ruth candy bar. Tonnie reached in his pocket, found his knife, unwrapped the candy, then carefully cut it into three equal pieces. He distributed the candy to each child, giving Dorothy her piece first because, as he always said, "Dot's the baby."

On the second Sunday in August, the family attended church. No matter how much they worked and played during the week, Sundays were always different. Opal did not believe in doing any work on Sunday. She did not sew or wash clothes, and she would never dream of allowing the children to work in the fields on the day that was set aside for worship. Tonnie, Opal, and the younger children went to Willow Grove, and the rest of the children attended Oakview Church. After service was over, they came home to more gospel singing and preaching on the radio. As soon as they got in the house, Opal found the radio station WDIA out of Memphis. The Negro disc jockeys, Nat D. Williams and Ford Nelson, played music by black artists. Opal did not allow secular music played in the house on Sunday, so after church the house was filled with the voices of the Five Blind Boys, the Dixie Hummingbirds, the Soul Stirrers, the Mighty Clouds of Joy, the Caravans, Mahalia Jackson singing "How I Made It Over," and Clara Ward and the Ward Singers singing "Surely He's Able to Carry You Through."

Grandpa Jim had come home with Tonnie and Opal for dinner. Sunday dinner was always special, but even more so when they had company. One thing that Opal allowed herself to do on Sunday was cook. The house had been cleaned real good on Saturday. The weather was hot, and the black fan oscillating in the window only blew hot air. Opal had two of the children stand over the table and fan flies. When everyone was called to the kitchen table, they knew they were in for a huge meal. Grandpa Jim was the main source of conversation throughout dinner. When he finished eating, he pushed back from the table, unfolded his long legs, stretched them out, and crossed them at the ankles. Then he laced his fingers together, laid them over his stomach, and leaned back in his chair. The thick mustache he still wore was now almost completely gray. He got a twinkle in his eye, and everyone knew he was ready to start telling jokes. The children loved to hear their grandpa tell stories. He began to chuckle even before he started.

"There was an old lady who was hard of hearing," Grandpa Jim said. "The man who had just finished having dinner with her said, 'I've dined sufficiently,' but she didn't understand him." Grandpa laughed at his own story, "She said, 'you say you been to fishing?' He tried again, 'I said I got a plenty.' This time she said, 'you say you caught twenty?'" Now everyone in the room was laughing. Grandpa Jim continued, "He said, 'I'm full to the soul.' The old woman said, 'you say you broke your pole?'" By the time Grandpa Jim finished telling his jokes, the children had laughed so hard their stomachs ached.

When dinner was over, they all moved outside. The summer heat combined with the heat of the stove from Opal's cooking made it too hot to stay inside. They sat around on the front porch and under the large hickory tree in the yard, waiting for the ice cream to freeze. Opal had made a pan full of custard by cooking milk, sugar, and eggs and adding lots of vanilla flavoring, which she got from the Watkins man who sold her liniment. She let it cool before pouring it into the aluminum bucket. Lois used a pick to chip pieces from the big solid block of ice Tonnie bought from the ice man who came by the house. They brought the old hand-crank freezer and pan of ice outside, and the children alternated turning the handle to freeze the ice cream. Old Black lay quietly on the ground nearby. Tonnie had tried to get rid of the dog twice by taking him all the way across town and leaving him, but both times the dog was back in the yard the next morning. He had gotten old and was now like a member of the family. The grownups and children sat outside, savoring the afternoon and eating the homemade ice cream as it melted in the bowl and soaked the slice of caramel cake. Opal thought it did not matter how nice any other day of the week was, there was something about the Lord's day that was special. Before Grandpa Jim left, he asked, "Sis Opal, are you getting ready for the fourth Sunday?"

Later that evening, when the sun was fading in the west and the moon was a dim silhouette in the sky, the family still sat outside trying to catch a summer breeze. As always, August was hot, but the temperature at night was beginning to get a little cooler. The mosquitoes were terrible. Opal and Tonnie sat in the swing but barely moved. Every now and then she hit her arm and leg to ward off the pesky insects. Some of the children sat on the front porch and on the steps, with Old Black nearby, while the younger children ran around in the yard chasing lightning bugs. They were trying to catch them in Opal's small Mason jars, but the bugs were fast. By the time the children reached the place where they saw the light, the bug had flown away. Lights were all over the front yard. Sometimes the children got lucky and grabbed a bug before it could escape. With the bugs' tails shining on and off in their cupped hands, the children quickly transferred the bugs to the jar and fastened the lid. They were fascinated by these creatures that lit up the night, and they would sit and watch them for hours.

The fourth Sunday in August was the beginning of revival. This was the one time of the year when the whole family looked forward to attending Willow Grove Church. Opal spent several days preparing food, making sure that she cooked enough to feed the family and all the other people who would come to church. She knew that on revival Sunday family came to visit from out of town, and there would be people coming who had not been inside a church all year.

The odors from the kitchen traveled down the hallway and filled the house. As usual, Opal baked her egg custard and chocolate meringue pies. Dinner was not complete without a piece of Opal's chocolate pie. She separated several chickens earlier in the month and put them in the chicken coop. The children fed them corn to "clean them out." Opal thought her chickens tasted better than those taken right from the yard and eaten. She boiled a pork shoulder roast and fixed another standard, her coleslaw, which she made differently from most people. After finely chopping the cabbage, she added lots of mustard, turning the slaw yellow. She served the slaw with the pork roast, and it was everyone's favorite.

Finally, the day they had all been waiting for was here. Church services started at eleven o'clock, and they needed to get there on time. Opal first made sure the children were dressed. They sat on the davenport in the hallway and waited for Tonnie and Opal. They wore cotton dresses that Opal had made them for Easter. The dresses had gathered skirts and long tie belts that tied in a bow behind their back. They each had on black patent leather slippers, which were only worn on Sundays. Before getting dressed, the children broke a biscuit in half and rubbed a piece on each shoe. When they wiped the crumbs away, the shoes shined like new. Opal carefully packed the food for transportation, and Tonnie loaded the cardboard boxes into the car.

They heard the out-of-tune piano playing as they arrived at the church. Tonnie found a spot under a tree to park. The church was already crowded. On the fourth Sunday they had to get to church early if they wanted a good seat. The Willow Grove Baptist Church was a little, but long, one-room wood building. One aisle ran from the front door to the altar, separating the pews on each side of the church. Two pews at the very front of the church faced each other from against opposite walls. Tonnie and Opal always entered from the back of the church. Tonnie sat in the pew on the left side of the church, and Opal always sat in the pew on the right side. The children sat with the rest of the congregation in the pews on the right side of the aisle, facing the pulpit.

Tonnie sat with Uncle Brown, Uncle Dan, and some of the other regular churchgoers: Mr. Prentis Thomas, Mr. Clay Currie, and Mr. Daley Walker. Since Grandpa Jim was a deacon, he sat on the first bench on the left side of the church with the other deacons: Mr. Ike Walker, Mr. Buddie Pirtle, and Deacon Allen. Opal was seated with the mothers of the church. There was Miss Josie Walker, Miss Pearline Currie, Miss Minnie D. Walker, Cousin Ada "Little Sister" Averyheart, Miss Anna Walker, Aunt Lucille, and Aunt Crettie Mae.

The choir stand was full. Although Willow Grove did not have a large choir, a visiting choir had joined the regular choir for revival Sunday. They were singing "Amazing Grace," and as the preacher appeared, everyone in the church stood. "Amazing grace—how sweet the sound—that saved a wretch like me! I once was lost but now am found, was blind but now I see."

The preacher, Reverend Clay, entered from the rear left door and walked passed the deacons and up the steps to the pulpit. He was accompanied by the ministers visiting from other churches. The choir continued singing, dragging out every syllable of each word: "'Twas grace that taught my heart to fear, and grace my fears relieved; how precious did that grace appear the hour I first believed!"

When the ministers were seated, the whole congregation sat down and continued singing the third verse: "Thro' many dangers, toils and snares

I have already come; 'tis grace hath brought me safe thus far, and grace will lead me home." By the time they had reached the fourth verse, one woman in the church was shouting, and she was quickly joined by a second woman. Two ushers went to each woman and tried to restrain them from waving their arms in the air and yelling. Even after the women were calmed down, the ushers stood over them, fanning. The fans were constructed of stiff cardboard, and painted on them was a black family. A flat wood handle was stapled to the board. The ushers held the handle tightly as they fanned the women, back and forth, back and forth. After the choir and the church finished singing, one of the older deacons got down on his knees and faced the pew. Leaning over the bench, he began to pray out loud. Every time he said a few words, the church answered with "Amen."

Ushering at every service was a man with a bad limp. Opal said the limp was from a bad car wreck he was in with a white man and another black man years ago, not far from the church. The children played with the fan he gave them. Opal Ree, Betty, and Dorothy shared the fan, twirling it around and around and looking at its front and back. The Rawls Funeral Home was advertised on the back side of the fan, along with a poem. "It's up to you," the poem began, "You can do what is good or do what is bad." It said that God gave you the day and that it was up to you what you did with it. Since the poem was easy to understand, the girls read it over and over as they listened to the flapping sound of the broken fan of the woman next to them. The adults enjoyed the church service and the children endured the ritual. The choir sang another song:

> What a friend we have in Jesus, All our sins, and griefs to bear!
> What a privilege to carry Ev'rything to God in prayer!
> O what peace we often forfeit, O what needless pain we bear,
> All because we do not carry Ev'rything to God in prayer!

Opal never shouted like some women in the church, but whenever she heard this song she would open her purse, take out the little white handkerchief with the purple flower in one corner, and dab at her eyes. The children watched their mother, confused about why she was crying.

> Have we trials and temptations? Is there trouble anywhere?
> We should never be discouraged—Take it to the Lord in prayer.
> Can we find a friend so faithful? Who will all our sorrows share?
> Jesus knows our ev'ry weakness—Take it to the Lord in prayer.

The Mourning Bench

After the preaching and about the time they were ready to take up the collection, Rev. Jimmy Lewis addressed the congregation. He did not have his own church, and every year he came to Willow Grove for revival. Before the service was over he would sing one of two songs. This time, instead of singing "Before This Time Another Year," he sang, "I'm a Baptist born, and a Baptist bred. And when I die, I'll be a Baptist dead."

Fried chicken, ham, green beans, two slices of white bread, and a piece of coconut cake and chocolate pie: the people were set. It was now thirty years, over a quarter of a century, since Opal first came to Willow Grove as a young bride. Not much about revival had changed. There were a lot more people driving cars than wagons, but the fourth Sunday was still all about fellowship, family, and food. The church ground bustled with people going from one family's box to another. Those who attended revival on a regular basis knew where they could find the best food. Family members who had left Willow Grove and moved up north came back to visit on revival Sunday. Some of Tonnie's sisters returned for the occasion. Aunt Vernise came up from Memphis, and Aunt Louise and Aunt Meg came from Decatur. A. D. Springfield, who was now living in Cleveland, Ohio, was there. They visited with Tonnie and Opal, Brown and Crettie Mae, and Dan and Lucille. Grandpa Jim walked around the church ground greeting everyone. He was still the undisputed head of his clan. People still joked about the revival Sunday when Grandpa Jim closed his eyes to pray over a long table full of fixed plates. They said when he opened his eyes, he discovered people had taken all the plates, and he had the most embarrassed look on his face. The women fed the men, the women visitors, and the children before they took a break themselves. During the course of dinner on the grounds, some of the men gravitated across the street to Willow Grove School, where they were filled with a different kind of spirit. Tonnie knew that some men, like one of his cousins, brought bootleg corn whiskey to sell just for the occasion, but he did not imbibe and he never mentioned to Opal what went on before the afternoon service. Everyone laughed and talked and joked and ate.

Sunday services were just the beginning of revival services, which were scheduled for the rest of the week. While most of the people at church on revival Sunday did not participate in the rest of the services, the faithful members came back every day. For them, revival was what this was really about. Church members renewed their commitment, and young converts who professed their willingness to follow Christ were baptized.

On Monday evening, Tonnie, Opal, and the children arrived at church as the choir sang, "Savior, Savior, hear my humble cry. While on others Thou art calling, do not pass me by." Most of the people worked in the fields all day, so they drifted in and the ushers directed them to seats while the choir continued to sing. "Standing at the thorn of mercy, 'tis a sweet relief. Savior, Savior, hear my humble cry. While on others Thou art calling, do not pass me by."

A visiting preacher carried on revival for the whole week, and there were people from other churches, though not nearly as many as had come on revival Sunday. The deacons prayed and the preacher delivered his sermon. Then the preacher extended an invitation for visitors to join the church as the congregation sang: "Come to Jesus, come to Jesus, come to Jesus just now." They sang the line over and over, swaying from side to side, then continued: "He will save you, He will save you, He will save you, just now."

As the congregation sang, the preacher raised his voice above the singing and appealed to the young people. Children between the ages of eight and twelve began to get out of their seats and make their way to the mourner's bench. The singing continued: "He's able, He's able, He's able just now. Come to Jesus just now."

Some people began to moan when they finished singing the last verse, and the preacher said: "When you moan, the devil don't know what you talking about." While this was going on, the preacher instructed the young people to go get their mothers. Each child got up and found his mother, who came to the bench, kneeled, and prayed with their child. After they prayed, a couple of the young people went up and shook the preacher's hand.

Tonnie, Opal, and the children returned to church each night, and the ritual was repeated. On Thursday night, a large crowd gathered for the last night of revival. The children in the church, around eight or ten years old, sat on the first pew in front of the preacher. After the sermon, the preacher again instructed the children to get their mothers and pray with them. They got down on their knees and prayed, and some of the mothers and their children cried. Now another child got up and went to the preacher, with tears running down her face. Opal was down on her knees, crying like the others, so Betty thought she was supposed to cry too. She wondered why whatever it was that had taken place with the other children had not happened to her yet. She was not exactly sure how she would know when it did. Since this was the last night, and she knew what was expected of her, she got up and began to cry as she joined the others standing with the preacher.

The Mourning Bench

On Friday afternoon, the children stood near the front entrance of the church, waiting to be led outside. They wore white shirts and blue jeans, and the girls had towels wrapped around their heads. The only service today was for baptizing. They marched in a line to the pond in the field next to the church, singing: "Take me to the water. Take me to the water. Take me to the water to be baptized. None but the righteous, none but the righteous, none but the righteous shall see God."

The children stood in a line on the bank of the little pond. The families and the other church people stood in the grass nearby. One by one, the children waded into the dark, murky water and stood between the preacher and his assistant. With the water at her chest, pushing her shirt up, the small child tugged at her shirttail to pull it down. The preacher raised his hand, repeated the words that he said for all the others, then, placing his hand over the child's face, he dipped her backward until she was submerged in the water. The child came up gasping for air and hitting at the preacher's hand to remove it from her face. As the next child waded into the water, those on the bank began singing again: "Take me to the water, take me to the water, take me to the water to be baptized."

The children came out of the pond with their feet soaked and with water dripping from their pants, shirts, and the towels on their heads. Most of the towels had come undone, and the children's hair was wet underneath. The mothers met the children and led them to get dressed. On the ride home, they talk about revival week. Opal said, "Lord, some of them children came off that mourning bench shoutin' just like old people." She knew they were young, but she thought it was important for them to show they were willing to accept Christ. Tonnie said, "Dot, it'll be your time next to sit on the mournin' bench." The new convert, still damp, sat with the air blowing on her through the car window. She knew that the next time they had the "Lord's Supper" she didn't have to let it pass by. After hearing people talk all week, and now listening to her mama and papa, she still did not understand why everyone called it the "morning bench."

In the fall of 1957, Gloria Sangster, Aunt Arizona's stepdaughter, telephoned Opal with news. Aunt Cloria had been in an automobile accident in Anniston, Alabama, but she was in the hospital in Birmingham. She had moved to Alabama some years back, after she married Reverend William Baskerville and left Brownsville. Her husband was driving the car at the time of the accident. Opal wanted to see her sister, and Tonnie took Opal and Aunt Arizona to town to catch the Greyhound bus to Birmingham. It was the first time Opal had ever been away from the children, or even away from home. In Alabama, they were met by one of the members from Reverend Baskerville's church, who took them directly to the hospital. Opal was not expecting what she saw. Aunt Cloria was in critical condition. Her eyes remained closed the whole time they were there. She never acknowledged their presence. Opal felt helpless—there was not anything they could do.

While Opal and Aunt Arizona stood by the bed, they looked up to find several ladies from the church. "We know we're not suppose to be here," they said, "but we sneaked around the back way so we could see Sister Cloria." Opal was not surprised. Aunt Cloria was more outgoing than her sisters and was always smiling. When they stopped at the church on their way back to the bus station, they stayed in the car while their driver took care of some business. As people learned their identity, they started gathering around the car. "These Sister Cloria's sisters," they said. "Y'all come here and meet Sister Cloria's sisters," they yelled to the others. Everyone made a big fuss over Sister Cloria's sisters. Opal found it reassuring, in a way, to know that all her life people had always "been crazy about Cloria." She thought about this later, when they told her that Aunt Cloria never regained conscious.

Opal and Aunt Arizona sat with Aunt Cloria's only child, Herbert Taylor, in the First Baptist Church on Jefferson Street in Brownsville. Aunt Cloria had died on November 4, 1957, shortly after their visit to Birmingham. Reverend Baskerville had recovered from his injuries, and he was seated nearby. As Opal mourned the loss of her sister, she listened to the choir sing the song she had requested:

> Oh, when I come to the end of my journey, Weary and tired from the work I have done,
> Be not dismayed if friends don't believe you, He'll understand all about it and say well done.
> Oh, can't you hear his voice calling . . .

As the choir continued, Opal suddenly realized what her recent dream had meant. In the dream, Opal and Arizona were sitting together at some place—where, she was not sure—but a white woman came out and talked to them. The white woman showed them a pink dress she had made. As she showed the dress, she said, "and I had enough material left to make some pink curtains." Opal had the dream before the wreck occurred. She thought the pink dress meant death, but she could not figure out what the pink curtains could mean. Now she sat on the front pew reserved for family, staring at Aunt Cloria lying in the casket in a pink dress. Draped over the casket was a thin pink curtain.

Aunt Cloria was laid to rest in the Rosenwald Cemetery, next to her former husband, Dan "Boy" Rawls. Later that day, when Opal got a chance to speak with Reverend Baskerville, she told him about her dream. Then he shared with her Aunt Cloria's dream. Reverend Baskerville said he had been visiting a church outside of the city when he called home and spoke with Aunt Cloria. She told him that she dreamed he was in a "real bad car wreck." She was very concerned and warned him to "be sure to be real careful" returning home. Reverend Baskerville then added, "It sure was meant to be." He explained that the ladies in the church had picked out another dress, but they could not agree; so they changed their minds and chose the pink dress.

The next year, Tonnie decided to sell their house and land and purchase Miss Emma Tyus's place on Key Corner. Her husband had died and her children were gone, so she was selling the place and leaving Brownsville. It had been over sixteen years since they moved to the Oakview community, and they had seen the family change a lot over the years. Over half of the children had grown up and left home, and Tonnie had resumed most of the work on the farm. The new place had a lot fewer acres, but each year Tonnie's workforce would continue to diminish. This time Opal did not mind the move. After all the years they had lived on Winfield Lane and all the work she had done to make the place home, she had never particularly cared about living there. She was also aware of the rumor throughout the community that no one had ever kept the place very long because of a problem with the title. The land had previously belonged to Mr. Jute Tucker, an old black man, and people said a white man had somehow taken the land from him.

Tonnie decided on his own to buy the house on Key Corner, but Opal was quite pleased with her new home. The little white house was well maintained, and it sat on a very nice lot right outside the city limits. The city sidewalks began just a short distance up the road, where the large homes, in which whites lived, lined both sides of the street. Since there was self-imposed segregation in housing, no blacks lived there. The only neighbor was Mr. Commage, who lived with his family in a little red house about a half mile down the road.

We Are Not Afraid

Mr. Commage sat in the front room, with the children around him rapt in his storytelling. "This man was riding his horse down a country road at night," he said, "when all of sudden, a woman with long flowing black hair jumped on the horse behind him, put her arms around his waist, and clung to him as he rode. He turned 'round and looked, and the woman had these great big teeth hangin' out her mouth, then he knew it was a hant. The man made his old horse go faster and faster, but she kept hangin' on." As the children sat a little closer to each other, some two to a chair, Mr. Commage continued. "One night these men were out huntin' in the woods," he said. "They were running and shooting their guns, chasing this coon until they finally caught it, and one of the men reached down to turned the coon over. When he turned it over, the coon had the face of a woman and it looked at them and started to grin." The children did not make a sound, and Mr. Commage moved on to his next tale without skipping a beat.

The front room of the house on Key Corner Street was used as a sitting room. It was called the front room because it was the first room off the front porch. In the room was a cast-iron wood-burning stove strategically placed to heat the house during the winter months. Opal's radio sat on a small table against one wall, with a few eight-by-ten pictures of her favorite gospel singers hanging above it. Several chairs were placed around the room. Opal and Tonnie's bedroom was to the right. On the left was the "company room." This room had the new couch Tonnie bought Opal when they moved, but it also had a double bed, because the house was not large enough for a separate living room. Opal kept the room straightened up for company that might drop by, and it was there that Lois and Shirley entertained their boyfriends who came calling on Sunday evening. But the family always gathered in the front room. Since Mr. Commage was no longer considered company, he joined the family in the front room whenever he visited.

A thin, brown-skinned man a few years younger than Tonnie, Mr. Commage began regularly coming by the house soon after they moved to Key Corner. His visits had become routine; in the evening he regaled the children with one ghost tale after another. He sat with his back straight as a rail and his hat on one knee. "Y'all know," he said, "they say if you bury somebody when it's stormin', they gonna go to hell. Well, there was this one time the people were at the cemetery gettin' ready to bury a man who was supposed to have lived a real bad life, and it come to stormin' and lightnin' so hard, that the lightnin' hit the coffin and stood it straight up in the ground." By the time he finished, the children were so scared they lay in bed, covers over their head, too afraid to go to sleep.

The children had gone from living in a community where there were lots of children to play with to having just one other black family that had mostly teenage boys. Although the boys visited quite often, there were many times when Mr. Commage came alone. On those occasions, instead of talking with Tonnie, he entertained the children. They thought he was kind of strange. He always talked about ghosts, and sometimes he talked about the things he did not believe in because he was religious. When the children got brightly colored hula hoops, he said it was a sin because the girls had to gyrate their hips to keep the hoop from falling. After Shirley discovered how he felt, she played with the hula hoop whenever he came by, just to see his reaction.

When the family moved, the younger children had to transfer to Carver High School on Jefferson Street, where Lois, Clarence, and Shirley were already attending. The high school actually taught the first through twelfth grades. All the children from the city went to school in town for their full twelve years. There were separate classrooms for each grade, and sometimes there were two classrooms for the same grade. The children, excited about their new home, soon found a whole new set of friends.

In the summer of 1959, Tonnie continued to farm even though the new place had less land. He planted a few acres of cotton in one field behind the house, but he still planted most of his cotton down on Winfield Lane, on the land he rented from Miss Lily White. He sold all of his cows except one before moving, but he kept all his hogs and his mules, which he needed for plowing. Since the new place had a hen house, Opal transported her chickens from Winfield Lane to Key Corner. She did not want to be without her chickens. So, although they were living almost in the city, little changed when it came to Tonnie's farming. And, as usual, Tonnie always found time to make trips into town to talk with other black men and the local white merchants and to keep up with news around Brownsville. That July, everyone in town was talking about what happened to the sheriff of Haywood County. It would remain the topic of conversation for the rest of 1959.

Sheriff J. S. "Jack" Hunter was shot and killed by a Negro, Willie Jones, on July 24th.[1] Sheriff Jack Hunter and his deputy, Duarwd Crouch, had gone to the home of Willie M. Jones armed with a warrant for Willie T. Jones for nonsupport. When the sheriff drove into the yard, he called for Jones to come to the car and go with him. Jones, who was an older, church going family man, tried to tell the sheriff that he had the wrong person. He knew the sheriff's reputation and was not eager to get in the car with him. "Goddamn nigger," the sheriff cursed, and he got out of the car as Jones ran inside his house. The sheriff rushed around to the back of the house, still cursing, "I'm gonna get that black son of a bitch," he supposedly said. When Jack Hunter got to the back door, he attempted to poke his pistol through the door, but by then Jones had gotten his double-barreled shotgun. People said the deputy, who was a little man, heard the shot and said, "The sheriff done killed that nigger. The sheriff done killed that nigger." But when he got around behind the house and saw the sheriff lying on the ground with his brains blown out, he took off running back to town. Tonnie laughed when he told Opal that he heard that after the deputy had gone some distance, a man stopped to pick him up. The deputy kept asking the man, "Am I dead? Am I dead?" They said that when he got back to the office, he took off his gun, threw it down on the desk, and said, "There's a crazy nigger out there. He done shot and killed the sheriff."

Tonnie and everyone else who lived in and around the county knew of the reputation of Jack Hunter and his brother Tip Hunter. For nearly twenty years they had alternated in the role of sheriff of Haywood County, with one serving as chief deputy for the other. Jack Hunter had just been declared the Democratic nominee for another term as sheriff when he was killed. The turnout for the funeral of the sheriff killed in the line of duty was so large that all the people could not get inside the Brownsville Funeral Home. Among whites, he was mourned and praised as a man widely known and respected. However, he had developed a terrible reputation when it came to the treatment of black people. Few if any of them mourned his passing. They were still shocked at the news, though, along with the city of Brownsville, the rest of Haywood County, and west Tennessee. The people could not believe that a black man in Brownsville had actually killed the sheriff. What was even more surprising to most was that there was not an immediate lynching of the man responsible. People said it was a tense moment when Jones was brought into the jail. Tip Hunter made a move for his gun, but the other men at the jail stopped him. Some claimed the black funeral director had to sneak Jones out of town in the back of a hearse after the decision was made to transfer him to the jail in Memphis.

Tonnie and Opal could feel the winds of change that had been blowing across other parts of the country for decades. They knew that a couple of years earlier, Currie Boyd, Ph.D., had returned home to Haywood County and started speaking at churches to generate an interest in voting rights. In 1959, he had contacted James Franklin Estes, a black attorney in Memphis to help organize the movement. That May, they learned that Dr. Boyd, Mr. Odell Sanders, the Turners from the New Hope community, and others had organized the Haywood County Civic and Welfare League in order to obtain voting rights and obtain factory jobs for blacks in Haywood County.[2] In July, the paper reported that Estes led a delegation of Haywood County Negroes to Nashville to testify before the State Election Commission. The group representing the Civic and Welfare League informed the State Commission that they had not been allowed to register and vote, having been told that the county registrar had resigned and no new appointment had been announced. Although they requested that the state appoint an election commission in Haywood to grant them further hearings, a few were determined to maintain pressure on the locals.[3]

"We never registered any here," said Mr. Moore, the county court clerk. Dr. Boyd had tried to dress down on purpose—wearing a shirt, jeans, and a baseball cap. He casually stood around, not wanting to draw attention to himself, until someone finally asked if he needed help. Dr. Boyd explained to the registrar that he wanted to change his voter registration from Decatur County, and she, not being sure how to handle the situation, referred him to the clerk. Mr. Moore kept his head down as he instructed Dr. Boyd that he needed to take his papers elsewhere, and he mumbled again, "we never registered any of them here."

Dr. Boyd said, "I knew the reference to 'them' meant colored people," but he was undaunted. He wrote to the U.S. Department of Justice in

Washington and inquired as to how he could register to vote. When he received very little response, Dr. Boyd sent a second letter, informing the department that the people in Brownsville were "sitting on a powder keg." He said, "my people got old rusty guns and Molotov cocktails and they are ready to fight." He warned that unless something was done soon, "there'll be blood in the streets and it won't be all black blood either."

Tonnie, like most other blacks residents of Haywood County, knew that, as things stood, blacks could not stay at the little motels in town; they had separate and much less attractive waiting rooms at doctors' offices and at the Greyhound bus station in town; and they could not eat at the town's restaurants or small diners. If they wanted to place an order for food, they were told to go around to the back door to pick up the food prepared by black cooks. They were not permitted to drink from any water fountains that whites drank from, including the nice wrought-iron fountain in front of the courthouse, next to the Confederate monument. That fountain had sign stating "Whites Only." For Negroes, there was a small stone water fountain at the back of the building. Its sign read "Colored." The black community knew it was not right, but for a long time they did not bother to ask questions. Even now, Tonnie never considered becoming involved with the voting rights efforts. He was a member of the majority, which welcomed progress, but he left the fight to the young folks.

"I've never had any white water," Dr. Boyd told one white man at the courthouse that he thought might be receptive to doing something about the water fountains. "And I will probably live if I don't ever have any," he added. But he explained that he did not like the fact that whites still expected people to drink from separate water fountains. He knew all whites in the county were not evil, and he thought perhaps the time had come for someone to stand up for change. The white man told Dr. Boyd that it was up to Sheriff Tip Hunter, but he offered to speak with the sheriff about the matter. On his next visit to the courthouse, Dr. Boyd noticed the nice water fountain for whites was no longer out front; Tip Hunter had taken care of the matter by tearing it down.

What happened next in Haywood County made Opal appreciate more than ever that they owned their own place and that Tonnie was not sharecropping a white man's land. As Dr. Boyd, Odell Sanders, George Graves, Thad Turner, Melvin Dotson, Norvell Turner, and others began an all-out effort to secure the right to vote, white landowners in Haywood County began sending certified letters to black tenant farmers and sharecroppers.

The letters notified tenants of their eviction and gave them a deadline for getting off the land. Ostensibly, the evictions were due to increased mechanization; however, once Negroes were evicted, most of the whites put the land in the "soil bank." Opal heard about whole families of black people who were put off the white man's land with no place to go.

The same things happening in Haywood were also going on in neighboring Fayette County. A group of blacks there established the Fayette County Civic and Welfare League shortly after the league was founded by Dr. Boyd. They had also begun a voter registration drive for the almost nine thousand eligible blacks in that county. The success of their efforts led to a court ruling that the county's all-white primary was illegal; however, for their victory the people soon faced harsh retaliation from the local whites. First they imposed a trade ban against blacks, then later, after the cotton had been picked, they instituted wholesale evictions of black tenants and sharecroppers.[4] As blacks were forced off the white man's farms for registering to vote in Fayette County, they set up living quarters in tents.

In 1960, "Tent City" followed in Haywood County as white farmers forced more and more blacks off their land. Opal heard about Tent City from both Tonnie and the children, who had classmates living in tents. She also read the newspaper articles and saw pictures of families with tents set up on one black man's farm. With some thirty or forty families living in tents in Haywood County alone, efforts to assist those evicted were heightened. Some local churches provided food but had little money to help the homeless families. People moved all their possessions into tents with cardboard floors, and they hauled their water from nearby farms. They made do with what they had.[5] To provide some relief, people from Brownsville traveled to places like Washington, Detroit, and even to California to raise money and find any other assistance. As a result of their efforts, the Congress of Racial Equality (CORE), out of California, sent food, clothing, and money. When Opal's church took up a collection to help the families, she gave what little she could.

Opal saw that once again national attention was focused on Haywood County due to its treatment of blacks. And again the local people called on Washington to help. But by the time the U.S. Department of Justice finally sent two men from the Federal Bureau of Investigation to Brownsville, crosses had already been burned in the yards of black families, and nothing had been done to counter the action. Not all black people in the county ascribed to passive resistance. Dr. Boyd told of an exchange he had with the FBI men. He told the investigators what he would do if the Klan came to his house to burn a cross. "I have a good aim," he said. "I don't smoke and I don't drink coffee, so I'm not nervous." He went on to state, "I can shoot a squirrel's left eye at fifty yards, and I will shoot to kill." The FBI man, who could not endorse violence, asked, "Why don't you just call the sheriff?" "What if the sheriff is leading the mob like he did when they killed Elbert Williams?" Dr. Boyd replied. "After I kill all them I can, may be I'll call you then. If they want me, they better come to my house between nine and five," he said. Dr. Boyd stayed up at night waiting with his M1 carbine, a banana clip holding thirty rounds, and two fifteen-round clips, but no cross burners came. He figured the FBI men must have passed the word on to the sheriff about what he had said, and the locals decided he was one of those "crazy niggers" that they would leave alone.

For Opal and others who well remembered the lynchings in 1940, the question persisted of whether the climate of fear and resistance would again prevail in Haywood County. Although it had been nearly a century since they had obtained their freedom, almost forty years since women gained the right to vote, and close to twenty years since Elbert Williams lost his life to the struggle, blacks in this county were still denied the right to participate in the election process. The situation became even more real for Tonnie and Opal when they discovered that some of their relatives and Willow Grove Church members were forced to move from the farms of white landowners for going to the courthouse in an attempt to register to vote. Among the black people evicted were Tonnie's cousin Lee Andrew Perry and his family.

While the whole town dealt with the fallout from the eviction of black families, Opal had concerns of her own about housing. She was sitting in the front room sewing one day when she heard a knock on the door. She opened the door and found a middle-aged white woman standing there. "I'm here to see the house," the woman said, explaining her presence. She said Tonnie had spoken to her about selling the place. Opal was caught completely off guard, and she did not try to mask her surprise. They had been in the house for less than a year. Although Tonnie had made the decision to purchase the place without consulting her, Opal and the children liked the house and its location closer to town. Opal thought to herself, "Here I and the children are sitting up here in this house and he's about to sell my home out from under us." She told the woman, "I don't know anything about Tonnie selling the house." The woman apologized to Opal and said she was not interested in the house if Opal was not aware of it being for sale.

When Tonnie learned the white woman was not going to buy the house, he simply found another buyer. This time the buyer was a white man and, as Opal feared, her house on Key Corner was sold. Opal was not sure exactly what was going on. Even after selling their home, Tonnie still talked very little about his plans. From what she could understand, Tonnie was upset that Grandpa Jim was considering selling a portion of his land to a church member who was not part of the family. Tonnie did not want to see the land sold to someone outside the family. He thought it was even worse that his papa was planning to sell the front of the place where Springfield School had been located. Tonnie decided that if a portion of the land were going to be sold, he would buy it himself; but first he needed to sell the Key Corner place and use those proceeds. After selling the house, the family moved, temporarily, to a little house on Fairground Road.

About the only good thing Opal could say about living in their temporary quarters was that for the first time since she married, she was living near her sister. This was also the first time they lived in a house not surrounded by farmland. The houses were lined in a row on one side of Fairground Road, across from the large field where the Haywood County and the Negro Fair were held. All the houses looked the same: small, white box-shaped homes with red shutters. The small lots were probably no more than a half acre. There was very little yard for the children to play, although they were becoming too old to spend a lot of time playing outside. And, since the children discovered that Aunt Arizona and Uncle Gilbert had a television set, they much preferred going next door to visit their cousins.

Aunt Arizona's older boys, Robert, Gilbert, and Howard, were in Michigan, and the older girls, Minnie L., Margaret, and Survern had also left home. The only ones left at home were Armex, Hazel, and the two younger boys, Manuel and Melvin, who were the same age as Opal's two youngest children. Every Saturday afternoon the children gathered at Aunt Arizona's house, where they sat in the room with the curtains drawn. The only light came from the small black-and-white TV. For hours at a time they watched every Western that came on: *The Rifleman, Wanted Dead or Alive, Maverick, Have Gun Will Travel, Roy Rogers,* and *The Lone Ranger.* The one show they watched every week that did not have cowboys was *Perry Mason.* The theme music was so dramatic that it captured their attention and held it until the defense attorney succeeded in getting another witness to confess to murder from the stand. Sometimes Aunt Arizona would sit in the big arm chair and watch *Perry Mason* with them. The children quickly adjusted to the new location. Just when they became comfortable spending time with their cousins and walking to school with other children in town, they learned they were moving again.

In 1960, Tonnie and Opal found themselves back where they had started, at Grandpa Jim's house on Springfield Road. It had been thirty-four years since Opal first arrived there as a young, shy girl of sixteen. She had been taken with the big house and its beautiful grounds full of trees and gardens and animals. "My, how the old home place has changed," she thought when they moved back. The long road, lined with trees, that led up to the front of the house was now closed. The whole area from the edge of the front yard to Springfield Road was a big field, with the old schoolhouse in the middle long abandoned. The house that had looked so splendid when they approached in the horse and buggy was now anything but grand. The once-white paint was now a dull gray, and there were large areas where the paint had chipped, exposing bare, weather-worn wood planks underneath. The wood on the porches had turned dark gray, and the screened-in porch, where the family had gathered around the big table for meals, was in disrepair. Even the green tin roof had been dulled with the passage of time. Grandpa Jim lived there by himself for a number of years and had neither the interest nor desire to fix up the place. Opal was not particular about bringing her family back there, but she did not complain. She thought it would not matter if she complained or not, because they had already moved back. Opal told herself this, too, was temporary.

Tonnie had purchased a plot of land on North McLemore Street in town and was having a house built. He had abandoned his plans to try to keep all of the old home place in the family when potential buyers became upset that Grandpa Jim had changed his mind. They said he had already made a promise to sell the land. Rather than cause more dissension, Tonnie decided he would let his papa do what he had originally planned. The only problem was that he had already sold their home. Tonnie contacted Miss Ceily Lanier, who owned several acres of land about one block beyond the city limits on the north side of town. Her husband had just died, and she sold Tonnie the place. They spent the next few months at Grandpa Jim's, waiting for the workers to finish building the new house.

During this time, the children got to know their grandpa better. They spent more time around him than ever before. They found Grandpa Jim easy to talk to, whereas Tonnie did not spend a whole lot of time talking to anyone. Grandpa Jim quizzed the children on the Bible and gave them a nickel when they got the right answer. Sometimes he gave them a quarter. While Opal had thought she hated Tonnie's father when she first met him, her feelings had long since changed. She carefully monitored his diet when she cooked, making sure he did not get too much sugar. She had come to admire Grandpa Jim as a good Christian man.

The children did not like living in the country again. They especially hated it on the mornings they had to walk more than a mile to Jackson Highway to catch the school bus. Opal and the children were happy when later that year they moved to 1005 North McLemore Street.

Opal saw 1960 as the year for change, not only in the family but also the nation. For the first time since she could remember, the country had a young, handsome, charismatic presidential candidate. She and Tonnie liked President Dwight "Ike" Eisenhower and his wife, Mamie, but she thought the Democratic candidate and his wife were certainly different. She held out some hope for the future when in September the news media reported that John F. Kennedy had begun an all-out effort for the Negro vote. He had met with a group of Negro lawyers and promised that, if elected, he would appoint more Negroes to federal judgeships. "With more than 4,000 [Negro] lawyers in this country," he said, " there are many outstanding Negroes from whom to choose future judges." The Democratic convention's civil rights platform was aimed at eliminating all remaining traces of racial segregation. "Our purpose will be to assure to each American his full constitutional rights and to 'make equal opportunity a living reality for all Americans,'" Kennedy had said.[6] He promised what the black people of Haywood County had for so long struggled. It was important to blacks that they be able to vote in the November election.

Tonnie and Opal had never voted in an election, local, state, or national, though they were aware of the continuing efforts of some to register in Haywood County. They heard people talking about what happened when Dr. Boyd, Odell Sanders, and others traveled to Washington to testify before the Civil Rights Commission. While he was in Washington, Dr. Boyd also spoke with John Doar, an attorney with the Justice Department, about the actions of some whites in the county. "If you catch me with ten gallons of whiskey, would you arrest me?" Dr. Boyd asked.

"Yes," Doar responded.

"Why?" Dr. Boyd asked.

"Because you would be breaking the law," Doar said.

"Aren't these white people in Haywood County breaking the law by not allowing blacks to vote?" asked Dr. Boyd.

"Yes," Doar again responded.

"Then why don't you arrest them?" Dr. Boyd inquired, having made his point.

Doar's response was to explain that a person accused of a crime has a right to a trial by jury.

"In Haywood County, who's the jury gonna be?" This time Doar was the one asking the question. Doar said that under the circumstances, he thought the better approach was to file for an injunction since the decision would be made by a judge.

Tonnie also heard folks talk about what happened when a representative from Washington came to town to investigate the situation. As a result of testimony before the Civil Rights Commission, the man was sent to Brownsville to conduct interviews. On his arrival in town, the man went to the courthouse to speak with local officials there. The whites were reluctant to cooperate with anyone who was perceived as aiding the Negro and his cause, so he learned little information. The story spread that as the man was leaving, Sheriff Buddy Sullivan struck him on the head. People swore it to be fact that the city of Brownsville rewarded Sullivan for his "act of bravery" by giving him $150 and a new suit.

Opal later learned that on September 13, 1960, the attorney general of the United States had petitioned the federal court in Memphis for a temporary and permanent injunction against twenty-seven white landowners and two banks in Haywood County to prevent any further evictions of black tenants. The purpose of the injunction was to restrain them, individually and collectively, from engaging in any threats, intimidations, or coercion, whether economic or otherwise, for the purpose of interfering with the right of any other person to register to vote and to vote for candidates for federal offices. Although the court could grant the temporary restraining order before the hearing, it could not grant the permanent injunction without a hearing. A U.S. marshall had come to Haywood County to serve summons on the defendants, who, if found guilty, would be forced to comply with the injunction or be fined or imprisoned or both.[7]

The local paper listed all the defendants named in the release: A. T. Beaty, Samuel Clifton Buchanan, Jimmy E. C——, Edmund Taylor, and Joseph Shelby Dixon of Stanton; Joe Richard Gibbs, Alex H. Gray, and

Samuel Russell Hawkins of People's Bank; Taylor "Tip" Hunter, sheriff; John M Jackson, First State Bank; Murdock Hudson Johnson, Harold Kelso, James A. Kurts, and Herbert Martin of Dancyville; J. B. Matthews, Lloyd McCool, and Floyd Qualls of Koko; Charles W. Scott, Stanton constable; James H. Shelton, Fayette County trustee; Alvis Stuart and Lofton K. Stuart of Stanton; Walter Stewart, George W. Sullivan, deputy sheriff; Mary Ware, Tommy B. Willis, Paul M. Windrow, and Frances Moore Woodson of Nashville.[8]

If those involved in the movement thought having the federal attorneys obtain the injunction was the appropriate course, most whites did not share this sentiment. On September 16, 1960, after the federal injunction was sought, the *States-Graphic* ran a front-page editorial in which it credited the Thursday's *Commercial Appeal* with publishing the following: "How far—if at all—the United States has traveled on the "police state" road might be determined by the outcome of a Federal civil rights suit filed against two banks and 27 citizens of Tennessee.... The suit, instigated by the Justice Department's Civil Rights Division, charges that the defendants conspired to prevent voting registration of Negroes and accuses them of threatening and taking economic action against Negroes." The editorial went on to state that the allegations had "been investigated ad infinitum" and had been "repeatedly and vigorously denied." It stated that the defendants should insist that the allegations be proved in court, as if that were not already the case, and that they make sure there was "no unnecessary delay in the Government's handling of its case." It set out the specific charges against the twenty-seven defendants: "Specifically, they are accused of terminating sharecropping and tenant farming relationships with Negroes; of refusing to sell necessaries, goods, and services for either cash or credit; of refusing to lend money to some of the Negroes; of circulating lists of names of Negroes who were leaders in registration and voting activity; of inducing suppliers of merchants not to deal with such merchants; of inducing merchants, landowners, and others to penalize economically the Negroes; inducing the wholesalers not to deal with Negro merchants."

Noting that the suit was said to be the first of its kind filed under a clause of the 1957 Civil Rights Act, the editorial said what was described as a "simple suit" was anything but for those who were "put to the expense and trouble of defending themselves." It said that after "all the legal gobbledygook has been stripped away," what the suit inferred was that the federal government had both the right and power to tell the banks and private citizens "to whom they should lend and sell, whom they shall house and feed, and whom they shall employ." The editor made it clear that "We do not believe that day has arrived—or ever will." And he questioned whether the "Civil Rights Division is trying to impress the people of Haywood County, or large segments of the voting populations in New York, Chicago, Detroit and Los Angeles."[9]

The fact that the cities singled out were those with large Negro populations was not lost on Opal or any of the other black people who read the article. The newspaper was staking a position that it knew was compatible with its white readers. This kind of reaction was nothing new to the black people in the county. Having lived in a place where they were denied certain basic rights all their lives, they had come to know what to expect from local officials. Almost anywhere else such an injunction would have been a "simple suit." There was hardly a black person in the county who did not know firsthand of someone who had been forced from the white man's land, denied credit by the bank or a white merchant, turned down for services and the shipment of goods—all because of their attempt to register to vote. Blacks thought whites in Haywood County had exercised total control over them for so long that they were just determined to cling to the last vestiges of their system of injustice. The only difference now was that some blacks in the county were even more determined to change things—to the way they should have been all along.

The presidential election was held two months after the injunction was filed, and this time Opal and the rest of the family watched the election news on the newly purchased television set in the living room They had also watched the debates between a composed Kennedy and a nervous-looking Nixon, and they kept up with the last days of campaigning. The Kennedy-Johnson ticket carried Haywood County with a margin of 683 votes in what had been a light turnout. The paper reported that some 3,345 voters of Haywood County gave the new president of the United States, John Fitzgerald Kennedy, the Democratic nominee, a margin of 683 votes in contributing to his narrow popular-vote margin over Richard Nixon.[10] The family was pleased with the outcome.

The state of Tennessee had favored Nixon, but Haywood County had continued a tradition voting Democrat that extended from post–Civil War days. The Democratic victory in the county was attributed, in part, to some 860 Negroes, the majority of whom "voted in their first Presidential election," according to a news report. It was speculated that the margin of victory could have been larger if not for the religious issue involved in the election.[11] As for the number of votes alleged to have been cast by Negroes, blacks knew the number was highly inflated. Only a few Negroes had been allowed to register. Open resistance to the efforts of black people to register and vote continued unabated.

Tonnie and Opal knew Mr. Norvell Turner because he was a member of the singing quartet of Turner brothers in Brownsville. Opal had first heard them sing at Oakview Church when the family was living on Winfield Lane. Mr. Norvell was one of the leaders in the group, and Opal liked to hear him sing. She had come to believe that all the Turners could sing, so whenever she met another Turner, she asked, "Can you sing, too?" Mr. Norvell, his wife, Nettie, and their children were tenants of a white man who owned land in the New Hope community. He and his wife were two charter members of the Haywood County Civic and Welfare League, who had participated in the voter registration efforts. When this was discovered, they became the targets of local whites who were evicting black tenants, but before they received their letter they were paid a visit. The "old boss man," the white man on the farm in charge of the Negroes, came by the house to issue the warning personally. "If you don't stop tryin' to register 'n' vote," he said, "you gonna haf ta move." He had his own interest to consider, since he could be forced to move if he failed to convince Mr. Norvell to heed his warning. Trying harder to make his message clear, he added, "Cause we can't have that." Mr. Norvell told the "boss man," "You just gonna have to make me move then."

Mr. Norvell said he considered himself fortunate, even after he was forced to move. He knew a "wealthy colored man," Mr. John R. Bond and his wife, who lived in Decatur, Illinois, who owned about two hundred acres of land seven miles out of Brownsville on the old Memphis Highway. They allowed Mr. Norvell and his family to move into the big ten-room house on the property and farm the land. The family thought it was great. The house was very nice and things were better than before. However, the following year, when they needed money to buy fertilizer, seeds, and other supplies to plant their crops, no one would loan them the money. Mr. Norvell went to the merchants who he had done business with in the past and they refused to allow him credit; then he went to the banks in town and was turned down for a loan. Everywhere he went, he was told, "I'm sorry we can't do that." Finally, he said he saw in a dream one night to whom he could go to get the money he needed.

Mr. Norvell said he "sat straight up in bed." The Lord had told him to go see Mr. Pat Mann for a loan. Mr. Pat Mann was a local white merchant who owned a store on Ripley Highway. Mr. Norvell went to see the white man and explained his situation. He told Mr. Pat Mann that he needed to grow his crops, and, he said, "I have a wife and I got these children." Having estimated what he needed to get by, he asked for a loan of $300. When Mr. Pat Mann handed him the check, he saw the amount entered was for $600. Mr. Norvell went right to the bank to cash the check, but the teller had to get approval before she would cash it. People in the bank started staring at him. After the bank finally gave him the money, he walked outside and saw Mr. Pat Mann waiting beside his truck in front of the bank. He did not know that he had been followed to the bank.

"Did you get your money?" Mr. Pat Mann asked.

"Yes, sir, I did," Mr. Norvell said, pleased that he had the money he needed.

"That's all I wanted to know," his lender said, and he got in his truck and drove away. The people in the bank did not know what to make of what had just taken place. Mr. Norvell knew they would be even more astounded to learn that never before, in his entire life, had he done business with this white man. But Tonnie had known Mr. Pat Mann for a long time, and had been doing business with him for years. He had always found him to be fair in his dealings.

From the talk around town, the filing of the federal lawsuit did nothing to curtail the retaliation against blacks for registering. With Brownsville being so small, everyone heard what was going on and they all knew the people involved. They said that Mr. Odell Sanders was targeted by local whites because he was one of the main leaders in the voter registration drive. Mr. Odell owned a small grocery in town and was well known. His wife, Marge "Sis" Sanders, was a beautician and worked out of their home. Opal and some of the girls went to Miss Sis Sanders, as everyone called her, to get their hair fixed.

Tonnie was told that after Mr. Odell became involved in the movement, he stopped receiving supplies for the store. The companies that had been making deliveries were told that if they delivered to Mr. Odell's store, the white merchants would no longer do business with them. Soon, the only product on the shelves was Wonder Bread, who continued to deliver. Unable to operate the store with only bread to sell, he was forced to close the store. Although he had been put out of business, he was determined to continue the voter registration efforts. The Klan burned crosses in his yard to scare him into giving up his struggle. When this also failed, they made the first of what would be three attempts on his life.

One day Jones Funeral Home telephoned Miss Sis Sanders, and the white man on the other end of the line told her he had gotten a call and was "going to pick up a dead nigger." Miss Sis Sanders and her children were inside their home some time later when they heard a loud thump at the front of the house. She sent the children to the front door to investigate the noise. They found their father, Mr. Odell, lying there on the front porch. They later learned that some unidentified white person had run him off the side of the road and left him for dead. Instead of calling one of the two Negro-owned funeral homes in town, someone called the white funeral home, which gave the family more reason to believe there was a conspiracy. The funeral home went to pick up the body but discovered that the victim was not dead. They took him to his house and dumped him on the front porch. Since Mr. Odell had sustained contusions and injuries to his head and leg, Miss Sis Sanders took him to the Haywood County Memorial Hospital in town. The hospital refused to admit him because they knew of his involvement with the voter registration efforts. She was forced to travel twenty-six miles to the hospital in Jackson.

After Mr. Odell and Dr. Boyd had begun operating Boyd and Sanders B&S Laundry on Jefferson Street, Mr. Odell would often spend the night there to watch the building and make sure the whites did not burn it down. He slept on a small cot near the front entrance of the building. One night someone entered the laundry and fired several shots into the cot. Unbeknownst to the intruders, a man who owned a business in a nearby building had offered to let Mr. Odell sleep there. The word always spread whenever someone was out to get a black person. On this particular night, Mr. Odell had taken the man up on his offer to sleep in the back of his business. Still, the momentum for change both on the local and national levels showed no signs of waning.

By 1963, Tonnie's days of planting large crops were gone for good. He no longer had the help he needed to continue farming. Lois, Clarence, and Shirley had left home in 1960. For the next couple of years, he planted large acres of cotton, but he had to hire workers at picking time. Now, Opal Ree was getting ready to leave home. That meant twelve of his children had grown up and left Brownsville. His brother Brown still had all his boys at home. Mr. Tom Bond's boys still farmed with him down on Winfield Lane, and he knew other men whose boys had stayed on the farm. Tonnie's children wanted something different. As they left, one by one, he never said anything and he never tried to convince one to stay. But he knew there was no way he could make a living farming with just the two youngest girls. He was going to have to start over, perhaps look for one of those factory jobs. Tonnie would be sixty in January. His primary concern was keeping his family fed and a roof over their heads, but he found the world around him was going through lots of changes.

The first Saturday in August of 1963, Tonnie went uptown as he always did. Before the day was over, he witnessed events on the streets of Brownsville that he never thought he would see in his lifetime. That morning, a group met with two representatives from CORE in the upstairs of the B&S Laundry on "Negro Street." The young Jewish man, Eric Weinberger, and his wife had met with this group on previous occasions. There had been others who came to Haywood County from up north, all Jewish, many of them staying with Mr. Odell and his family. These northerners had been meeting with people at churches in different communities, planning strategies for voter registration efforts. As they made plans for organized protests, they trained in the principles of nonviolence. They stressed that any protest by them had to be compatible with the teachings of Dr. Martin Luther King Jr. and therefore peaceful. They sang each song of the freedom movement until everyone had memorized all the words. Finally, the time had come to implement their plan.

They stood in a circle, holding hands, their heads bowed, praying. When they had finished praying, they were ready to face whatever awaited them. They anticipated trouble, so Eric Weinberger left his wife behind in case she had to contact Washington with urgent news. The group left the B&S Laundry and marched up Jefferson Street toward town. They walked rapidly, carrying their homemade signs and singing all the way. At Jefferson and South Washington, they turned right and proceeded past the U.S. Post Office, right of the square, and marched one block to East Main. Upon reaching the wide main street, which ran directly in front of the courthouse, they found their paths blocked. For a moment they stood across the street and assessed the situation.

The tall Confederate soldier rose above the faces of the crowd, which the marchers estimated at between five and six hundred: all white, all male, and all angry. They covered the courthouse lawn, the surrounding sidewalks, and they spilled out into the street. The town had turned out in a show of force. The marchers saw white men in their work overalls and khaki pants and others in business attire waiting in the afternoon heat, prepared to do almost anything to prevent the Negroes from coming to the courthouse. White city police officers positioned themselves between the marchers and the crowd. Just three weeks earlier, the city had announced the hiring of its first two Negro police officers, Robert Lewis Wiley and George Lewis Delk. They were assigned to the "Negro business district" and had no authority to intervene in the situation at the courthouse. The white officers stood in front of the marchers, holding onto three large German shepherds.

There were only eleven of them. Eric Weinberger, who was about thirty, and Edna Jones, in her twenties, were the spokepersons for the group. The others—Wilbia Turner, Lee Wilson Turner, James Turner, Willie Lewis Turner, Jeanette Turner, Mamie Turner, Norma Ballard, Mary Alice Pearce, and Lettie Price—were mainly teenagers, many still in high school. Although they were outnumbered by a staggering ratio, their resolve to complete their mission never wavered. Walking head on toward the policemen, the dogs, the men holding fire hoses, and the feral crowd, they began to sing:

> Ain't gonna let nobody turn me round,
> Turn me round, turn me round.
> Ain't gonna let nobody turn me round.
> Keep on a walking, keep on a talking,
> Marching on to freedom land.

As the ten blacks and their out-of- town visitor began to cross the street, all hell broke loose. Yelling and cursing, the crowd readied for the assault. It soon became obvious what the group already knew: the sheriff and the officers were not there to protect them from harm or danger. Instead, the policemen turned their dogs loose to attack the marchers. What ensued took on all the elements and character of a mob. The men in the crowd spat on the young marchers; they hit them; they used a cattle prod to shock one of the boys; and they turned the city fire hoses on the teenagers with such force that the water all but lifted them off the ground. Deputy Sheriff Buddy Sullivan had ordered his men to turn the water hoses on the picketers when they refused to leave. The townspeople continued their mayhem as some whites leaned from windows on the upper floor of the courthouse and dropped acid on the marchers. They called Eric Weinberger a nigger lover and doused him with acid, which ate through his clothes and burned his skin. The man that ran the blacksmith shop in town confronted Edna Jones as she came on the courthouse lawn. He struck her in the face, and when she was not deterred, he struck her again. "Stop Daddy," the son said to his father, trying to keep the older white man from hitting the young black woman a third time.

Somehow the marchers maneuvered through the crowd; not once did they consider turning back. They did not curse anyone or lift a hand to fight their attackers. Regardless of the manner of abuse, they kept reminding themselves that their protest was supposed to be nonviolent, and they continued to sing. By the time they made their way one time around the courthouse, things had gotten ugly. Having finished what they had set out to accomplish, they decided to head back to their meeting place before one of them was killed. Haywood County had just experienced its first civil rights demonstration.

Tonnie did not see the entire demonstration, but he was with a crowd that had gathered in the Alley. He was watching when the ten indomitable but battered freedom marchers made their way down East Main, returning to the B&S Laundry. They were missing the white man, Eric Weinberger, and they had to hurry to let his wife know what had happened so she could call for assistance. Edna Jones had two black eyes from being struck twice in the face. She had also been bitten by the dogs. Some of the other marchers had a few cuts and scratches and bruises, and they were all soaking wet from the fire hoses. Tonnie saw the two black officers standing nearby, looking at the young folks as they walked by. He knew that under the circumstances, there was not much the officers could have done.

Sometime later, they learned that the police had arrested Weinberger, calling him a "self-styled Caucasian leader" who represented the Congress of Racial Equality. The officers took particular note of the fact that the out-of-towner was bearded, and they charged him with assault and battery, disorderly conduct, conspiracy to commit an act injurious to public health and welfare, and obstructing justice and due process of law. Buddy Sullivan claimed Weinberger tossed a cloth soaked with "some kind of gas" on the ground in front of the officers and that he refused to move along as instructed. With acid burns over one-third of his body, he was taken to jail and held overnight on a fifteen-hundred-dollar bond.[12]

The following Monday, the children told Opal that two men from the FBI came to school to question the freedom marchers. Although the principal tried to keep the FBI presence quiet, they learned that most of the marchers were their classmates. The visit was part of the FBI's continuing investigation into certain activities in Haywood County. The men wanted to know details of the demonstration: how the marchers were treated, what specifically was done to them, and the names of the whites who had attacked them. They asked questions and received some answers, but the Justice Department took no action against the city or any of the local whites involved in the attacks. The authorities made no other arrests. Many blacks were left wondering exactly what justice had been obstructed.

What Tonnie and the others witnessed in Haywood County was similar to incidents in other parts of the country. Blacks had seen the success of the boycott in Montgomery, Alabama, that followed the December 1955 arrest of Rosa Parks for refusing to give up her seat on a bus to a white man. Organized protest intensified after the 1961 sit-ins took place in Greenville, South Carolina. During the summer of 1963, civil rights demonstrations and protests, along with resistance by whites, took place all over the country. Opal said it seemed that every time she turned on the television or read the paper, there was something about marchers and sit-ins.

On the evening of June 11, 1963, Opal and the children watched as President Kennedy addressed the nation on civil rights. The president thought he should speak to the country after the Birmingham crisis developed, and television flashed pictures all over the country of Gov. George Wallace standing in the doorway at the University of Alabama to prevent a black student from entering. They paid particular attention as President Kennedy said the time had come for America to remove the blight of racial discrimination. He promised to ask Congress "to make a commitment it has not fully made in this century to the proposition that race has no place in American life or law." The next night, the family heard the news that NAACP field director Medgar Evers was shot and killed by a sniper in front of his home in Mississippi.

By August 1963, Opal thought it seemed clear that this time not even killings were going to stop blacks from demanding equal rights. She heard reports almost daily of how their efforts had successfully forced thousands of restaurants, hotels, swimming pools, and schools to desegregate in hundreds of cities, and the demonstrations continued. In Chicago, the city called out police and clergymen in an effort to curb the violence of the city's worst racial outbreak in a decade. Four hundred and fifty National Guardsmen in Cambridge, Massachusetts, were ordered to stay through the cutoff date for filing petitions to block a proposed city charter amendment requiring equal accommodations for Negroes and whites. In Danville, Virginia, last capital of the Confederacy, Negroes charged that the court-ordered injunction against those who demonstrated against segregation and discrimination would not halt the racial conflict there, so they carried on with their protest. Demonstrators picketed businesses and restaurants from Alabama to Pennsylvania and from Louisiana to New Jersey.[13] Closer to home, students organized sit-ins in Knoxville, Nashville, and Memphis. The civil rights movement steadily gained momentum.

Civil rights leaders planned the "jobs and freedom" March on Washington for August 28, 1963. In New York, movement leaders revised upward the projected numbers of those expected to participate. They planned the march, in part, as a show of unity for President Kennedy's civil rights proposals. When the date finally arrived, an estimated 250,000 persons gathered in the area around the Lincoln Memorial. It was the largest single demonstration of a movement in history. The young and old and all those in between had traveled from every part of the country to the nation's capital. Somewhere among the thousands that had come were the ten young freedom marchers from Brownsville. They arrived in Washington, their first visit to the city, on a chartered Greyhound bus, having received the free trip for their brave contribution to the movement. Because the large crowd prevented the ten from getting anywhere close to the podium, they listened to the message over loudspeakers on the Mall grounds. Opal and her family, and thousands more like them, sat around their television sets at home, caught up in the inspirational message of Dr. Martin Luther King Jr.

The March on Washington was the first time most blacks had ever seen an event sponsored by their people receive such respect and attention. It left them even more committed to the struggle for equal rights. The theme of providing new jobs for blacks struck a cord for those in Haywood County, where new industry was locating and bringing with it hundreds of jobs. So far, the plant personnel had refused to hire blacks to even work as janitors. If whites thought their behavior at the courthouse had discouraged further demonstrations, they were mistaken. It had been just the beginning. The demonstrations that followed grew larger and larger.

The next time the group of blacks gathered at the courthouse, they arrived before the doors opened and waited to register to vote. People doing business at the courthouse came and went as they glanced at the group that was still there. Some of the workers at the courthouse gave them angry looks every time they walked passed the men and women still there in the afternoon.

However, blacks in the county were demanding not only the right to vote, but also jobs. As farming lost its predominance as a primary source of income, blacks demanded jobs in order to earn a decent living to support their families. Some had also gone to the handful of restaurants and small diners in town and demanded to be served. They wanted equal treatment, so they continued standing, although the city had placed benches on the lawn. There was no sign; it was just understood that colored people were not allowed to sit down on the benches reserved for whites. And, lest they forget, some whites put acid on the benches to remind them. One man had gotten tired and sat down, only to have the seat of his pants burned off. The long line continued to form at the courthouse. Blacks stood all day long, waiting. At the end of the day, one person had registered.

Eric Weinberger was no longer a spokesperson for the black marchers. In October, the man branded as a "racial agitator" appeared in court along with his Memphis attorney, R. B. Sugarmon Jr., to answer the charges against him. In exchange for agreeing to "vacate himself from the jurisdiction of this court," the charges were retired from the docket. The judge sternly warned Weinberger that if he ever returned to Haywood County, the charges would "reappear on the docket."[14] Blacks were not too bothered by the ruling. After the first march, they had not needed as much convincing to participate.

The next month, for a brief period, most of the citizens of Haywood County were saddened. Friday, November 22, 1963, began as a gray, overcast day. As students arrived at Carver High School, they took their seat on the bleachers in the gymnasium to wait until the eight o'clock bell rang to signal the start of the first period class. After a while, the students started to notice that the teachers were acting a bit strange. They kept going to the door to the parking lot and peering out, and they huddled together and talked. Something was wrong. The students began to whisper among themselves that something had happened. Putting together bits and pieces of what they had heard, they discerned that one of the buses had not arrived as scheduled.

The students could not recall exactly when their fears were confirmed. They just remembered the chaos, the crying, and the effort to console each other after they got the news. The bus bringing students from Stanton had been struck by a truck on Highway 70 in the Hatchie bottom. The big truck, loaded with gasoline, crashed into the rear of the school bus, causing the driver to lose control of the bus and careen into a deep ditch, where the rear end of the bus was submerged under water. The brakes on the truck had failed and the truck plunged into the ditch along with the bus. Several rescue workers tried feverishly to free the thirty-five students from the bus, but three students died: Neal May, 19; Joseph Brewer Jr., 17; and Joe C. Malone, 15.[15]

Practically the entire Carver enrollment knew the three boys, all of whom had been at school the day before, when Betty and her friends had joked with Neal in the cafeteria. Students spent the whole morning crying, many keeping their heads on their desks all period. When the bell rang to change classes, the students walked down the halls with puffy, red eyes and tear-stained faces.

Later that morning, a few students who had been on the bus from Stanton came to school, and the others learned more details of the wreck. One boy, who had been seated at the back of the bus, saw the truck coming upon them at a high rate of speed. "That truck is going to hit us," he said as he got up from his seat and walked to the front of the bus. This act saved his life. After the crash, other students pulled their classmates and friends from the water. One student used his Red Cross training and administered mouth-to-mouth resuscitation to save his classmate's life. Several injured students were rushed to the Haywood County Hospital. Hearing again about the three that could not be saved only upset some of the students more. It had been a horrible morning for everyone. By midday, the students did not think they could take hearing anything else about the accident.

It was shortly after noon when the principal, Mr. Roy Bond, made the announcement on the intercom: President Kennedy had been shot. Already frayed emotions were now overloaded. Lots of students and teachers started to cry all over again. Since it was obvious that no one would be able to accomplish anything for the remainder of the day, Mr. Bond announced that school was closing early.

Opal had the TV on when the children got home. For the rest of the day and most of the night, the children sat in the living room taking in all the news. It seemed the whole nation had come to a standstill. Even after the news was finally broadcast that the president had died, the family sat glued to the television set, watching Lyndon Johnson being sworn in as the new president, with the grieving widow, Jackie Kennedy, at his side. They watched the nation deal with the assassination of its fallen leader. The coverage continued all weekend. On Sunday morning, the children dressed for church and were watching television again when Opal heard them discussing what had just happened. Right on national TV, Jack Ruby had walked up to Lee Harvey Oswald, Kennedy's accused assassin, and shot him as officers were leading him from jail. After church, they watched the solemn viewing of the flag-draped casket that lay in state as thousands filed by. All schools were closed on Monday, and the nation watched as the country buried a president.

It was said that America lost its innocence when President Kennedy was assassinated. Many lamented the loss of the fifties morality, when citizens generally held a certain respect for authority. The sixties would bring turbulent years. The Vietnam era brought with it years of unrest and protest. This time when young boys marched off to fight in yet another war, they did so without the support of the majority of their country. Many boys from Haywood County fought in the war, and several did not return. Most black people considered the problems with this country's system of injustice to be magnified by the fact that a disproportionate number of young black men lost their lives in Vietnam when they could not vote or enjoy other basic rights at home. The blacks in Haywood County continued their quest for equal justice under the law.

In May of 1966, Opal saw pictures in the paper of the aftermath of acts of violence that had again shaken the people in this rural west Tennessee county. In one night, there were gunshots, cross burnings, and two explosions in Brownsville. The shots were fired and the crosses were burned on Jefferson Street, where a white couple from up north was staying with a black family. A short time later, one bomb damaged a new garage, while the other bomb ripped an entire side off the home of Mr. Odell Sanders. The explosion blew away the living room, dining room, and kitchen, but the family, asleep in the bedrooms at the time, felt fortunate that no one was injured. Their next door neighbor was not as fortunate. After witnessing the damage to the Sanders home and sustaining cuts from flying glass when his own windows were blown out, Pete Bradford suffered a heart attack and died.[16] "It was not done by any of our members," the local members of the Brownsville KKK said. However, less than a month earlier, the Klan had held a large rally at the courthouse in town.

In this climate, the black people in Haywood County continued their struggle. Opal and Tonnie were not players, but they, unwittingly, were advanced along with the movement. They understood that "there could be no change without struggle," although they had never read Frederick Douglass. As one young freedom marcher said when asked why she protested, "I didn't see any difference between me and them." She added that the conditions they had been subjected to "just weren't right." Once they recognized this fact, they knew that America had not lived up to its claim of democracy, not as written by Winston Churchill in 1944, when he said: "At the bottom of all tributes paid to democracy is the little man walking into the little booth with a little pencil, making a little cross on a little bit of paper."

So it was in the 1960s that blacks in Haywood County decided the time had come to force America to live up to its claim as the greatest democracy. And they joined others all over the country who faced, in the words of one anonymous writer:

>Billy club swinging, white
>Policemen on feet
>fire hoses
>Klansmen
>attack dogs
>mob attacks
>cattle prods
>bombings
>jailings
>killings
>Still they marched, staged
>Sit-ins, went to jail, stood
>up to being cursed
>Spat on, beaten, and
>even killed, saying
>"We Are Not Afraid."[17]

10.

Hull's Dinner

January 1967. The times they were a changing.

On January 10, Tonnie turned sixty-three. He had been simply "Tinnie" or "Papa" to the family for so long that no one really thought about him getting old. Tonnie was the husband, the father, the disciplinarian, and the provider. For a couple of years now he had been one of the few hundred workers employed at the Winter Garden in Bells, where he worked five days a week. Opal had dinner ready every day shortly after noon, and they sat down to their main meal of the day. Sometime around three o'clock, Tonnie put his hat on, stuck his pipe in his mouth, then climbed in his truck and headed northwest of Brownsville. Most days he drove alone on the twelve-mile route through the countryside to neighboring Crockett County. At times, he stopped and picked up one or two people who caught a ride to work with him. They arrived in time to clock in for the four-to-midnight shift.

The Winter Garden processed fresh vegetables that were frozen, packaged, and shipped to various parts of the country. The company owned large farms, and it shipped to the plant big trucks loaded with turnip greens, black-eyed peas, lima beans, okra, snap beans, and bell peppers. The women and men stood in a line on both sides of long conveyor belts, picking out trash as the vegetables passed before them. Their job was to catch any foreign object to make sure it did not end up in some housewife's pot of frozen vegetables. On a few occasions, a frog would leap from the pile of vegetables, and one time a snake scurried from the belt and onto the floor, sending the women running and screaming. The boss man got mad and cursed them for calling attention to the reptile. Tonnie worked on the lines sometimes, but he mostly kept bins filled with okra for the women who spent the night cutting off their stems. Although there were few blacks employed at the factories in Brownsville, most of the people working with Tonnie were black. He worked hard and never slacked off like some of the younger ones. When quitting time came, he drove his truck home, trying mightily to keep from running off the road. All the neighbors were sleeping by the time Tonnie made the turn from Thomas Street onto McLemore.

Mr. Cal Davis, his wife, Miss Mattie, and her mother, Miss Deely, lived in the house on the north side of Tonnie. About a year or more after moving there, Tonnie sold a couple acres of his land to Mr. Cal. Since the Davises never added a separate driveway when they built their house, they shared a common drive with Tonnie. Mr. Shine Horton and Miss Ethel lived on the other side of Mr. Cal and Miss Mattie. Until she married Mr. Shine, Miss Ethel lived across the street from where the Davis house was now located. Her sister, Miss Ione, and the grown children of both women still lived in the house. Miss Ida White lived in a small, box-shaped house on the south side of Tonnie and Opal. Next door to Miss Ida was Mr. Ed Curie and Miss Lily. Mr. Blair Macklin and the other Miss Ida lived in the house across the street from the Curries. Miss Katherine was on one side of the Macklins, and on the other side a vacant lot separated the Macklins' house from Mr. Gene. They were all around the age of Tonnie or older, and, like most neighborhoods, there were a few interesting characters.

Miss Mattie, who was several years older than Opal, spent most of the day sitting on the front porch with Miss Deely. She was still doing some work when they first moved to McLemore, and some of Opal's children picked cotton with her. Now, the small, somewhat frail woman sat and watched the neighborhood children and everything else that went on up and down the street. Miss Mattie was someone who believed in going to church on Sunday and living right the rest of the week. If she saw a young boy or girl doing something wrong, she would say, without raising her voice, "Com'ere. You com'ere, now." When she got the youngster over to the porch, she would then quietly straighten the child out. She always spoke softly, with what sounded like a lisp, but could actually have been due to the big dip of snuff she kept in her mouth while periodically expectorating into a tin can. She was just a bit jealous of Mr. Cal. Opal did not know whether she had cause. Since she had known Cal, he left home early every Sunday morning to teach Sunday school. Opal enjoyed Miss Deely's and Miss Mattie's company when they got a chance to visit, and she could not think of anyone else she would rather have as her next door neighbors.

Miss Ida White talked all the time. Much of the time, no one else was around to carry on a conversation with her, but that did not keep her from talking anyway. Opal thought that perhaps she developed the habit from living by herself for so long. She looked as though she was probably very attractive as a young woman. Now in her late sixties or early seventies, she was quite bony, with weathered skin and almost completely white hair that she kept pinned up behind her head. On any day she could be found walking the street, always taking extra long steps as if she were in a hurry to get somewhere. When she came to visit Opal, she simply walked through the few scattered trees and tall grass along the slightly raised property line that adjoined their yards. Miss Ida would come by and volunteer to help Opal shell peas and butter beans or whatever else Opal may have been doing. She always worked fast and finished in a short time. She was really a harmless old woman who got along with almost everyone in the neighborhood. One time she came by the house and said, "Miss Opal, you got any peas you want me to shell for you?" After she had finished the peas, she kept sitting and sitting. Finally, Opal figured out that she was too scared to go home because of a rumor she had spread about the other Ida. Then there was her nemesis, Mr. Gene.

Mr. Gene, who most only knew by just one name, was short and bald. The children in the neighborhood thought he was real mean. Staying to himself most of the time, he sat on his front porch looking menacing. About the only time he bothered to speak to anyone was when a young girl walked up the street wearing a short dress, then he would raise his head with a semblance of a smile on his face. The rumor was that he had mistreated his mother, who used to live with him. To the good people in the neighborhood, this was the ultimate sin. He now lived alone, directly across the street from Miss Ida. For some reason, which no one understood, he was constantly badgering her about one thing or another. If he had failed in his efforts to completely intimidate her before, he succeeded when he went uptown and had the poor woman arrested. He told the police that Miss Ida had come by his house bothering him and had poured sugar around his house. Opal could not believe the police actually picked the old woman up on something Mr. Gene said. Miss Ida was so upset that she cried. Some of the neighbors got together and went to the jail and told the police that what Mr. Gene said was not true. She was released, but Mr. Gene had solidified his reputation for being a mean, ornery man who none of the neighbors liked.

Miss Ida Macklin was nothing like the woman who shared her name. Ida Macklin was a stout woman with a brown complexion and big eyes that showed an abundance of white when she looked at you. Opal had started calling the women "Big Ida" and "Little Ida" in order to distinguish them. Opal knew that Big Ida could be as mean as she wanted to at times. She was sewing and looking out the window one day when she saw Big Ida "setting her husband out" about something. Mr. Blair just kept working in the garden and never opened his mouth. So when Opal saw Big Ida head over to Mr. Gene's house that time, looking as though she could roll right over anyone who got in her way, Opal decided that this was probably worth her putting her sewing down so she could find out what had prompted the visit.

All her life, Opal had been prim and proper, shunning gossip and never wanting to do anything that would in any way involve getting into someone else's business. But for Mr. Gene, she made a conscious exception. When Big Ida went strutting across the open field that separated her home from Mr. Gene's, Opal said to herself, "I'm just going to be nosey." She did not want to be too obvious, so instead of going out the front door, she went out into the backyard. Trying to look nonchalant, in case someone was watching, she sauntered over to the side of the house next to Little Ida. From her vantage point, Opal could see Big Ida standing facing Mr. Gene with her hands on her hips. She was shaking her head and giving him a piece of her mind. "I done told you to keep your chickens out of my garden," she said. She called him mean and a lying SOB. Then she took a few steps closer, until she was right in his face, then said, "You know you been a ——— ever since you left your Mama's womb." Mr. Gene stood there with his eyes diverted to the ground and did not even say one word. Seeing him looking like a child who had just been scolded, Opal was convinced of the truth of what she often heard a lot of old people say: "No matter how bad a person might think he is, there's always somebody else that's badder."

By the end of March 1967, Tonnie and Opal had settled into their routine for another year. Now that spring had come, Tonnie was again busy working outdoors. Since he could never sleep late, even on nights when he went to bed past midnight, he was up early each morning and dressed to start the day. He never sat around the house doing nothing. Instead, right after breakfast, he loaded his lawn mower and gas can in the back of his pickup truck and headed in the direction of town. At the end of the street, he turned left on Key Corner and then on toward the first of several houses where he mowed the lawns for the owners on a regular basis.

When he finished one lawn, he went straight to the next one. By the time he finished working most of the morning in the scorching summer sun, his khaki pants and shirt were soaked with perspiration. The band around his straw hat dripped sweat down his face. Still, he never thought about slowing down. Opal was used to him being on the go all the time, and she always said he could never sit still.

Although he was not farming any longer, Tonnie continued to plant his truck garden. He grew okra, tomatoes, and peas, but his main money crop was turnip greens. He rented a patch of land up the road on Key Corner, where he had planted his crops. When the vegetables were ready later in the spring, he would get the same two women that he always hired to help do the picking. While the women were busy working, Tonnie rode in his truck. Just as he had done for years now, Tonnie sold some vegetables off his truck and took the rest to the stores in town. There were not too many days when he returned home without doing some shopping. He evenly split his business between the two main stores, Kroger and Big Star, and he was always pleased when he found a bargain. Tonnie was a smart consumer, and he found buying in large quantities to be less expensive. Toting his paper sacks in the house, he sat them on the dining room table, where Opal could have a better look at each item.

"Come here, Kid," he called out as soon as he sat the bags down. "Come look a here at what I got you." He unwrapped the white paper to show her the fryers that he got for twenty-five cents a pound and the cartons of large eggs that were on sale at three dozen for a dollar. Since they used so much, he always bought a one-pound block of margarine. He also bought the largest jar of Maxwell House Coffee that he could find and a ten-pound sack of sugar. It had been some time since he brought home a twenty-five-pound sack, like he did when all the children were at home. Tonnie always made sure that he remembered to get the Quality and Top Value stamps from the cashier when she gave him his grocery receipt. "Here you go, Kid," Tonnie said to Opal as he gave her the long row of trading stamps.

Opal put the stamps in the drawer with the others and the stamp books, some of which were already filled. When she had the time, she would sit down and paste the stamps in the small paper books. She always kept a catalogue for the Quality and Top Value stamps, and she carefully went through both catalogs to see which items she wanted and how many books she needed to get them. Once Opal filled enough books, she got Tonnie to take her over to Jackson, where she exchanged her stamps for merchandise. With her stamps, she had purchased a set of bed sheets, pots and pans, several lace tablecloths, the large clock on their living room wall, and several other items.

If things had changed for Tonnie, they were certainly different for Opal. Whenever she was not preparing meals, she spent most of her time sewing. She prepared much smaller meals now that she no longer had a crowd coming home after school. The last two girls to graduate from high school had left home and gone away to college. Opal could hardly believe the day had come when all the children were gone except the youngest child. Now, instead of sewing just for the children, she sewed for other people in town. Quite a few people had become regular customers, including several teachers at the Eastside Elementary School and some women in the neighborhood. Uncle Dan often brought material by the house for Aunt Lucille's church dresses. Opal's customers were always pleased with her work. For someone who had learned to sew on her own, out of necessity, she was quite good at the trade. She had even made suits for some of the local men. When the table was not being used for eating, Opal often turned back the tablecloth and spread out her pattern in order to cut out the material. Sometimes people showed her a picture of a dress or pantsuit they liked. Opal would take a piece of old newspaper and cut a pattern just from looking at the picture.

For Opal, the house was quiet all the time now, but her sewing kept her busy. She had come to look forward to the occasional interruption of the ringing telephone. It was usually one of the children calling to check on them. Opal enjoyed hearing what was going on with the children, and they liked to get news from home. She always told them who had come to visit, who was sick, and who had died recently. They would ask her how she and Tonnie were doing, and they asked her about who she was sewing for. They wanted to know how much she charged, and they tried to convince her that it was much less than what her labor was worth. Other seamstresses in town charged much more than Opal. She made dresses for as little as four dollars and pantsuits for eight dollars. The children would explain that if the item was purchased at the store, it would cost fifty or sixty dollars or more, but she would not listen. Opal was aware that some of her children thought she was too nice, but she figured as long as she was able to save money from her sewing, she would stick with her price list. After all, there was not anything she really wanted that, by praying, she could not find a way to get.

While Opal was busy with her work, Tonnie often headed back to town again. Although he was taciturn most of the time at home, Tonnie never missed a chance to talk with some of the local men, including the white merchants in town. They discussed most anything. At the times when Tonnie was not part of the conversation, he was within earshot. The men stood around and talked about how things were changing. According to a recent report, Haywood County was steadily losing its population. Since the men knew people in the county were still having their share of babies every year, they figured the loss had to be due to people leaving. They tried to come up with an answer for what was taking place in their county, especially in light of the fact that the overall population for the state had increased significantly. Only ten other counties out of the ninety-five had experienced an actual loss in population in the past few years.[1] They were afraid the trend in Haywood County would likely continue. This raised some serious concern among the locals about the future of farming in the county, especially since farming had always been the primary source of income for Haywood Countians.[2]

Tonnie agreed that the population decline was probably due to the lack of jobs and other opportunities for young people upon graduation from high school. He knew that was the reason his own children had left home after finishing high school. Opal always said that the children would have an opportunity to find better jobs if they left Brownsville. If they got an education, they could find a job that paid more money and gave them a chance to make something of themselves. She had seen many others who had stayed around town and were unable to find decent jobs. As far as she was concerned, there was no future for young people in Brownsville. Although her children had to leave home to get an education, she never doubted that it would be worth it in the long run. If they did well, they would be in a better position to help their own children one day. Opal felt the farm no longer offered any kind of life for a young person.

Farming in Tennessee had undergone profound changes over the past four years since Tonnie had left the business, and even more startling changes were expected in the future. There was now a greater degree of specialization with higher capitalization, which yielded higher production efficiency. The big farmers in the county were able to adjust to these radical changes. Since the decrease in farm operations, the big farmers had actually improved their individual income and now had a higher standard of living. Since the more highly efficient production was also more profitable, the large landowners had little reason to complain. However, the impact felt by the advent of the spectacular change in agriculture was palpable. Not only were there fewer farm workers, but the small farm, operated by families like Tonnie's, which was unable to afford costly machinery and keep pace with the changes, had all but ceased to exist.[3] Many either sold or lost their land. They left the country and moved to town, or they left Brownsville and went north.

Locals realized the trend in Tennessee was toward fewer, larger, and more efficient enterprises. Because of improved technology, farm production rates had been steadily rising in both crops and livestock. Even as the individual farm became more specialized, farming in the state remained highly diversified. A popular combination among farmers in Haywood County was cotton, corn, and soybeans. While the other two crops showed a gain, cotton had the lowest yield in the past four years.[4]

Still, the trend toward greater specialization continued, because along with it came a reduction in the cost of machinery and a more profitable total operation. At the same time, there was a parallel downward movement of total land in farms, but an increase in the average size of the farm, causing land values to climb with unprecedented rapidity. While the state had lost over 100,000 farm workers over the past few years, and close to the same number of farms, the changes in operation resulted in the income of farmers going up each year. In Haywood County, there were now a lot more farmers who held full-time jobs in industry. This contributed greatly to the level of living for the farm people. With all the commiserating about the changes in farming, few of the locals could argue with the fact that recent trends accounted for the gain in the general standard of living among farmers.[5] Tonnie still thought he had done the right thing when he quit farming four years ago.

Another thing the men talked about was the recent lawsuit the Justice Department had filed against the Haywood County and Brownsville City school boards for noncompliance with the Civil Rights Act of 1964. They thought the freedom-of-choice plan, where parents could sign for their children to attend all-white schools was sufficient. The notice from the Justice Department had requested an order directing the school boards to eliminate the city school system and have only one county-operated system.[6] Teachers were now to be hired without regard to race, and a teacher could not be dismissed or refused promotion because of his or her race. The men grumbled about how much it was going to cost. They would have to discontinue use of the old substandard school buildings that the black children had been using and offer equal facilities, equipment, and courses to all students. They did not discuss the notion that the county had discriminated against blacks because of their race.

Severe inequalities between the schools for blacks and for whites in Haywood County had continued for years. Even funds allocated for black children went to improve the education of white children, which widened existing disparities.[7] Black teachers had routinely complained of the inequity in their salaries compared to the salaries of white teachers. They also complained of having to teach black children from old text books that the white schools had discontinued. But the county spent money drawn from black children not enrolled and from money saved on the operating cost of black schools in order to provide better schools for whites.[8] Those familiar with the history of the county did not readily believe claims made by whites of their current efforts.

The Justice Department complaint raised obvious questions about the city's claim that it had done everything it could to achieve integration of its school system. It warned the locals that federal financial assistance would be deferred for noncompliance with the Civil Rights Act. Dr. John Thornton Jr., who was on the city school board, responded by saying they "had extended every effort in operating the freedom of choice plan of school integration for the past two years."[9] However, everyone knew that despite what was said to the federal government, few parents had exercised the option. The fact was the local school system had remained virtually unchanged.

Tonnie found it interesting to hear some of the local white people talk about how they really felt about integrating the schools. Although he was not surprised, he had difficulty trying to understand the hard line that some expressed. These were the men he had been doing business with for as long as he could remember. They usually greeted him with a smile whenever he went into their store and when he saw them on the street. They would say, "Hi, Tonnie," then add, "You doing all right today?" The store owners always recognized Tonnie's children and would say, "You Tonnie's boys." Then, they would let the children have whatever they wanted. But when it came to their children attending the same schools, Tonnie said that was a different story. He told Opal about the conversation he had with Mr. Harbert Thornton, partly because he could not believe what the man had the audacity to say to his face. They were talking one day when they somehow got on the subject of integration. Mr. Harbert said to Tonnie, "I'll rather die than let my grandchild go to school with a nigger."

Opal read the notice printed in the Brownsville newspaper with only marginal interest. She had seen the same notice in the paper for the past three or four weeks. It informed the public about the school desegregation plan, claiming that reading the notice would answer any questions the people might have about school desegregation. The Brownsville City public schools, the notice said, was being desegregated to eliminate from the school system the racial segregation of students and all other forms of discrimination.[10] Each student or his parent was required to choose the school the student would attend the next school year. The choice period was to begin on April 30, 1967, and they had thirty days to decide. Under the plan, no choice was to be denied unless it would cause overcrowding. All school-connected activities, facilities, and programs were to be open to all. The faculties would also be desegregated, and no one would lose a position because of race. Opal already knew some of the black teachers were considering retirement because they feared losing their jobs. Choosing a school was not a difficult decision for Opal to make. Since Dorothy only had one more year left in high school, Opal knew she would want to stay at Carver, and that was all right with her. She was not too concerned about having her go to the white high school anyway.

Tonnie had gotten Dorothy a job working with him at the Winter Garden during the summer. The two of them rode to work together in his truck. He had stopped buying cars a long time ago; now every time he came home with a new vehicle it was another truck. He had owned a Ford, a GMC, and a Chevrolet and had gotten good use from all of them. Opal was never interested in trying to learn how to drive, and none of the children ever drove his trucks. As Tonnie and Dorothy headed to work, neither did much talking. For the most part, they rode to work in silence. Although Tonnie had never been demonstrative when it came to showing affection, he was, nevertheless, very proud of all his children and liked to talk about what they were doing. He had always been especially fond of his youngest child. He was pleased to have her along when they rode to and from work.

Tonnie loaded large bins with okra while Dorothy joined the group working with the green peppers. They stood on each side of the conveyor, picking out bad peppers as they passed in front of them. They had worked about half the evening when a bell pepper went by Dorothy that had a big green worm on it. She quit her job right on the spot. Tonnie was not surprised, since every single one of his girls had expressed the same fear. He thought that by growing up on the farm and working in the field like they had, they would be used to worms. After all, he had never seen a field that did not have a worm in it. Not too many things had made him angrier than when he went to the field when the girls were picking cotton and found his cotton stalks broken, all because they had seen a worm. Using one foot, they pressed the stalks on both sides of the row down and away from them until they were leaning almost to the ground. There was also the time when one of the girls embarrassed him by coming out of her clothes because she discovered a worm on her shirt. Tonnie knew that while Dorothy may not have cared much for working, her fear was real. Later on, he talked to one of the men in charge and had him change Dorothy's assignment so she could come back to work.

The first Saturday of April 1967 was also the day before Easter Sunday. Grandpa Jim and Little Jim, Uncle Brown and Aunt Crettie Mae's boy, along with one of Cousin Booker's sons, were returning from Decatur, Illinois, to Brownsville. Although the nickname had stuck with him, there was nothing little about Little Jim. About the same age as Opal Ree, Little Jim was the tallest and probably the biggest of Uncle Brown's six boys. Opal had a theory that whenever people call someone "Little so and so," they grow up to be large. She avoided calling any of her children "little" the way so many other people did.

On this Saturday Little Jim had driven almost to Memphis when a white woman pulled into their path. He could not avoid colliding with the other vehicle. Little Jim and Cousin Booker's son were thrown from the car. Grandpa Jim, who had been riding in the front passenger seat, was knocked down onto the floor, partially underneath the steering wheel. The impact sent their car plummeting into a ditch. When Grandpa Jim finally got his bearings, he realized that the car was in a ravine. He was thankful to know that he was still alive. To the amazement of those who assisted in freeing him, Grandpa Jim walked away from the wreckage. He walked only slightly less erect than usual and made his way to a nearby telephone to call Uncle Brown. Cousin Booker's son also walked away from the accident, sustaining only minor injuries, but Little Jim suffered serious injuries. They were transported to the hospital in Memphis, where Little Jim was admitted. The doctors worked on him, doing all they could, but they were unable to pull him through.

They brought Grandpa Jim to the house, and Opal put him in the front bedroom, off the living room. She pulled off his shoes and helped him lay down on the bed and stretch out his long body. He told her how the car went off the road and he ended up trapped inside the car in a ditch "as tall as that door." He said that he was not hurt and was able to walk from the wreck. When Tonnie got home, he helped his papa take off his clothes. Tonnie told Opal that Grandpa Jim's side was completely black and blue.

Tonnie looked after Grandpa Jim while he stayed with them, and Opal took care to prepare his meals just right. He was diabetic and did not eat foods cooked with sugar, but he liked grapefruits and grapefruit juice. He had always been very strict about his diet, which was why he was still in such good health. Every morning he administered his own insulin injection. A few weeks before the accident, he went to the doctor for a checkup. The doctor, who gave him a clean bill of heath, said he could probably live to see one hundred. Despite his being so strong, he had been in a serious accident, and the family and church members were concerned. During the two weeks that he was at the house, many of them came by to visit.

Opal heard sounds coming from the front bedroom and said to herself, "I wonder what in the world is going on." Laughter roared from the front bedroom and vibrated throughout the house. Some of the deacons from the church came to visit Grandpa Jim. If they had expected to find a sick old man confined to his bed, they were disappointed. Instead, they found their old friend in as good of spirits as he had always been. And, as on many previous occasions, he was entertaining them. Opal knew he must have told them something really funny this time because the men were enjoying what she called a good belly laugh. They laughed so hard that they heaved and leaned forward as they slapped their thighs. This had been going on for a while now, and Opal was curious about what was happening in there.

Tonnie had escorted the men to Grandpa Jim's room, where he was seated in a chair by the bed. As was custom at Willow Grove Church, some of the members visited those on the sick-and-shut-in list on Sunday mornings. The minister read the names of the sick so he could pray for their healing. Depending on how sick the persons were and how long they had been sick, the church sometimes took up a special collection for them. When church members were sent out to visit the sick, they took with them a small gift of money. On occasion, they would also bring food, especially around holidays. The church sent a box filled with such staples as flour, sugar, and meal, along with a few canned goods and bags of fruit. The visitor would pray with the sick, read the Bible with him, and try to cheer him up. This day, these men were not having their usual visit.

Tonnie brought in more chairs from the dinning room table until everyone had a chair. They sat in a sort of half-moon formation, facing the "sick" one to whom they had come to pay their respect. Grandpa Jim was telling a

Hulls Dinner

story with all the dignity of a scholar discussing a great literary work. No one else could possibly match him. He expressed himself using his hands, captivating his audience. "Talking with his hands" is what Opal called it. He described what had happened to him one day a while back when he was uptown. "I had been doing a bit of shopping," Grandpa said. "I decided to stop in the little colored market before going home." He explained that he had only been in Mr. Odell's store for a short amount of time when all of a sudden he just passed out. He attributed this to his blood sugar, having gone too long without eating. "When I came to myself, I was lying there stretched out on the floor," he said. Then he chuckled a little, not giving any hint to what happened next. "As I was coming around, I could hear all the ladies calling my name, and I could feel them fanning me and they were rubbing me." He said, "I opened my eyes and one was leaning right over my head." Now some of the men were beginning to get the picture. "She was really busy working on me," Grandpa said. "Then she realized that I had come around." Spreading his hands and imitating the lady, he shared what she said, "Mr. Jim, you ready to get up now, Mr. Jim?" Grandpa said he lay there and looked up at her and very politely said, "Yes, ma'am, I can get up now." It was the way he implied what was left unsaid that had all the men dying laughing.

Although Grandpa Jim did not act like he had been in an automobile accident, people started trying to convince him to go to the hospital. First, Uncle Dan came by to see him and said, "Papa, you need to go to the hospital in Jackson." Like many other black people, he did not trust the hospital in Brownsville. Next, one of his cousins on the Bond side of the family came by the house. The man took a seat on the floor by Grandpa Jim's chair. Opal suspected he had taken a couple drinks too many. "Uncle Jim, you need to go to the hospital," he said. Then every few minutes he would repeat himself, "Uncle Jim, you need to go to the hospital." Tonnie talked to Grandpa, and they decided he would talk to the doctor to see if perhaps he should be in the hospital. Tonnie contacted Dr. Thornton Sr. and arranged for him to come out to the house.

The two elderly gentlemen, one black and one white, sat there at the table in the dining room. Grandpa Jim had been sitting there when the doctor came in, and Dr. Thornton sat down near him. They talked about how Grandpa was feeling and his concern that he should check into the hospital. He said that the family thought it best if he were admitted so he could be thoroughly examined. Opal was in the kitchen working, and since no wall separated the two rooms, she could not help but hear their conversation. As she watched the men sitting there talking, she thought it was kind of odd in a way. Dr. Thornton had delivered almost half of her children, but this was the first time that she had looked on him like one of the other men that had come to visit "Old Man Jim." But the doctor was on call. "You're not going to like it," Dr. Thornton said. "You're gonna get tired sitting around that hospital, but I can arrange for you to go in." Grandpa Jim agreed to let the doctor make the necessary arrangements.

Uncle Brown and Aunt Crettie Mae came by for a visit not long after Grandpa decided to go into the Brownsville hospital. "Papa, you need to go in the hospital down in Memphis," Uncle Brown said, and Aunt Crettie Mae agreed. "You know Vernice is down there, and she can look after you," he added. He continued, telling all the reasons why he thought Papa needed to go in the Memphis hospital. Grandpa finally relented, having been convinced that he should not follow through with the arrangements that had already been made. They made the trip to Memphis, but because of some problem concerning how Grandpa was to be admitted, he did not stay. Opal was surprised when they brought him back home. He explained that the hospital down in Memphis would not accept his insurance and wanted him to pay cash. Grandpa, who the family had always said was tight with his money, refused. By the time he got back to Brownsville, the time that was scheduled for him to check into the hospital had passed.

"Papa, you should go to the hospital in Decatur," said Aunt Lee. She had been living in New York for so long that she had acquired an accent from that part of the country. She had also adopted the belief of many northerners that their services were somehow superior to the South's. She was the latest in the almost steady stream of family, friends, and church members who had come by the house since Grandpa had been with Tonnie and Opal. Grandpa Jim was about as well liked as he was well known in the various communities throughout Brownsville. Not only was he actively involved with the Willow Grove Church, but whenever they hosted or visited other churches, Grandpa was always one of the men to address the congregation or lead them in prayer. Local people thought highly of Grandpa, and they came to visit and offer their well-intended advice. "You know, they got the best doctors and the best hospitals up there," Aunt Lee said. Then she offered him a way to get there. "Brown and Crettie Mae are going to Decatur, and you can go with them." To further persuade him, she added, "And you'll have Louise, Meg, and Ada there to check on you."

Opal thought that one thing was for sure, there had been no shortage of advice dispensed in her house lately. But then she said, "if anything ever happens to me, I sure hope my children will come together and decide the best thing to do." As for "Old Man Jim," which she fondly called him, it seemed that everyone in the family was telling him something different. But Aunt Lee convinced him that he would receive better treatment up north. When Uncle Brown and Aunt Crettie Mae got ready to make the trip, Grandpa was packed and ready to go with them. Grandpa Jim rode with them on the Greyhound bus to Decatur, Illinois.

Grandpa Jim had been staying with Aunt Louise at the time that he and Little Jim took the trip to Brownsville. So he returned to her home when they reached Decatur. He made the bus trip without any problem, but his side was still awfully bruised. Although he had been carrying on like his usual self since the accident, he experienced pain at times. Tonnie had seen him wrench in pain when he changed his clothes, but Grandpa had done a good job of masking the pain from most everyone else. He saw the doctor in Decatur as soon as they could schedule an appointment. The doctor examining him could tell right away that his side was causing him a great deal of discomfort. Grandpa Jim had sustained three fractured ribs in the accident, and, so far, his injury had gone untreated. The doctor put him in a back brace and ordered him to take it easy. When Uncle Brown and Aunt Crettie Mae left for Brownsville, they had to leave him behind.

Someone in the family told Opal, "After Brown and Crettie Mae left, Papa Jim began to worry himself about coming home." Opal did not know if he had worried or not, but some others did say that Grandpa Jim wanted to come back to Brownsville. They said, "That's the reason for what happened, cause he was settin' around worrying himself." One day not long after he got back to Decatur, he and Aunt Louise were sitting around the house. It was just the two of them at home. He got up and went to the bathroom, and a little while later, Aunt Louise heard a noise. "Papa, Papa," Aunt Louise called out as she went to check on him. She found him lying there on the bathroom floor, where he had fallen. As she leaned over him, he looked up at her and smiled. Grandpa Jim was transported to the hospital, but he never regained consciousness. He had suffered a stroke. On April 20, 1967, nineteen days after he amazed everyone by walking away from the automobile accident, he died from a cerebral hemorrhage. He was eighty-seven.

After Grandpa died, the word of his death spread to family in Washington, New York, Michigan, and other faraway places. The news reached

Brownsville right away, and a day or so later his body was returned home. Over the next several days, family came in town from all over the country, most of them staying with family members who had never left. There were all of Tonnie's sisters, Aunt Lee, Aunt Meg, Aunt Louise, Aunt Vernise and Aunt Ada. Uncle Charles came from Decatur and Uncle Avery from Memphis. Tonnie, Uncle Brown, and Uncle Dan were the only ones that had remained in Brownsville, where they had farmed just like their papa had done. Many others came to pay their respects, including the members from his church, people from the Springfield community, and members from other churches. There was also a large number of grandchildren who returned home for the funeral.

Opal Ree boarded the Greyhound bus in Washington for the almost twenty-four-hour trip home. After finding a seat on the crowded bus, she commenced talking to the little boy standing on the seat in front of her. She was more outgoing than some of the girls, and she never had a problem engaging strangers in conversation. As she started telling the child, who looked to be no more than two or three years old, that he was a "cute little boy," his mother, whom he was standing beside, turned around. It was then that Opal realized she had been playing with her nephew. Cloria had boarded the bus in New Jersey, where she was now living. They kept each other company for the rest of the day and all night, talking the whole time without sleeping. As the bus rolled down Highway 70 and into the city limits of Brownsville, Opal and Cloria watched out the window as they passed a long line of cars heading in the opposite direction. The two of them stopped talking and stared as each one of the cars went by. The procession drove slowly, with headlights on, behind a big black hearse.

The cars traveled on Jackson Highway, and one by one the cars followed the hearse up the little hill to the church grounds. They packed the little church on the hill. The pastor of Willow Grove, Reverend Allen, delivered the eulogy. Reverend Allen talked about how early on Grandpa Jim had dedicated his life to serving God. He was devoted to the church and brought up all his children there. Aunt Vernise was, as usual, the most emotional. She did not jump over the bench like she had done over twenty years earlier at Grandma Ada's funeral, but since she had not made it to Decatur before Grandpa died, she kept screaming, "Papa, I was coming. Papa, I was coming."

Everyone felt the tremendous loss. Although he had made a lot of people laugh, the family knew he had some trials, especially after he lost

Grandma Ada. He remarried, to a much younger woman named Mariah Bond, but that marriage was so brief some had forgotten it ever occurred. Then, in his later years he stayed with some of his children. Through it all, one thing never changed, he loved the Bible and he always read it. Sagacious, schooled more by life than a formal education, he impressed all those he met with his keen intellect. He once offered to pay the first of Tonnie's young children who could tell him the answer to an old riddle that asked, "What is it that walks on four legs in the morning, two legs at noonday, and three legs in the evening." It was only years later, after they had studied literature, that they could fully appreciate his knowledge. The minister described him as a faithful servant, and his words were not hollow. Grandpa served as deacon at Willow Grove for several decades, and he taught Sunday school for fifty years. He had a remarkable life. As Opal viewed his body for the last time, she said to herself, "That sure looks like a smile on Old Man Jim's face."

Grandpa Jim was buried in Rosenwald Cemetery, next to Grandma Ada. Later, everyone gathered for dinner. There was an abundance of food on which to feast: fried chicken, ham, potato salad, several different kinds of vegetables, cornbread and rolls, and an assortment of cakes and pies. Some food had been prepared by the family and some food was brought to the house by the church members and other people in the community. After the funeral, having dinner was the next order of business for the day. This was also a time to visit and catch up on news in the family. Most of the aunts ended up at Uncle Brown and Aunt Crettie Mae's that evening, and Tonnie, Opal, and some of the children joined them. The gathering was just as it always was whenever a group of Springfields got together. Most of Tonnie's sisters were large, healthy women, with great big legs and big hips. In fact, people around town always said they could tell a Springfield woman by her legs. These aunts loved laughing and joking as much as their brothers. As visitors came to pay respect, they could hear the sound of loud laughter emanating from a room in the back of the house.

Everyone greeted each other with big hugs, including the ones that they did not recognize right away. "Now, who is this?" the aunts asked, and "Which one are you?" Then they would turn to one of the other sisters for confirmation and say, "Lord, this child here looks just like Opal, don't she?" They usually agreed, regardless of which one of the children it was. It was not uncommon for them not to recognize the younger ones. It had been many years since the aunts had seen most of Tonnie's children. On some of their trips to Brownsville, they might visit their brother Brown and not see Tonnie. Opal thought it was probably because Brown's children liked to laugh and joke with them more than her children. While the aunts tried to identify the children, the children tried to identify their aunts. After they finally discovered who everyone was, the aunts gave them a bigger hug, followed by an even bigger laugh.

This may have appeared odd to an outsider who happened upon the scene. Even some of the younger members of the family had difficulty fully comprehending the dynamics. Family members who had been weeping in such sorrow a short time ago were now exhibiting behavior that was the diametric opposite. The gathering was more akin to a celebration: people, food, talk, and laughter. Everyone enjoyed himself, celebrating a life without ever saying so. None had forgotten the occasion that brought them together. With time, they would all reflect on Grandpa Jim's life and begin to grieve. It takes a while to feel pain after a cut, and that night the wound was too fresh to hurt deeply. The act of coming together was the comfort they provided each other. Jim Springfield would have enjoyed the occasion more than anyone there.

Later, Opal remembered what her Grandma Tamar told her years ago. "I was nine years old when all us slaves from different plantations got together for this great big celebration. They called it Hulls Dinner," she said. "Mama combed my hair and put me on a pretty little purple dress." Isabel fixed her and the other children up so she looked real nice. Isabel and the rest of the women folks had cooked all kinds of good food, and there was lots of singing, praying, and praising the Lord. From the oldest on down, people were walking around laughing, talking, and having a good time. "I didn't know some of those folks had that much life left in them," she said. "Ain't never before seen some of 'em look that happy." Funerals and weddings were about the only other times the slaves came together. Grandma Tamar never forgot that day. Years later, she still got excited whenever she talked about the big dinner they had to celebrate their freedom.

Opal had come to think very highly of Grandpa Jim. She knew the feeling was mutual, and she had long ago accepted his teasing, like his calling her "Sis Opie," as good natured. It was good for the family to get together, have a fun time, and enjoy each other after they buried Grandpa. She felt it was appropriate to celebrate his life and the fact that now he was free again.

11.

Hope for Reunion

Three years later, in May 1970, the family began planning for their summer trip home. The last of Tonnie and Opal's children had finally left home, and everyone was scattered all over the country. Though some of them had been away for over twenty years now, they still said "going home" when they talked about visiting Brownsville. In the past, they had always visited at different times during the course of the year. This made it difficult to see each other, and some of the children had not seen each other in several years. For the first time, they decided to coordinate their trip so they would all be home at the same time. Over the next few months, they made plans for the homecoming. Finally, in the last week of August, their planning came together.

The house on McLemore Street was full to capacity, taking all three bedrooms and the living room, and still a number of the children stayed at the motel in town. Most of them had children of their own now, so Opal had lots of young grandchildren. There were toddlers, a few who were just learning to walk, and even younger babies, with the youngest grandchild at the reunion being only three weeks old. But they were not going to miss the opportunity to see everyone. They all came, except for Salathiel, Lois, and Aaron, who was in a veteran's hospital in Marion, Indiana. The sisters helped Opal in the kitchen and kept after the little children. The brothers ran errands uptown, but spent most of their time sitting under the shade trees in the front yard, laughing and talking and reminiscing.

The big pecan trees had grown tall, and their long limbs almost enveloped the white house with black shutters. One of the big trees stood in front of the house, next to the road, and the other two were on the north side of the house, near the driveway. In the past, the trees had borne their share of tasty nuts. Each fall, the yard was covered with pecans. Tonnie had the younger children pick up the pecans, then he would take them uptown to sell them to different store owners. For some reason, which he had yet to determine, the trees had gradually stopped producing. Now he only saw a few pecans in the fall, scattered here and there over the yard. But the trees still served the very useful purpose of providing shade during the long hot Tennessee summers. Tonnie and the boys sat outside, surrounded by the pecan trees, the weeping willow Opal had set out near the front south end of the house, and the not yet full-grown oak she had planted close to the front of the house. The shade trees made the temperature outside seem much cooler than it was. With all the cooking going on inside the house, the heat was almost unbearable, and everyone spent as much time as possible sitting outside in the shade.

Tonnie was so proud of all the children. Whenever one of them happened to accompany him to town, he bragged to the storekeepers and other people about what his children were doing. He especially liked to point out that his boy and girl were teaching school. Although he never told the children how he felt, he did not have to say what they could see in his eyes and on his face. It was not easy on him when all the boys first left home and the older girls went off to college, but no one was more pleased with what they had accomplished than Tonnie. He still did not often join in conversations when the children came home, but he would always take a seat nearby, where he could take in everything that went on around him. They knew he listened to what they said, because when someone told a joke he would laugh out loud. But any attempt to pull him into the conversation was, for the most part, gently rebuffed.

After talking for a while, Lee or Tony would call out to him and ask, "What you think about that, Pops?" Sometimes they tried to get him to agree with them by asking, "Ain't that right, Papa?" Tonnie just laughed. Once one of the boys said, "Pops, they tell me you voted in the last presidential election. You didn't vote for Nixon did you?" They knew that Tonnie and Opal had registered and voted for the first time in the 1968 election. They both voted for the Democratic candidate, Hubert H. Humphrey, but the boys asked anyway. It was part of their effort to bring Tonnie into the conversation, which like always was not very successful. Tonnie would smile and laugh at their jokes, but he would not say much. They would continue talking while Tonnie closely observed everyone.

Hope for Reunion

The children were interested in what was going on with the school system in Brownsville. Earlier, a group of them had driven down Jefferson Street just to see the old school. In May, Carver High had held its last commencement, graduating over two hundred students. The school was now closed for good. They drove by slowly to get a good look, and memories flooded their minds: friends and teachers, study hall, eating in the cafeteria, sock hops and basketball games in the gym. The school had a good team, and Carver had won the district tournament last year. The girls remembered boys that they liked but never dated because Tonnie was too strict. They pointed to the aging building and told the small children, "That's where your Mommie went to high school." It seemed strange that no other child in Brownsville would ever feel the pride of having graduated from Carver High School. The city had designated the building for vocational education classes.

Most local blacks were not eager to close the doors of their high school, and they blamed the desegregation plan for what had happened to Carver. After all the meetings of the school board, which had merged, the trips to court, filing of answers and talks of appeals, the decision concerning the school system was finally made. The federal court ordered complete school integration, with the choice of two plans. The court said the county could either divide into two geographic zones, with one for each school, or the two schools could be paired, with one taking the ninth and tenth grades and another taking the junior and senior classes. Either way, the court held that neither school would be identified as Negro or white. The county finally resolved the issue by constructing the new Haywood High School, which was now ready to open. For the first time, all the black and white high school students in the county would attend the same school this August.

Opal found out from some of her customers at the Eastside Elementary School that they had been asked whether they wanted to transfer to the Haywood County Elementary School, which was all white. The plan that had been adopted called for the two schools to exchange some teachers and students, rather than closing the schools. Opal knew a few black teachers who had finally volunteered to go to the white school. She thought it was probably inevitable that along with the change there were some who were unhappy. A number of black teachers were concerned about the status of their jobs. Others were apprehensive about the move but reluctantly accepted the change. Still, there were a number of black teachers who opted to retire, thinking it was in their best interest. Opal told the children about the teachers who had retired. They all thought it sad that some of their old teachers' teaching careers had come to an end this way. Some questioned why it had to be their people that always ended up with the worse end of the deal. Later, they went by to see the new school that spread out over four acres. They hoped it was a start for the people of Brownsville to come together.

The reunion was three full days, and longer for some, of family, fun, food, and activities. It had been almost like the old times, when all the children were at home. Opal started cooking early, baking cakes and pies and putting them in the deep freezer until her company came. The house was full once again, and she was in the kitchen cooking a big breakfast, with homemade biscuits and steak and gravy. But now the children did not want breakfast as early as they used to, and Opal had some difficulty accepting that some of the girls did not eat breakfast anymore. She tried to get them to eat anyway. After having no success with the girls, she would talk to them about feeding their husbands and children. Opal reminded the girls, "Y'all feed your husbands now." She would say, "You need to fix your husband his plate first." She sensed the girls did not feel nearly as strongly as she did about this. Opal decided the only thing to do was accept the fact that she could not impose all her ideas on the children. She knew that things were changing, but she wanted the children to remember the important things in life. She firmly believed all her children were good Christian folks who believed in living right.

Immediately after the first meal was over, Opal started putting on dinner. The house was usually quiet now, and she had almost forgotten how it was to have the children and grandchildren home. She was reminded of how much she missed the sound of loud talking and laughter as the children held discussions on different topics, sometimes agreeing and sometimes having heated debates. It was the same every time they came home. Opal was pleased that whenever her children got together, there was no drinking, no drugs, and, now that Tonnie no longer sported his pipe or cigar, there was no smoking, except for Jim Howell, who sometimes lit up a cigar. Opal liked to see the kids enjoying one another, but before she knew it, they were saying goodbye and going back to their own homes. The family had never been demonstrative when it came to showing affection, and that did not change. Instead of hugs and kisses, they waved to each other as one yelled, "If you can't be good, be careful." And most of them jokingly opted to be careful. With the rest of the family standing in the front yard, the ones leaving tooted their car horns as they headed up the road toward town.

Hope for Reunion

By the first of the next week, the children had left and Tonnie and Opal returned to their daily routine. Tonnie was still working at the Winter Garden and Opal was still sewing, only now she had more customers than ever before, and several were local white women. Although Opal was an experienced seamstress, she never made the buttonholes for any of the garments. Instead, when she finished a dress or coat or any other item that called for buttons, she had Tonnie take the garment to Reese's Fabric Store. When she needed to purchase material, match thread for someone's fabric, or look for a pattern, she rode along with Tonnie. The woman who ran the store made her buttonholes, and she was also the person who referred most of Opal's white customers. Opal was in the fabric store one day when a middle-aged white woman she had not met before asked what she charged to make a dress. Opal quoted a price of four dollars. "Well, I got me a good Christian lady that do all my sewing," was the woman's response. "And she don't ever overcharge me," the woman added. Opal didn't bother to say anything to the woman, but she did think to herself, "You can let your good Christian lady keep right on doing your sewing, too."

As time went by, Opal received more and more customers. The women brought their material and patterns and Opal took their measurements: around the bust, around the waist, and around the hips. Some brought pictures from magazines to show how they wanted their dress to look. Opal figured she could make the dresses without any problem; she just could not make the women look like the models in the pictures. There were times when she felt like telling the women that she was a good seamstress, but not a miracle worker. Sometimes husbands dropped off fabric for their wives, and sometimes men brought material for themselves, wanting Opal to make them a shirt or suit. Since Opal seldom got the chance to go out, visits with customers were occasions for her to catch up on news in town. Although she still would not join in idle gossip, it never stopped her from listening to what her customers had to say.

Opal heard that her neighbor across the street, Mr. Gene, had a problem with the title to his land. One man said that he asked a white person whatever happened to Gene, and the person told him, "If he hadn't been so mean he would still be here." Mr. Gene was supposed to have moved somewhere up north. There was another time the previous year when a woman commented to Opal about the recent news reports, "You know ain't no man walked on no moon." After going on and on about how she did not believe such thing was possible, the woman added, "That's the reason it been raining like it is, 'cause man been messin' with the moon." She said, "If they don't stop what they's doing, ain't no tellin' what gonna happen."

Except when she was preparing Tonnie's meals, Opal spent the day sewing. She started early, before breakfast, spreading out material and laying out a pattern on the dining room table. She worked until Tonnie woke up, and then she stopped to fix the first meal of the day. Each time, she carefully rolled the material and pattern together and removed it from the table so Tonnie could sit down to eat. No matter what she was doing, when it came to breakfast and dinner, she followed the same schedule every day. Tonnie had to have his meals on time. Since he worked at night, supper was the one meal she did not have to rush to get ready on time. Most evenings she worked as late as she could stand to stay awake, pinning material, cutting, and sewing. The next day, she would get started all over again. The small fee she charged for her service added up sufficiently, and it was the means by which Opal was able to purchase most of the things she wanted.

Tonnie's salary at the Winter Garden was now supplemented with his monthly Social Security check. Although the amount of money he brought home in one month would be considered meager by most, he was able to manage his finances quite well. When he went grocery shopping, he still bought food in large quantities, as he did when the children were at home. They never did without anything they really needed, and he was even able to regularly make small deposits in the bank. They were able to make ends meet without Opal's Social Security check. Each month, year after year, Opal sent her entire check to Dorothy until she graduated from Tennessee State University in 1974.

Around this time, Opal decided that she wanted to add another room to the house. The living room, dining room, kitchen, and three bedrooms were more than enough for her and Tonnie, but she was thinking about when all the children came home. She wanted a sitting room so the children could spread out, the grandchildren would have a place to play, and every one could relax. This new addition would also serve as her sewing room. Whenever her customers brought their work by the house, they could come directly to her new room instead of walking all through the house. The room would extend from the north end of the house, and it would have its own separate entrance. She wanted a nice-sized room with a big picture window facing the street, so she could see what was going on while she sat at her sewing machine. She worked it all out in her mind

Hope for Reunion

before she told Tonnie about her plan. All that was left for her to do was to figure out how she was going to get it done.

"You don't need to build another room," Tonnie said. He was totally convinced that Opal's proposal would result in a waste of money. She suggested using the money that she made from sewing, not asking him to pay anything on the room. No matter what Opal said, he could not be sold on the idea. But Opal wasn't about to give up on her plan so easily. She thought about how he had reacted years ago when she had wanted to make another purchase. She had saved her egg money for some time, and in the Sears and Roebuck catalog she found a bedroom suite she wanted to buy. When she told Tonnie that she wanted to order the new bedroom suite, he became so angry that he took the catalog and walked across the yard, tearing out pages until their front yard was littered with paper. "What all that pretty paper doing all over the yard," Grandma Ada asked when she happened up a short time later. Opal did not try to explain, but as soon as Grandma left, Opal went out in the yard. She took her time, picking up page after page until she found the one page she was looking for. It had a picture of a bed, dresser, and chest of drawers. She continued picking up pages until she came across the second page she needed. Opal went right into the house and copied all the information from the first page onto the order form, and the next day she sent off for her brand-new bedroom suite.

"I'd about given up on building my new room," Opal told the children. "Then, one day when I was sitting there sewing, it seemed the Lord spoke to me and said, 'you can get that room.'" After that, nothing Tonnie said, and he talked plenty, could change her mind. Opal firmly believed that the husband should be the head of the house. She respected Tonnie, she fixed his food on time, and she always served him before any of the children. And Tonnie made all the business decisions when it came to the family. No one would dispute the fact that Tonnie was the head of his household. He would not have stood for it being any other way. But, this was one of the few occasions when Opal stood her ground for what she wanted. She decided on the size of the room, where she wanted it, and where she wanted the windows, doors, and the outside steps. Opal worked it all out by herself, and the men built her new room just as she had envisioned.

In 1975, the family began making plans to come together again. The following year marked a special anniversary, and they agreed that it called for a big celebration. That May, Tonnie and Opal would have been married for fifty years. Everyone decided to come home in late summer, as they had done the first time. During the last week of August 1976, the house was once again filled with the children, grandchildren, and spouses. In the six years since the last reunion, all but one of Opal's eight girls had provided her with at least one more grandchild, and some had added more. This meant there were more children running around the house, in the yard, and playing in Tonnie's truck. With more people than before, it also meant nonstop cooking and serving.

Jim, Tony, and Lee barbecued. They grilled steaks, ribs, hamburgers, and hot dogs. The girls prepared potato salad, coleslaw, corn on the cob, and other vegetables. Like always, Opal fixed coconut pies, chocolate pies, and several cakes. As with any Springfield gathering, there was more food than any family could possibly consume. When dinner was ready, only the adults sat around the main dining room table. It took lots of explaining and instructions before all the children were finally seated at a second table against the wall. Before the rest of the crowd spilled over to the living room and outside to the picnic table under the tree, everyone became quiet long enough for Tonnie, in his usual place at the head of the table, to bless the food. It was just like old times, with everyone laughing and talking and telling jokes. Someone started telling the favorite joke that Grandpa Jim almost always told after finishing a big meal. By the time the person got to the part about having dined sufficiently, which the old lady mistook for having gone fishing, some of the others had joined in to help finish the story. They had all heard it many times before, but everyone laughed anyway.

The grandchildren's program began shortly after everyone finished dinner. The children sang, read a scripture and a poem, and paid tribute to the guests of honor. Then Lee, who was seldom serious with the other children, decided to deliver an impromptu tribute. He thanked "Mama and Papa for everything they did in raising us, and for all their hard work and sacrifice." He gave them credit for his success in life and for what he had been able to accomplish. Lee had received his master's from Memphis State University and was teaching in the Memphis school system and at one of the local colleges. He reminded the others, who now had good jobs, that none of them would be where they were if it were not for the "moral values and strong work ethics that Mama and Papa instilled in us." The children had always appreciated the sacrifices their parents made, but until now they were not sure if any one of them had ever expressed their gratitude. So, when Lee finished, he and most of the others were teary eyed.

Later, the girls went for a ride around Brownsville, going to Key Corner

Hope for Reunion

and to Winfield Lane, in the country. An old black woman was sitting on the front porch of the house on Winfield Lane when the car loaded with five of the girls pulled into the driveway and parked near the road. With a little explaining from Cloria about whose children they were and why they were there, the woman said it was okay for them to look around. Although the old house was only a few miles from town, this was the first time the girls had been back to see it since they moved. They surveyed the little wood house with the scattered flecks of faded red paint. It was the right location—the weather-worn tin roof still topped the house—but somehow it appeared much smaller. They walked across the front yard, now covered with grass that needed cutting, and around the left side of the house. The pump that Mr. Clay Evans's father installed after the old well fell in had turned rusty with age. There was a flash of two young children at the pump, one working the handle while the other child put her face down under the water and drank. Once they were behind the house, it was clear that none of the outdoor structures had been maintained: the smokehouse, hen house, and the barn were all dilapidated. They associated a story with everything they saw.

The sisters remembered the boys cutting wood and stocking the wood piles, which reminded them of the time Clarence lost an eye while chopping wood for the kitchen stove. They pointed to the patch of ground on the hill behind the orchard where Tonnie had grown some of the biggest watermelons in town. As they recalled the many days they had caught supper, they were barely able to see the outline of several children walking across the pasture with their fishing poles and tin cans in hand. One girl ran with a long pole that was used to prop up the clothes line in the backyard; she and her brother were trying to herd the cows into the barn. They sat on a little stool with a bucket in front of them and pulled the cows' teats for milking. It felt good to recall the old times that after more than twenty years had become fond memories.

Three of the youngest girls remembered playing underneath the house with sticks they had named. They squatted in the dirt, dressing the sticks in scraps of material their mama had discarded. With the children's help, the sticks carried on animated conversations. They played for long periods of time, totally oblivious to what was going on outside their shelter. Eventually, they would scramble from under the back porch, which was high off the ground. Now the women noticed that the back porch seemed to have been lowered at least three feet. None of them let on about their surprise. But this was not the first one of the day. Before stopping at the house, they had driven down to Oakview School. They anxiously awaited the big curve they used to sprint around every day on the last leg of their walk home from school. They never came to a big curve, and it became clear to the sisters that they viewed things differently when they were young. The curve in the road was barely noticeable.

The old woman was trusting enough to allow the complete strangers to take a tour of her home. There was clutter everywhere, but the children ignored it as they walked from room to room, trying to see if the house was the same as they remembered. The first bedroom and the large open area they called a hallway still had the floral wallpaper their mama had pasted and hung. In her old bedroom, Opal had taken great care to paint the bricks around the fireplace rose pink. Then she painted bright blue flowers that she stenciled from a piece of cardboard. The girls searched the fireplace for some sign of the pastel colors, but there was nothing left that resembled her work. They opened the door to the adjoining bedroom and there were the two old beds, pushed against opposite walls. Each night, three girls crammed into each bed—two at the head and one at the foot. There was no heat in the room, but each bed was weighed down with so many blankets and handmade quilts that the girls exerted great effort just to turn over. They could hear the sound the springs made each time they moved.

Poking their heads into the kitchen door, they were greeted by the heavenly aroma of fresh strawberry preserves cooking on the wood-burning stove. Cousin A. D. walked over to the stove, looked in the pot, and commented on how good they smelled. He was there visiting their papa, as he did every time he was in town, and he was staying for supper. Opal was taking a pan of hot biscuits out of the oven, and she had just finished frying two chickens from the yard. The big, sturdily built, rectangular wood table that her Uncle Bishop made had the same red and white oil cloth spread over it. The table was surrounded by old chairs with slat backs and worn cane-bottom seats. Opal called everyone to the table, and the family gathered around and waited for Papa to bless the food. The sisters did not eat supper anymore. In the city they had lunch at noon, and when they called their children to eat in the evening, they made sure it was for dinner. Somewhere deep down inside, though, they thought it was a pity that not many people ate supper anymore.

The sisters thanked the old woman for indulging their desire to travel back in time, if only for a brief period. Someone asked about taking pictures, but they had not remembered to bring a camera. They had not thought they

Hope for Reunion

would want a picture of the old rundown house. They walked to the car, passing three young girls in the yard playing a game with an old red rubber ball. The girls wore little checked shirt dresses that were buttoned from the neck to the waist and were loosely gathered. Their hair was fixed exactly the same, with one plait on the top and one plait behind each ear. Two were jumping up and yelling, "chunk it, chunk it," and the other one threw the ball; innocent play without a care of how others viewed their world. They wanted their own children to meet those three little girls one day.

On the drive back to town, they talked about how much the town had changed since they left home. Most of their classmates who stayed in Brownsville worked at the factories in town, and a few worked in Jackson. Since they were usually only home for a few days, they seldom saw anyone other than family. The same was true for this trip. They stopped at two of the old stores in town, Suzanne's and Miss Rankin's. The latter was a little grocery store that Tonnie often took the children to when they were young. The square had changed, and a number of stores had gone out of business. No one went uptown on Saturday nights anymore because all the stores closed early. The old Ritz Theater, where they used to pay a quarter to watch movies from the balcony, was still open for business. Only now, blacks and whites sat together.

Before everyone left home, they talked about why it was important for them to come back to Brownsville to spend time together. Now that Opal and Tonnie's children were scattered all over the country, they did not want to lose touch. They felt it was important for their children to know their grandparents and each other. They agreed that in the future they would have family reunions on a regular basis.

Aaron Springfield, ca. 1949, before he left for Liverpool, England.

Salathiel Springfield, ca. 1986.

Lois Springfield, ca. 1961.

The Springfield family reunion in 1970. From left, Clarence, Lee, Tony, Jim Howell, Opal, Asalean, Cloria, Wallis, Shirley, Opal Ree, Bettye, and Dorothy.

Tonnie Springfield, ca. 1968.

A. D. and Catherine Springfield, 1966.

Avery Springfield, ca. 1955.

Dan Springfield, ca. 1980.

12.

The Storm

On a Sunday afternoon in the summer of 1980, Opal sat on the same pew against the wall that she sat at every Sunday. Willow Grove Church was having all-day service, and she was listening to her second sermon of the day. Down through the years, she had seen ministers come and go. The current pastor, a young man named Thomas Averyheart, was the son of Tonnie's first cousin Ada. Reverend Averyheart was in his mid-thirties, but he was still young to Opal, since most of her children were older. The minister for the afternoon service was visiting from another church. She could tell he was nearing the close of his message because his voice had elevated several decibels. He made unintelligible sounds, and the church shouted back, "Amen." Having grown up in the Methodist church, Opal had taken a long time to become accustomed to all the hollering and shouting that the preachers at Tonnie's church did; but she realized long ago that most Baptist preachers did the same thing.

Although she tried to focus on the service, her mind wandered. Opal kept watching the door to the right of the choir stand. Whenever they had service that lasted all day, Tonnie always sent one of the church ladies to let her know when he was ready to go home. It was getting late, and he had not yet indicated that he wanted to leave. She thought this was unusual, but service was just about over, so she continued sitting until the preacher sat down. The other ministers gave talks, the choir sang another selection, and finally they all raised their right hand and sang the benediction in unison:

> 'Til we meet, 'til we meet.
> 'Til we meet at Jesus' feet.
> God be with you, God be with you.
> God be with you, 'till we meet again.

As soon as the last word had been sung, the people began to congregate in small clusters, greeting one another, laughing, and talking. Opal did not take the time to stick around. She left through the side door and made her way around those few who had already reached the little room in back of the church. She knew how impatient Tonnie was and had been all his life. He never liked to be kept waiting under any circumstances, and she did not want to see him getting upset at church. When they had a large number of visitors like this Sunday, Tonnie moved his truck to the highway in front of the church after the first service. That way, no one could block him in when he was ready to leave. Opal went to where the truck was usually parked, quickening her steps because she did not know what had happened to Tonnie. She was much relieved when she met Tonnie coming toward her before she made it down the hill.

"C'mon, lets go," was all Tonnie said. Opal thought he seemed a little upset, but he said very little on the drive home. They pulled into the driveway and, as always, Max was there to greet them. He had lost all his friskiness, and in dog years he was almost as old as his master. Next year they would both turn seventy-seven. The ever-faithful Max slowly walked with them as far as the front steps, then he laid down while they went inside.

"Where my bucket?" Tonnie asked.

"What you want, Tinnie?" Opal asked. "Your what?"

"You know, my bucket," Tonnie said, sounding frustrated as he looked through the house.

"You had it," he said. Opal was trying to help, but she didn't have any idea what he was talking about. "That's okay, I done found them now," Tonnie said as he picked up the pair of pants Opal had earlier stitched for him.

Monday morning, Tonnie and Opal were both up early. Neither one had ever slept a minute passed six o'clock a day since they were married. While Opal was in the kitchen starting breakfast, Tonnie told her that he was going to pick up his lawn mower that a man across town was fixing for him. He was mowing yards on a regular basis now that he was no longer working at the Winter Garden. One night when he was at work at the plant, some young men tried to tell him, "Tonnie, you gonna work with us tonight. You gonna help us tonight." Tonnie told Opal that when he ignored them, they went to the little white straw boss, who supported the young men. He said, "Tonnie, you gonna help them tonight." These younger guys thought they could pick on Tonnie because he was an old man and would not say anything. They did not know Tonnie Springfield. He had not mellowed with age. Tonnie cursed

The Storm

out the little white boss, told the others what they could all do with that job, and walked straight out the door and drove home. They later tried to get him to come back and work as a night watchman at the Winter Garden, but he turned down the offer.

People who knew Tonnie considered him one of the most honest and decent men that could be found anywhere. If he had one vice, it was his temper, and as long as no one made him angry, there was nothing to worry about. When someone tried to take advantage of him, he did not hesitate to give the other person a piece of his mind. His message was generally peppered with words the recipient was shocked to hear from a mild-mannered man. Whenever the children let their temper get the best of them, they said it was the "Tonnie Springfield" in them. He had spent his whole life not allowing anyone to treat him the way they did some blacks in Brownsville. So, rather than go back to work at the Winter Garden, he took a job as janitor at the Golden Age Center, a place for local senior citizens. The bus picked up senior citizens from all over Haywood County and brought them to the old Haywood High School building. There the seniors socialized, made ceramics, had Bible study, and ate dinner. Tonnie saw Miss Mattie eating dinner there some days while he was working. He stayed busy with his work at the center, and he mowed lawns every chance he got. He never slowed down. Opal's sewing kept her busy, too, and she never thought about going to the center, nor did she think she ever would.

"You know, I couldn't find that man's house to save my life," Tonnie told Opal as soon as he walked through the door. It was the middle of the day when Opal heard Tonnie's truck pull into the yard. He had told her he was coming right back, and she had expected him hours ago. She knew where the man lived, but she asked anyway, "Doesn't that man live right over there on Haywood Street?" She couldn't think of what the problem was. Tonnie had left the lawn mower at the man's house himself, and it was not very far from Carver school. Tonnie explained that he had gotten lost trying to find the man's house and said he had just been driving around and around. When he was not able to find where the man lived, he finally gave up and decided to come back home. He said, "The only way that I knew my own house was because of that dog out there."

"Come on, Tinnie, I'll go with you," Opal said. She knew that what Tonnie told her did not sound quite right, but she was not too concerned. Tonnie had always been the strong one, taking care of all the business and making all the decisions. She had no reason to believe that things would ever change. She just thought she should ride along with him this morning since he seem to be having a little difficulty finding where he wanted to go. Opal got her purse, which she never left the house without, closed the house, and the two of them climbed into the truck and headed up the road in the direction of town.

"Who live there?" Tonnie asked, pointing at the little gray house as he slowly drove past Mr. Ed Currie's. When he passed Miss Catherine's house, he asked, "Who live there?" After they had gone a short distance farther, Tonnie pointed to the large white house that belonged to a white man named Mr. Haynes. Again he asked, "Who live there?" He wanted to know who lived in all the houses on McLemore Street. Before they reached the end of the street, Opal knew something was wrong. Tonnie was asking her about houses he had passed hundreds of times before. This was strange. He knew more about the people who lived in these houses than she did, but she figured he was just "talking out of his head." "Turn around, Tinnie," Opal said, "lets go back home."

On Tuesday morning, Tonnie told Opal he was going to have another man from the center work for him for a few days. He did not know how to contact the man, other than going to his house. The man lived only a few blocks down the street, on Fairground Road. After breakfast, Opal rode along with Tonnie. He drove straight to the man's house. While Tonnie went and knocked on the door, Opal sat in the truck and waited. She was encouraged that he was able to find the right house with no problem. The man's wife answered the door and said her husband was not home so Tonnie stood on the porch and spoke to the woman for a few minutes. When Tonnie returned to the truck, he looked somewhat puzzled as he asked Opal, "Didn't that man look kind of funny to you?" For the first time, Opal realized that whatever problem he was experiencing was not going away. As soon as they got home, she called the doctor.

Dr. White's office was located in the same area as the Haywood County hospital on Bells Highway. Tonnie drove his truck to the doctor's office this morning just as he had done on previous occasions. The nurse asked Opal questions about Tonnie, who had been a patient of the doctor for a while now. Opal described the type of problems Tonnie had experienced the last two days. "Has he been talking funny?" the nurse asked. Opal wondered then if the nurse knew what may be wrong. "Yes, he's been talking out of his head," Opal said. "Ever since Sunday, Tinnie hadn't called anything by its right name."

The Storm

"You been taking your medicine, Tonnie?" Dr. White asked. Not getting a response right away, he asked again, "Tonnie, have you been taking your medicine?" The doctor was referring to the medicine he had prescribed for Tonnie's high blood pressure, which Tonnie was to take daily. He discovered that Tonnie had missed taking his pills on Sunday. He had forgotten to take the bottle of pills with him when they went to church all day. Still, the doctor did not seem alarmed. As he wrote the prescription, Dr. White said to Opal, "Have him take these, he'll be all right in a day or so." That was all the doctor said, and he handed Opal a little slip of paper. He had not performed any physical examination, but it was clear that they had been dismissed.

The Kroger parking lot was arguably the largest parking area in the city of Brownsville. In this city's version of a shopping mall, there was Kroger, the apparent anchor tenant, and a series of smaller stores lined up in a row on Bradford Square. There were not many other places to shop, and everybody who came to town made a trip to Bradford Square. Opal had the prescription filled at the little pharmacy at the hospital, but they had to stop by Kroger before going home. When they got ready to leave, Tonnie had a problem getting the truck out of the parking lot. He kept shifting gears and trying to back up, but after repeated attempts they had not moved. He could not get the truck to go backward. Opal was becoming upset. She did not understand why they could not just leave. Before she had the chance to say anything to Tonnie, the truck jerked backward and they were finally on their way home.

Dr. White prescribed little white tablets for Tonnie this time. Opal made sure he took the pills, along with his high blood pressure medicine. She was eager to see if there would be any change in his condition, but she did not think it was serious enough to contact the children. Tonnie had been fiercely independent all his life, and Opal had always relied on him to handle any problems. Neither of them would consider asking for help, even from the children, unless it was absolutely necessary.

Wednesday morning, Tonnie got up early, as always, and got dressed. During breakfast, Opal reluctantly accepted the fact that there had been no improvement. Tonnie was still "talking out of his head." This time she decided to call James, one of Uncle Brown's sons, to take Tonnie back to the doctor. After the difficulty with the truck the previous day, she did not want to risk having Tonnie do the driving. For the second time in as many days, they were visiting Dr. White's office. The nurse was there, but she told them the doctor was not in yet; they would have to wait. Mr. Shine Horton, one of their neighbors, was sitting in the waiting room and overheard the conversation about Tonnie. "There's a good colored doctor down in Covington," he volunteered. Mr. Shine told them what he knew of Dr. Jesse Cannon and his reputation for being a very good doctor. "Why don't y'all take him down there," he said. Although Tonnie had been seeing Dr. White, Opal had heard other people question his treatment of some patients. She thought it may be worth the trip to find out what was wrong with Tonnie. So they set out south of town to Covington.

James waited with Opal and Tonnie to see Dr. Cannon. Tonnie enjoyed the time he spent with his brother's boys. Uncle Brown had been dead now for about ten years, but James and Jesse occasionally checked on "Uncle Tom," as they called him. Sometimes they took Tonnie out to their farm so he could see the horses. They usually kept lots of horses that they trained and raced up in Louisville, Kentucky. Tonnie got a kick out of watching the horses and laughing and joking with James, Jesse, and Brown's other boys. Unlike his children, who all left home for other cities, four of Brown's boys stayed in Brownsville. He had never said so to his own boys, but he would have liked it if just one had stayed around.

When Dr. Cannon heard Tonnie speak, he immediately told Opal, "He's already had a stroke." He said that the pills Dr. White prescribed for Tonnie were nothing but something to help him sleep. Dr. Cannon explained to them what had happened. He said that after Tonnie missed his blood pressure medicine, his pressure went up, doing damage to the part of the brain that controls speech. Although his blood pressure had gone back down, the damage was done. He said that once a patient had a stroke like this, "the only thing he could look forward to was another stroke." Dr. Cannon said he needed to know whether there had been any bleeding around Tonnie's brain. If so, it would be necessary to operate. Since Covington did not have the facilities to make this determination, Tonnie would have to go to the hospital in Humboldt. He needed to be checked out as soon as possible. On the ride back home, Opal had a lot of things to sort out in her mind. Her first decision was to call one of the children.

The next day, Lee drove up from Memphis and took Tonnie and Opal to Humboldt. Opal contacted Lee because he lived closer than the other children. She never had to call all the children to report news, because as soon as one heard anything, the word quickly spread throughout the family. They spent most of the day in Humboldt while the doctors thoroughly

The Storm

examined Tonnie. He underwent a battery of tests and a series of X-rays. After the first set of X-rays, the doctors let Tonnie rest while they examined the X-rays they had, then they ordered more. Several hours later, Opal was tired from sitting and waiting, and Tonnie was exhausted. The doctors announced that the tests revealed no evidence of bleeding on the brain. It appeared that surgery was not going to be necessary. However, they could offer little hope of Tonnie ever being able to completely recover the full use of his speech.

The thought that Tonnie may have suffered a stroke had never entered Opal's mind. It had been years since she had heard of anyone she knew having a stroke. She thought the problem with Tonnie talking out of his head was only temporary and that at any time he would be back to his old self. It did not occur to her that this could be a permanent condition. After a few weeks of trying to adjust to the idea, she still had a difficult time. She had to accept the fact that Tonnie would no longer be able to work or to take care of business. Opal felt that everything had fallen on her all of a sudden. Over the next few days, she started crying and praying, crying and praying. One day when she was crying and praying, she decided to have a talk with the Lord. She wanted to know how she was going to manage everything by herself. She prayed, "Lord, here I am seventy years old and I ain't never even bought a sack of groceries in my life." Distressed and not sure she would be able to handle things, she said, "I got Tinnie and myself to provide food for, and I even got a dog to feed."

Not long after that day, Opal woke up one morning thinking about Isaiah. She thought there must be a reason the Lord wanted her to read Isaiah. Since she had not read from that book in a long time, she knew it was going to take her a minute to find exactly where it was located. She reached for the Bible and opened it right to the book of Isaiah. Opal read for some time. After she finished reading several chapters, she was convinced that the Lord had heard her prayers. Laying the Bible on the table by the bed, she went into the other room to catch the program "Back to the Bible" on the radio before it went off. She turned the radio on just in time to hear the last few minutes of the program. The minister said, "Whenever you are in distress or going through a difficult time, you should read Isaiah 41:10."

Opal rushed back to the bedroom, picked up the Bible again, and quickly flipped the pages until she found the scripture. The passage read: "Fear thou not; for I am with thee: be not dismayed; for I am thy God." Upon reading the verse, Opal sat immobile on the side of the bed for a while. She read the verse for a second time, then she read it again and again. It seem as if the Lord was speaking directly to her; telling her not to worry. No one else was in the room, but she spoke the words out loud, "This is what the Lord wants me to know."

As the weeks passed and turned into months, Opal discovered to her surprise that she had not fallen apart. Her first experience at grocery shopping had been a real challenge, since she did not have any idea on what aisle to find most items. Although she felt rather strange, she made it through the ordeal with the help of Lee. She had written out her grocery list, like she had done for Tonnie all those years, and Lee helped her make selections. Together, they went down her list as she looked for the brand names that Tonnie usually bought. Tonnie had told her a long time ago that when he bought milk, he always got his gallon from the back of the shelf, and he always checked the date to make sure it was the freshest. The shopping was even more stressful because Opal had to rush to keep Tonnie from waiting long. When she was finally through, Tonnie helped her unload the cart and put the groceries in the car. And once they were home, he went through the bags of groceries, placing each item on the dining room table, checking to make sure that Opal had bought the right things.

After the first experience, grocery shopping slowly became easier. Most of the time Mr. Cal Davis would drive Tonnie's truck, and Opal would sit between the two aging men. She thought Mr. Cal was a little older than Tonnie, but he appeared to be in good health. Opal and Tonnie felt fortunate to have him living next door, because he was always willing to help. While Opal did the shopping, he sat with Tonnie on the bench in front of the store, waiting and watching the people go by. If Opal had only a few items to buy, the two men waited in the truck, with both doors open. When Opal was finished, the three of them would head right back to the house. They did not have time to linger uptown and engage in idle conversations. After Opal took care of the business that brought her to town, she and Tonnie returned to the place where they now spent all their time.

Sometimes Opal felt as if she had given herself an ulcer. She was always nervous and rushing to do everything, though her time restraints were usually self-imposed. She hurried to prepare Tonnie's meals on time, which was nothing new, but somehow this seemed more urgent after the stroke. Even when she had the children with her to help, she always rushed. Right after Tonnie had his stroke, almost every appliance in their house stopped working, one after the other. She relied on Lee to help handle the business matters, including taking her to the store and selecting new appliances. On each occasion, she quickly found the stove, the refrigerator, and the gas heater, and was ready to return home immediately. Opal continued to sew for a period of time, finishing work that she had already received or promised to do. But the demands soon became too much, forcing her to give up sewing for others and freeing her to devote all her time to cooking and being available to Tonnie.

Opal realized that things were still going on in Brownsville and across the country, but she simply did not have time to keep up with the news as before. She continued to receive her weekly copy of the *States Graphic*, thanks to one of the children who kept the subscription current, but it was difficult to find time to read it. When the children came home, they usually found stacks of old copies around the house, and they scanned them for the local news. Opal sometimes watched the evening news on CBS, but that was about the same time that she fixed Tonnie's supper. The one thing that she missed most was not being able to make church service on Sunday mornings. But taking care of Tonnie was now her priority. She thought that somehow the Lord understood.

If Opal was thankful for anything about Tonnie's condition, it was that the stroke had not made him physically weak. He helped Mr. Cal gather fresh vegetables from the garden. And since Tonnie was still the stronger of the two, he carried the heavy bushels into the house. In the fall, he worked in the yard, raking and burning leaves, but, unbeknownst to him, Opal tried to watch out for his safety. Before Tonnie got sick, Opal had seen him douse gasoline on a pile of leaves on many occasions. He would throw a lighted match on the leaves and hurriedly step back as the flames shot up in the air. But one day after the stroke, Opal happened to look out the window just as Tonnie was about to light a match to a pile of leaves soaked with gasoline. Knowing that the stroke had affected his mobility, Opal rushed to get to Tonnie before the flames could burn him. Luckily, only a small flame arose, and it immediately disappeared. Tonnie tried a second time, and the same thing happened. Opal watched in astonishment. She knew she would not have been able to reach Tonnie before the flames did, so she believed that another hand had intervened.

In the spring of that year, Tonnie made an effort to set out tomatoes and other plants. Opal had difficulty watching him, because Tonnie could not accept that he could no longer do many of the things he once did. He was determined not to give up easily. Following the stroke, he even drove his truck to town a few times. Coming home one day, he drove by Aunt Arizona's house on Wilson Street. She later told Opal, "I said, Lord, there's brother Tonnie in his truck again." She had noticed how slowly he was going, and she said he seemed to be having a difficult time at the wheel. It was his last attempt at driving.

There was no doubt about Tonnie's ability to drive again, and the truck sat near the front door steps. Perhaps keeping it in the same spot also meant the family did not have to fully accept the inevitable conclusion that Tonnie was never going to be himself again. The old Tonnie was a man who could not stay still for long before finding something to keep him busy. He would come home only to jump in his truck a short time later and leave again. His green and white Chevrolet truck had become an appendage; truck and driver were linked together, constantly going up and down the road. The decision to sell the truck was not an easy one for Opal to make, not so much because of the sale itself, but everything that it represented. Finally, after talking it over with some of the children, she decided this was for the best. Tonnie seemed to gradually let go of the inner turmoil of what he thought he was capable of doing and how his body actually responded. He settled into a new permanent routine: every weekday morning he watched "The Price Is Right" game show on television; on Saturday mornings, he never missed wrestling; and he especially enjoyed the fish dinner Opal fixed for him on Saturday afternoons. He also looked forward to Lee's visits every other week, when he came up from Memphis, and to seeing the other children whenever they came home.

One day in 1982 Tonnie had another visitor, whose name he was unable to recall. Since suffering the stroke, he had lost his ability to remember names, even of the people he had known most of his life, including Opal and the children. He recognized faces and knew exactly who persons were, most of the time, but the names escaped his memory. After a few moments, Tonnie remembered his cousin A. D. Springfield. Down through the years, whenever he came back to Brownsville, A. D. never once failed to come by and visit Tonnie. The smile of recognition spread across Tonnie's face until it became a big grin; then the grin faded, and tears welled up in his eyes. Opal remembered when Tonnie was the last person anyone expected to see cry, but now the tears came much more easily and

The Storm

more often. He became frustrated when he could not talk to A. D. the way he used to. Because they knew each other so well, it did not matter, they could still communicate. They sat in the living room and talked, with Cousin A. D., who patiently listened until he understood what Tonnie was trying to say. The two cousins had always been fond of each other, and it was obvious the years had not changed their feelings. They were glad to be together again, sharing laughs, almost like old times.

Opal watched the two men enjoying each other's company. A. D. had introduced her to Tonnie all those years ago, when she was just a young girl and they were not much older. She could not believe how fast the time had passed. Now they were getting on in years. A. D. was balding, and his remaining hair had turned mostly gray. Tonnie still had all his hair, and, surprisingly, it was only about 75 percent gray. Opal thought that A. D. still looked well. Except for being a little thinner, he had not changed much since the last time she had seen him. She felt badly that Tonnie, who looked healthy and had even gained weight since the stroke, could no longer express himself as he used to. What she did not know, because A. D. did not tell them, was that he was dying of cancer and had come by to pay one final visit.

Later that year, Opal was in the kitchen fixing breakfast when she realized that Tonnie was taking a lot longer than usual in the bathroom. Every morning, he showered and dressed while Opal prepared breakfast. The stroke that he had two years ago had not really affected him physically. Since he continued to do all the things that he needed to do for himself, she did not have to help him shower and dress in the morning. Before Opal had could stop what she was doing and check on him, he walked out of the bathroom. He was only partially dressed, and he was shaken and crying. Seeing him in this condition, Opal immediately dropped what she was holding. "What's the matter with you, Tinnie?" she asked. He said that he had been in there all that time trying to get dressed, but he could not figure out how to get his clothes on right.

The doctor said Tonnie had suffered a second stroke. This time the doctor admitted him to the hospital. Tonnie may have been sick, but he still could not stand the thought of being confined. After the first day in the hospital, he realized where he was. The nurse came in the room and asked, "How you doing, Mr. Springfield?" Tonnie replied by telling Opal to pay the woman so that he could go home. Throughout his short stay, Tonnie kept insisting that Opal pay the people so they could go back home.

The stroke had left Tonnie partially paralyzed on his left side. He now walked around the house with the help of a walker. Taking the walker in one hand, he would steady himself, then move the chrome object a few inches ahead of him every time he took a step. Over the next two years, he grew weaker as his heath continued to decline. When his walking became more and more labored, he advanced to a larger walker. It curved around in a half circle, which required Tonnie to grip the sides of the walker with both hands, raise it, and set it down a few paces in front of him. Only with the walker firmly in place was he confident that he could walk without falling. He took small unsteady steps, almost like a child learning to walk. Thus, he slowly shuffled from one place to another within his limited perimeter.

Every morning after breakfast, Tonnie made his way down to the sitting room Opal had added a few years ago. He sat for long periods of time in his oversized chair by the big picture window and stared at the rest of the world as it moved on without him. He watched the cars go by, the children play, and the people walk to and from the store. Many times he nodded off and made loud, irregular snoring sounds. After a while, he would awake, jerk his head upright, and resume looking through the window. He frequently delighted at little things. His eyes would light up and he would smile as he yelled to Opal to come watch the little children whose play sometimes strayed into their front yard. Other times he called, "Come here, Kid," adding, "look at those things there." Tonnie pointed to the squirrels running across the yard and up a tree trunk, and he would let out a big laugh. Then, even though he had told Opal lots of time before, he said again, "You know, you sho' did the right thing building this room."

Tonnie was lying next to Opal in bed one morning when he commenced to shaking all over. Frightened more than she had probably ever been, Opal called his name and shook him gently. She did not get him to respond. He was still shaking uncontrollably. Opal jumped out of bed and rushed to the telephone. First she tried to contact Mr. Cal, but she got no answer. Next, she called Jessie, who was now living a few doors up the road. Jessie was there in a few minutes. "Uncle Tom," Jessie said as he shook his shoulder. "Uncle Tom." When he was unable to get Tonnie to respond, he called for the ambulance.

The driver and attendant rushed in the house and straight back to the bedroom. Tonnie was sitting on the side of the bed facing the wall. He refused to leave. Jessie caught him by the arm and tried to coax him into going

The Storm

with the two men, but he jerked his arm away and turned his back to them. "I think Uncle Tom said one of them bad words," Jessie said. Though his body had been weakened by the stroke, Tonnie figured that as long as it had not bothered his mind, he could still decide some things for himself. All their efforts to get him to go to the hospital were useless. The men gave up and left. A short time later, they were called back. Tonnie had suffered another seizure. This time he woke up in the hospital. His eyes scanned the room until he spotted Opal. "You brought me here?" he asked her.

Tonnie's condition was not any worse. Opal was glad when he was released and the two of them returned home. Their morning routine now included Opal bathing Tonnie, shaving him, and brushing his hair. Except for shaving him, she repeated the routine every day. But once Tonnie was dressed, he stilled made his way around the house. Then one morning in early 1986, he did not get out of bed. The next day, it was the same thing, only now Tonnie had fallen into a deep sleep and would not wake up. Opal called for the ambulance. Tonnie came to himself as they were pushing him into the hospital. He opened his eyes and looked at Opal for a long while. She knew how much he hated being there, but this time he was not able to speak. As he closed his eyes, Opal thought about a song the choir always sang.

> Precious Lord, take my hand,
> Lead me on, let me stand,
> I am tired, I am weak, I am worn;
> Thru the storm, thru the night,
> Lead me on to the light,
> Take my hand, precious Lord.

It was the last week of February when the word circulated through the family that Tonnie was in the hospital again. This time when the children began gathering at home, things seemed different, more portentous. Lee and Wallis came first from Memphis, then the other children came from Nashville. They joined Opal at the hospital, where she had been by Tonnie's bed since he was admitted. She told them that he had been lying there sleeping ever since they brought him in. She looked weary and tired but refused to go home, as if she were afraid of what might happen if she left. So, the children talked quietly, keeping her company. Later that evening, Dr. Thornton Jr. dropped in to see how Tonnie was doing. He checked the patient briefly but did not tell the family anything about his condition. Betty stopped him at the door, introduced herself, and asked about the prognosis for her father. They were not prepared for the news the doctor delivered. He explained that Tonnie was in a coma; then he added, "I don't think he will last through the night."

> When my way grows drear, precious Lord, linger near,
> When my life is almost gone,
> Hear my cry, hear my call,
> Hold my hand lest I fall;
> Take my hand, precious Lord.

How do you tell a woman that the man she has been married to for three months shy of sixty years is dying? Everyone was at a lost for words. Opal was remarkably strong. She decided to spend the night at the hospital and ignored any suggestion of going home to get some rest. At about ten o'clock the next morning, Opal was there when Tonnie opened his eyes wide and looked toward the window, where bright light streamed through the slits of the blinds. The years all ran together: The boy at Springfield school becoming a young man and meeting the pretty girl on revival Sunday; buying those two little blue vases at the store as a Christmas present; buying his first place on Poplar Corner; plowing the fields behind his old mule that beat him to the house when the dinner bell rang; raising his young family on Winfield Lane; the children leaving home one by one; the khaki shirts dripping wet with his sweat and clinging to his body as he worked sunup to sundown; the faces of all the children, whose names, funnily enough, he could now remember; and, of course, Opal. There had always been Opal. He had only been looking toward the window for a few seconds, and the light was growing brighter. The years had passed so quickly he could hardly believe it, and he never told any one that he loved them. But his family was the reason that he worked so hard. That was his way of expressing how he felt, and he hoped they knew it. Opal was standing by his bed, calling his name and asking if he was trying to say something when, suddenly, he closed his eyes again.

> When the darkness appears, and the night draws near,
> And the day is past and gone,
> At the river I stand,
> Guide my feet, hold my hand;
> Take my hand, precious Lord,
> Lead me home.

The Storm

On Saturday morning the telephone rang at 1005 North McLemore. Lee called with the news. As some of the children rushed back to the hospital, they could not help but notice how beautiful and unseasonably warm the weather was for the first day of March. There was not a cloud in the sky. The look on everyone's face in the hospital room confirmed the news. Opal kept repeating that she had gone to the bed when Tonnie opened his eyes. She had held his head in her hands, but he had looked right passed her to the window. She thought he wanted to tell her something. It had been six years since he had the first stroke; perhaps he was thinking of the old Negro spiritual:

> Just look what a shape I'm in,
> Just look what a shape I'm in,
> Cryin' Oh Lord, give me more time to pray,
> I've been in the storm so long.

The next week was busy and hectic and one great big blur. Making the funeral arrangements fell on those of us who were already home. So, we children did the planning in an effort to try to somehow make this period easier for Mama. There were so many details to the planning that we had not envisioned. Our large family had been extremely blessed: none of us had dealt with the death of a close family member. Taking care of the business end of the funeral left little time for us to accept our loss and grieve. Sitting around the dining room table working on a draft of the obituary, we grappled for the right words to sum up Papa's life and character. He had been a devoted family man and was devoted to the church all his life, and he had been a farmer and a landowner, but those words seemed to fall far short of telling who he really was. Asalean wrote, "As the light flashed from birth to death, he was here and gone." That was the part with which we were having the most difficulty; Papa had lived on this earth for more than fourscore years, and it seemed like such a short time. After changing the initial date of the funeral, everyone finally agreed to set the service for Saturday, March 8, 1986, at Willow Grove Baptist Church. By late in the week, the house was filled with the children who had come home, bringing their families with them.

Saturday was another beautiful, unseasonably warm day. Sometime before noon, the family met at the house. There was Jim Howell, now the spitting image of Papa; Tony, no longer called Bubba; Lee Arthur; and

Clarence—who all came with their families. All the girls were there, with their husbands and children, except for Lois. Salathiel had moved back to Tennessee and was now living in Jackson. He could not attend the funeral because of recent injuries from an automobile accident. Aaron, who was still in the veteran's hospital in Marion, Indiana, was also unable to come. We gathered in the front yard and waited for the Rawls Funeral Home to send cars to transport the family to the church. No one did much talking, each one of us was occupied with our own thoughts of Papa.

As the funeral procession made its way down East Main and onto Jackson Highway, I thought about the many times Papa had made this trip: on his horse, in the wagon with his mules, in his first car, and in all of his different trucks. When we were growing up, he was always on the go—to the field, to town, to church, or to the children's school. The hearse drove slowly up the highway, past the place where Papa had been born in a little log cabin, which had been torn down years earlier, and past Springfield Road. We drove by Mulligan's Store, where Papa used to stop after church to buy a cold bottle of soda water. We traveled the last few yards up the highway then up the little hill to Willow Grove Church.

Outside the church, we formed another line. Jim Howell stood with Mama, while all the other children were placed in decreasing chronological order. With the grandchildren paired in line behind the adults, we followed the men who carried Papa. I do not remember much of what happened from the time we entered the church until we all went up to the front of the church to view Papa for the last time. I was concerned about Mama and how she was doing. And I thought about the fact that Mama and Papa were less than three months away from celebrating what would have been sixty years of marriage. Mama had requested that the choir sing "Precious Lord," but I cannot recall whether they did. Six of the grandchildren served as pallbearers: Tony's two sons, Lee's two sons, and one of Cloria's and one of Shirley's sons.

Interment was at Rosenwald Cemetery on Anderson Street. Quite some years ago, long before some of the children were even born, Mama and Papa had planned for this day by purchasing their plots at the cemetery from Al Rawls. The grave diggers had prepared the site for Papa right next to the graves of Grandpa Jim, Grandma Ada, and Uncle Brown. After a brief service, Papa's family and friends departed before he was laid to rest. Feeling the need to hold on to something tangible, I took a single yellow flower from one of the arrangements before leaving. Some of my sisters did the same.

From the cemetery, we went to the First Baptist Church on Jefferson

Street, where dinner had been prepared for the family. Later, all of the children, along with our families and other relatives, reassembled at the house on McLemore. In keeping with tradition, neighbors and church members had started dropping food at the house early that morning. So, even though dinner was served at the church, there was lots of food at the house when we returned. We spent time socializing, talking with the older family members, and sharing memories. Three of Papa's four surviving brothers attended the funeral: Uncle Dan, who still lived in Brownsville; Uncle Charles from Decatur; and Uncle Avery from Memphis. Aunt Louise was the only one of Papa's sisters who was able to attend. His other three sisters were suffering from a variety of illnesses. Aunt Arizona, who was now living in Memphis, was there for Mama.

The grandchildren separated into similar age groups. Many of them had not seen each other since the last family reunion. As the day wore on, there was lots of laughter and talk and food. And some took lots of pictures. To an outsider, our celebratory gathering might seem inappropriate for mourning a loved one. But nothing would have pleased Papa more than to see everyone together at the house on McLemore, the house he built. He was probably sitting somewhere quietly taking in everything, as he had always done. And I think he was pleased with what he saw. After all, he had lived a life that his family could celebrate.

Epilogue: Offering to the Ancestors

"Memory was given to man for some wise purpose. The past is . . . the mirror in which we may discern the dim outlines of the future and by which we may make them more symmetrical," wrote Frederick Douglass in 1884. I agree with Mr. Douglass, which is why I tapped the memory of many family members, who, eager to share their memories of the past with me, have provided much of the material for *The Legacy of Tamar*.

Growing up as the next to the youngest of Tonnie and Opal's fourteen children, with the large extended Springfield and Taylor families, I recall lots of occasions for storytelling. Tonnie and Opal were visited by all of Papa's sisters: Aunt Meg, Aunt Lee, Aunt Louise, Aunt Vernice, Aunt Ada, and the oldest sister, Aunt Cherry, who died when I was just a young girl. While Mama's two sisters, Aunt Cloria and Aunt Arizona, also came for visits, they were not nearly as loquacious and fun loving as the Springfield sisters. The Springfield sisters were usually loud and boisterous, but peppered in their conversations was talk of family. Since Aunt Cloria died in 1957, Mama and Aunt Arizona were the only ones around to talk about their mama and papa, Ora and Howell; Grandma Tamar and Grandpa Polk; and the dream Grandpa Polk had just before five family members died that winter. After my older sisters and brothers went off to college and to cities up north, they would return for visits. They talked about events in other places and reminisced about the good old days. Invariably, they always talked of the things they did while growing up. I listened with great interest and asked lots of questions as they described the way things were before I was born. My fondest memories are of Grandpa Jim's Sunday afternoon visits, when after dinner he told stories that made everyone laugh.

Offering to the Ancestors

Only later, after Papa died in 1986, did I seriously consider writing what would become this book. At that time, I was working in downtown Nashville at the state attorney general's office, within walking distance of the state library and archives, where I began spending my lunch hour and searching the circuit court records for Haywood County. The first roll of microfilm that I examined was the records for Trustees of Estates from November 1910 through September 1913. Down through the years, the family had always said Mama was three years old when she lost her parents and the others, which they remembered occurring in January or February. Since a guardian had been appointed for the children, there had to be a court record of the appointment. I knew that Mama had been born in November 1909; therefore, I figured 1913 would be a good place to start. I carefully scanned the first roll of film, looking for one of the names I had heard Mama talk about, but none of the names sounded familiar. A few minutes into the second roll of film, I discovered the first of many documents about the Taylor family that my search eventually revealed.

Recorded in the circuit court minutes for Tuesday morning, February 3, 1914, was the following: "In the matter of appointment of Thomas Lewis Taylor as Administrator of estate of Howell Y. Taylor, deceased, departed this life intestate January 31, 1914 at his home in #5 Haywood County, applicant and widow, Ora Taylor, request act." It is an unbelievable, almost indescribable feeling to come face to face with your ancestral past. Although I had expected to find something, actually seeing the names of Howell and Ora, the grandparents whom I had never known, and Thomas Lewis Taylor, who had to be Uncle Tom, unleashed a swell of emotions. I stared at the screen for a long time, reading and rereading the entry. Finally, I copied down the information, realizing for the first time that at least part of what had happened to Mama's family that winter, all those years ago, had been recorded for posterity. This initial discovery meant there had to be other documents about the family right there at the state library and archives. The discovery also showed how important it was to verify the information that I had received orally, because Mama had not been three years old when her parents died, but four.

My efforts to uncover more about the family history had begun not as a quest to make sense of the death of Sam and Isabel, Polk and Tamar, Howell and Ora, Jim and Ada, and all the others; instead, I wanted to learn the purpose of their lives, especially after Papa died. The conclusion that I reached was that they were placed here for a reason. This had to be true, for to think otherwise would mean they lived and struggled and laughed and cried, then died, and the world was no better or no different because they were here. The only way to perpetuate the essence and meaning of their lives was to preserve their stories. Taking time to ask questions and discover more about the older relatives never seemed important before Papa's death, which, though inevitable, seemed to have come too soon. Although he was eighty-two years old and had been sick for a long time, Mama and the children were not prepared that Saturday morning when he finally left.

Three years after Papa's death, in 1989, I learned that Aunt Arizona had been placed in a nursing home. From what I was told, it appeared she had some very serious ailments. I called Mama and asked if she would like me to take her to Memphis for a visit, feeling sure that she would not pass up such an opportunity. I must admit, in all honesty, that my offer was not entirely altruistic. I was partially motivated by the possibility of gaining more information about the Taylor family. Since Aunt Arizona was a couple of years older than Mama, I thought she might remember some things about Grandma Tamar, Grandpa Polk, and their mama and papa that I had not heard. Too, even though I had heard Mama and Arizona talk about the family, I had never asked Aunt Arizona any questions. Because Papa's death had taught me a lesson about mortality, I felt I needed to ask questions while there was still someone around who knew the answers. So, with Mama eagerly accepting my offer, I drove home for the weekend. On August 7, 1989, we took the one-hour trip to Memphis.

At around 2:00 in the afternoon, Lee, Wallis, Mama, and I arrived at the White Haven Care Center in Memphis. We found Aunt Arizona propped up on a pillow in bed. "Is that my sister?" she asked upon hearing Mama's voice. "Yes," Mama said. She went over to the bed, and the two sisters embraced. Mama, almost eighty, and Aunt Arizona, eighty-one, kissed each other and wiped away tears. Aunt Arizona was the hardest worker of the three sisters. She picked cotton for a number of years after her children left home. Now, only the strong resonance of her voice remained. She had gone blind, both of her legs had been amputated above the knee, and she was much more frail than I last remembered. But her spirit seem to lift because we were there, and she talked the entire time, almost without ceasing.

Aunt Arizona told us about her recent dream: "There was this old dug well in front of the courthouse," she said, " and all kinds of money was just coming out—dollar bills, lots of coins and even gold." Spreading her arms she said, "I then heard this voice. I didn't see anybody and I don't

Offering to the Ancestors

know where it came from, but it was a man's voice, and he said, 'This here money is for the heirs of Howell Taylor—and he only has two—that is Opal Springfield and Arizona Johnson.'"

Excitedly recalling events from three-quarters of a century ago as if they occurred yesterday, Aunt Arizona told us about Grandpa Polk's dream that had foretold five deaths. "Grandpa said he saw five white horses, and he said they were the prettiest, whitest horses that he had ever seen," she offered. She recalled that Grandpa Polk had said the horses were riding inside the house, which was a detail Mama did not remember. She talked about the winter of 1914 and what had happened to all the possessions that her mama and papa had accumulated before they died. "Papa had his favorite buggy horse that he called 'Old Lucy' and Mama's favorite buggy horse was called 'Old Annie,'" she said. "Papa had saved money to buy his own place and when he died every thing was sold and all the money was put in the bank with Lawyer Wills as trustee, and we lived off only the interest." Aunt Arizona thought there should still be money in some bank account that belonged to her papa. She believed her dream was a sign of this, and she wanted someone to check with the banks in Brownsville. Aunt Arizona also spoke, straightforwardly, about her condition and pain. It did not seem to bother her at all that she might not be around much longer. In fact, she seemed to welcome the idea.

The following year, some of my sisters and brothers, along with hundreds of other alumni of the Dunbar-Haywood Training School/Carver High School, gathered in Nashville for the all-class reunion on the July 4 weekend. The group came together every other year, and the number of attendees continued to increase. Most had looked forward to seeing all their old classmates and friends since the last reunion. As a member of the Nashville Alumni Chapter, I had been involved with the planning and was pleased to see it finally come together. People came from New York, California, and lots of places in between. For families like ours, this was not just a class reunion but also a mini family reunion. Everyone enjoyed the three- to four-day event. During that week, Mama called to say Aunt Arizona had died.

Mama had seen Aunt Arizona on one other occasion after our trip together. One of the neighbors had driven Mama and her first cousin Ora to the center a few months earlier. Aunt Arizona told Mama, "The next time you see me, I'm going to be in a box." Mama tried to assure her sister that this was not true, but Aunt Arizona insisted that she knew what she was saying. She repeated, "Ah, the next time you see me, I'm gonna be in a box." She explained that whatever her condition was that caused the amputation, she thought it was blood clots, had spread throughout her body. She said she was ready for God to take her away. She had dreamed just the other night that she and her grandson Ricky were together. Mama knew that Ricky had died as a young man, some time ago.

On Sunday, July 8, 1990, Aunt Arizona's funeral was held at the Farmer Chapel C.M.E. Church in Brownsville. Aunt Arizona, unlike Mama, had remained a Methodist throughout her life; but they both had shared a steadfast commitment to their religious upbringing. In the early afternoon, we assembled at Farmer Chapel for the short service. It followed the same general programming as funerals I had attended in Baptist churches. Before the eulogy, someone sang the solo "Precious Lord," and at the end of the service we viewed the remains. Aunt Arizona was laid to rest at Taylor's Chapel Cemetery, not far from Grandpa Polk, Grandma Tamar, and Howell, Ora, and the others who seemed to have died before their time. She was eighty-two.

Sometime later, on one of my trips home, I suggested to Mama that we ride out to the country to visit her old home site. Although I had lived in Brownsville until graduating from high school, I had never been out to the farm where Mama lived as a child. I even had to ask Mama the name of her mother and father. Now, I had a fervent desire to learn all that I could about her people and Papa's family. I had to discover exactly who these people were before it was too late. When we arrived, she said, "This is the Old Crossroads Place." She said, "Grandpa Polk and Grandma Tamar's house was right there," she pointed to a little hill several yards from the road. Indicating a distance in the same direction, but unseen from where we were standing, she said, "My Mama and Papa's house was back across the field there."

Both the home where she had lived until she was four and the house where she later moved into with Grandpa Polk and Grandma Tamar were gone. A pile of old bricks covered the hill where the latter had been. Mama walked a few steps toward the bricks, her feet leaving impressions in the cultivated field. She described the house that once stood on that spot. What had first caught her attention when we stopped the car was a little wood shed enclosed around an old well. When Mama realized what it was, she got excited, "This is that old system well," she said. The shed was painted white and appeared newly constructed. Mama said that back when she was a girl, there was a fence around the well to keep the children out. She could barely believe that the well was still there. "Grandpa used to come down here and get water and we children would laugh at how he would hold it in his mouth and rinse his mouth out."

We headed back down Highway 54, passing a huge open field across from where Mama had lived. She said all that land had been owned by her grandma's brother, Uncle Pack. We turned onto a little road that connected with Taylor's Chapel Road, and Mama explained that this crossroad was how the Old Cross Road Place got its name. We passed a few old houses still standing and occupied. Mama told me who had lived in each one when she was a girl. Then, we turned left onto Tabernacle Road and drove past the campgrounds right next to Tabernacle Methodist Church. She said the campgrounds were still used and that her cousin Ora cooked there every summer. She pointed to the dilapidated stone house on the other side of the church. Its windows were broken and it was almost completely overtaken by weeds and bush. "That's where the old white lady named Miss Emma Taylor use to live." She told me how Grandma Tamar often sent her to the old white woman's house with fresh vegetables. Repeating what I had heard her say before, she said, "Miss Emma said to me, you know, all the Taylors are kin, anyhow."

Not much farther up the road, we came to another church and Mama said, "Now, this was my people's church." The large white letters on the black wrought iron post in the front yard said, "Taylor's Chapel CME Church." This was the first time I had seen the church Mama talked about so many times. It was on the same side of the road as the church for its white neighbors, but it was constructed of wood instead of brick and it was much smaller. Mama told me that a large church bell once hung from the overhang extending above four concrete steps that lead to the double front doors. This is where she had gone to school, and she used to pick berries and plums on her way home from here. On Sundays, she came here for Sunday school and worship service. Looking at the little church, I could visualize children playing at recess and tolling the bell each time a funeral was about to begin.

We went past the campgrounds and took the narrow, bumpy dirt road to Taylor's Chapel Cemetery. "My folks were buried under a big tree," Mama said, but she was uncertain of the exact location. They had no headstones. She thought the family was buried under the towering sweet gum tree near the far side of the cemetery. We walked underneath the tree and all around the grounds. The cemetery was old, with stones dating back to the eighteen hundreds. Time and weather had completely worn away some names and dates, and several stones were overturned. As we walked, I read names from headstones. Amazingly, Mama recalled something about many of the people and shared with me whatever story she knew about each one. We visited the graves of Aunt Arizona and Uncle Gilbert and stopped there for a moment to read the markers. "Of all my people, I am the only one left, now," Mama said.

On lots of other occasions, and in an untold number of long-distance telephone calls, I asked questions about the family and Mama supplied the answers. Most of the time she started with the same disclaimer: It all happened so long ago that she was not sure whether she could remember. She would then proceed to recall details of events with such clarity that I found it incredible. Initially, I was reluctant to ask Mama some questions, thinking they may be painful for her. I soon realized how much Mama enjoyed talking about her family. Her face shined with renewed life when we talked about people and things she had not thought about in years. She wished she had asked more questions of some of the people in her family while they were alive. She gave me the names of people, verified the places they had lived, and supplied dates for many events.

Mama took me to see Papa's first cousin, Ada "Little Sister" Averyheart. At almost ninety-five, she was the oldest living relative on the Springfield side of the family. She was alert, in good health, and still lived alone in her own home. Her mother and Papa's mother were sisters, and they married Dave Springfield and his nephew, Jim Springfield. I was eager to talk with her to learn more about Papa's side of the family. Mama called in advance and explained why I wanted to visit. Never having been in her home, I felt a bit uncomfortable going in and recording our conversation. To my surprise, almost immediately after we sat down and Cousin Ada started to talk about the family, she said to me, "Honey, why don't you get you a piece of paper and write this down so you won't forget."

"My grandpapa was named Freeman Springfield, and he married my Grandmama Abbie," she said. "They were both slaves." She called the names from memory, without any hesitation, of Papa's great grandparents. As she told stories about the family, she gave me names of other Springfield relatives. "When I was a girl, I used to baby sit for Uncle Jim and Aunt Ada. Back then, they lived in a little two room log cabin on Old Willow Grove Road." She recalled stories that she had heard down through the years, some from Brown Wiley, the second husband of Papa's grandmother, Alice Shaw. Brown told them about things that happened when he was a slave there in Haywood County. "He told us when the slaves complained about their feet being cold in the winter, the whites would heat coals and make the slaves stand on the hot coals. And those slaves caught reading and writing, they cut off four of their fingers," she said.

Cousin Ada said her folks talked about the slaves' prayer meetings and how they turned over a large wash pot, raising it slightly off the ground, to catch the sound of their praying. She laughed when she thought about the slave parties held in the slave cabins. "If the overseer came through that door while the party was going on, one of the slaves would throw hot ashes in his face and this allowed the others to get away," she said. I asked her if she had heard of Hulls Dinner, and she got excited explaining what the family had said about the event. Mama joined in as they both talked about the big dinner that lots of colored people attended. They did not know any other meaning of the name Hulls Dinner, just that it was a celebration for the slaves after they were set free.

In the spring of 1995, I traveled to Decatur, Illinois, to visit Papa's family. With the exception of Cousin Ada, I had not interviewed any of the Springfields. Mama had been able to supply lots of information, but her knowledge was of what she learned after marrying into the family. In order to discover as much as I possibly could about that side of the family, I decided I needed to talk with Papa's sisters and brothers, who now were all getting on in years. Aunt Louise was the one with whom I had the most contact in recent years, and I arranged to visit her at her home. When I arrived at Aunt Louise's that Saturday, she had breakfast waiting. Although she had scheduled surgery on her knee, and had a noticeable limp, it did not stop her from making a fuss over me and my daughter during our entire visit. Aunt Louise is a great cook, and for our weekend visit she fixed pork chops with gravy, biscuits, chicken and dressing, green beans, cabbage, and cherry pies.

"Papa was always real strict on us girls," Aunt Louise said. "We would go to suppers down at Springfield School, he came along and stood around watching us while we were sitting there talking to the boys. When it got 8:00, he would say, 'Ya'll, come on, let's go,' then he walked us home across the field." She told us of going to Tom Wilson Cafe, down from Al Rawls Funeral Home, on Saturday nights and going to church on Sunday mornings. "If it had rained, we couldn't ride in the wagon because it would get stuck in the mud," she said. "So, we walked to church in our old shoes and carried our church slippers in a sack. Papa would be walking in front of us saying, 'Come on, come on,' hurrying us along." She said Grandpa Jim had to get to church in time to teach Sunday school. "He taught Sunday school for fifty years," she added. Aunt Louise told about working in one of President Roosevelt's New Deal programs and what life was like when they lived on Springfield Road. She also shared how Grandpa spent his last days in her home; having come there after his accident.

My cousin Geneva, Aunt Louise's daughter, took us to see Cousin Lizzie Taylor, who had been almost like a sister to Mama and who now lived in Decatur. We then visited Aunt Ada and Aunt Meg, Papa's oldest living sibling, who, at eighty-six, still attended church every Sunday. From there, we visited Uncle Charles and his wife, Margie. The only one in the family to leave the Baptist Church, Uncle Charles was at Mass when we arrived. He had recently been ill, but he attended Mass every Saturday.

When the time came for us to return to Nashville, Aunt Louise packed lots of food to take with us. My favorite was a jar of homemade strawberry preserves, and I made them last for several months. Every time I reached for the jar of preserves, I was reminded of Aunt Louise and her generosity.

I flew to Michigan over Labor Day weekend to see Mama's first cousin Clarence Taylor. My brother Tony drove me to Romulus, just outside Detroit. When I met Clarence Taylor for the first time, he said, "Girl, you look just like Opal." He was immaculately dressed in gray slacks with a perfect crease and a white sweat shirt with "Grandpa" printed on it. Although his remaining hair was mostly gray, his skin was smooth and wrinkle free. His wife, Florene, calls him "baby face." His smile, his agility, and his spirit belied his years. If I had not known better, no one could have convinced me that he was an octogenarian. For nearly two hours he entertained us with stories about his earlier years in Brownsville. He talked about the restaurant he had in town with his first wife, Alma; his friendship with the man he called "Santa Claus," who made nocturnal deliveries of bootleg whiskey; and his ride around town in the backseat of a police cruiser, being threatened by officers he figured were part of the mob. He knew that the police officers in town had earned a reputation for beating blacks, but he was not afraid because he had his gun tucked in his waist, under an old apron, and was prepared used it. "I just got in my car and drove out of town and left everything," he said of the day he left Brownsville. We also talked about the lynching of Dick Williams, and he reminded us that Dick's sister Julie had married his brother Meedie.

Before we left, Cousin Clarence led us behind his house to his backyard,

Offering to the Ancestors

where he proudly showed off his large vegetable garden. As we walked to the front yard, we passed two late-model Chryslers parked underneath his carport. He said that they still drove their own cars. He was a charming man and full of life and energy. Both he and Florene were friendly people. They invited us to come back to see them, promising to fix dinner for us the next time. We had a delightful visit. I was very glad that I had decided to make the trip.

A few months later, at work, I found a small envelope stuck in the middle of my mail, legal documents, message slips, and other papers. Inside was a note thanking me for the pictures I had sent, along with two ten dollar bills. "Here is a little change, get you some candy or flowers," Clarence Taylor wrote. The note made my day. I cannot think of any other gift that I have appreciated more.

I chose flowers, finding two dozen roses at a bargain price. The vase of Oceania roses sat on my kitchen table for a week, and the wonderful fragrance filled the room. Each evening when I came home tired from the day's work and entered my kitchen, I had to stop for a moment to enjoy their beauty. Every time I looked at the roses, I could not suppress the smile that spread across my face as I thought about the simple act of kindness that had brightened my day. And, of course, the fact that Clarence Taylor still lived up to his reputation as a ladies' man. He had, without knowing it, taught me an invaluable lesson. This is what family is supposed to be about, I told myself. For the first time, I thought about why we are on this planet: to share what we know and what we have so that we may bring joy into the lives of others.

There was something interesting about all the people that I interviewed in gathering material for *The Legacy of Tamar*. Although I had never had a conversation with most of these relatives, they welcomed me into their homes. As I sat with them, I searched their faces and was not surprised to find some familial resemblance. When talking with them, I felt as if we had known each other all our lives. I also made contact with a number of individuals who were not family, but who nevertheless took time to answer my many questions. I shall be forever grateful for all the stories they shared with me.

In recent years, I began to feel an urgency to finish *Legacy* while Mama was still here to fill in any missing pieces. Except for her diabetes, she was still in fairly good health, but a few things had changed since Papa passed. Twice a week now the bus picked her up and took her to the senior citizen center, where she made ceramics and shared a noon meal with other seniors. She made ceramic pieces for most of the children. To pass time at home, Mama also started quilting again. She made a beautiful quilt for every one of the children, giving us something to remember her by when she is gone. She will turn ninety this year on November 9, and she still recalls events much better than she gives herself credit. There were many, many times that I called on her and she supplied details about the family that she had stored in her memory for all those years. She was my primary source for most of the stories in *Legacy*.

Mama expressed much pride when she talked about the children. She said, "I didn't go as far as I would like to have gone myself, since I was never able to get a college education or anything." And she never had any idea that her own children would accomplish the things they achieved. "The one thing that was always my desire," she said, "was that my children go to church and go to school." She talked about her "bunch," which included teachers, government workers, a preacher, a lawyer, and a professor at Tennessee State University. "I am proud of the fact that my children had the mind to do something for themselves," she said. "It will help their children go further than their parents have gone."

Mama is even more proud of the grandchildren, and they are the ones she brags about now at her weekly visits to the senior citizens center. Both of Tony's boys graduated from the University of Michigan with degrees in engineering, and the older one later received his MBA from Massachusetts Institute of Technology. Lee's older son, at thirty, became the only dentist in the state, in private practice, to specialize in prosthodontics, and his younger son received his doctor of pharmacy degree this year. Asalean's only child is completing a master's program in hospital administration at Meharry Medical College. Cloria has a son and daughter who attended college. Wallis's one daughter graduated from Tennessee State University. Lois has several children who are college graduates, including one daughter who teaches and another who is a lawyer. One of Clarence's two sons attended college. Two of Shirley's sons graduated from Howard University in Washington, and the third attended Tennessee State University and co-owns a mortgage business. Opal's two daughters graduated from Carnegie Mellon and American University, and her son attended a local university before his death. Both of Betty's children followed in her footsteps; her daughter graduated from Texas Southern University and Northwestern University and is an attorney, and her son graduated from the University of Memphis Law School. Dorothy, the youngest child, has two girls, one still in high school and the other a student at Dartmouth. The two oldest boys, Jim Howell and Aaron, never had children. Mama and all of us are most proud of the oldest great grandchild, Salathiel's granddaughter; she graduated this year from Howard University in Washington. Mama said that her message to all young people is that they "should go as far as they can go."

In discovering the hopes and dreams of Howell and Ora, I discovered that family, education, and effort to make things better for the next generation are the themes of their many stories. What Mama told me about Grandpa Polk, Grandma Tamar, Grandpa Jim, and Grandma Ada revealed that, against seemingly insurmountable odds, they refused to give up. Regardless of what obstacles they faced, they prayed and held firmly to their faith. She said that some years after Grandpa Jim died she saw him in a dream. "Sis Opie," he said as he walked toward her, "hold on to what you got. It's gonna mean a lot to you one day." She initially thought he was referring to her insurance. Later she knew it was her faith.

"Of all my people, it's just me now," Mama has repeatedly said. Even though the others are gone now, I know they would want us to hold on to our faith, continue to work, and do what is right. It is my hope that we keep striving until one day we balance the scales of justice.

ABBREVIATIONS

BHCHS	Brownsville-Haywood County Historical Society
LC	Library of Congress, Washington, D.C.
MSLC	Manuscript Section Library of Congress, Washington, D.C.
NA	National Archives, Washington, D.C.
NAACP	National Association for the Advancement of Colored People
THQ	*Tennessee Historical Quarterly*
TSLA	Tennessee State Library and Archives, Nashville

PREFACE

1. U.S. Bureau of the Census, *Thirteenth Census of United States, 1910* (Washington, D.C., 1913, 1:243.

2. Ibid., 3:750.

3. Hazel O. Lander, Federal Writers Project, *Tennessee State Encyclopedia, Cities Towns and Villages,* July 17, 1939, Manuscript Division, TSLA.

4. Richard Wright, *12 Million Black Voices: A Folk History of the Negro in the United States* (New York: Viking, 1941).

1. OLD CROSSROADS PLACE

1. BHCHS, *History of Haywood County Tennessee* (Walsworth Publishing, Marceline, Mo., 1989), 237.

2. Ibid., 240. Weston Goodspeed, *History of Tennessee: From the Earliest Times to the Present* (Nashville: Goodspeed Publishers, 1887), 818–29.

3. BHCHS, *History of Haywood County,* 237–39.

4. See County Clerk Minutes, vol. 12, 1913–18, Feb. 3, 1914, microfilm, TSLA.

5. Ibid.

6. Ibid., Feb. 7, 1914.

7. See Inventory of the estate of Howell Y. Taylor, Sworn to and subscribed before the court at Brownsville, Tennessee, Feb. 5, 1914. Settlements, Guardians, Administrators, and Executors, roll 25, vol. 4, Jan. 1886–May 1926, 253, microfilm, TSLA.

8. Ibid.

9. Ibid.

10. County Clerk Minutes, Haywood County, vol. 12, 1913–18, Feb. 21, 1914.

11. Ibid.

12. BHCHS, *History of Haywood County*, 194.

13. Death certificates for Benjamin Franklin Taylor and the other four family members—Howell, Walter, Ora, and Polk Taylor—may be found in the Death Index, microfilm, TSLA.

2. KINFOLKS

1. The Tabernacle Historical Committee's *The Taylors of Tabernacle* (Jackson: McCowat-Mercer Press, 1957) was a primary source for this chapter. The work includes the diaries of John A. Taylor, S. Edmund Taylor, and Robert E. Taylor. The entries of John A. Taylor, who kept a diary from around 1840 until 1881, were especially helpful in documenting the Civil War period and in providing a vivid account of life on the Taylor plantation. Among the slaves on the plantation were a young Tamar, my great grandmother, and her parents, Sam and Isabel Taylor. I am grateful to the Taylors for providing in their recordings of family history and recollections of Kinfolks meetings some reference to Sam, Isabel, and Tamar.

2. Ibid., 4.

3. Ibid., 9.

4. Ibid., 361, diary of Robert E. Taylor. The surveyed land on Tabernacle Road that John A. Taylor gave to the Negroes as church property was recorded as "Beginning at the Southwest corner, running North 13 poles and 5 links, thence East 14 poles and 7 links, thence South 13 poles and 5 links, thence West 14 poles and 7 links to the beginning."

5. Eugene D. Genovese, *Roll, Jordan, Roll: The World the Slaves Made* (New York: Vintage Books, 1974), 472. Masters wanted their slaves to marry someone from the same farm or plantation because it was less disruptive and they would have rights to any children born to the union. They had no rights to children that their male had by a female on another plantation.

6. Herbert G. Gutman, *The Black Family in Slavery and Freedom, 1750–1925* (New York: Vintage Books, 1976), 270.

7. Genovese, *Roll, Jordan, Roll*, 475. Weddings received sanction from the master, who saw them as necessary for the preservation of social control.

8. Ibid., 480–81.

9. Ibid.

10. Gutman, *The Black Family in Slavery and Freedom*, 273. Tabernacle Historical Committee, *The Taylors of Tabernacle*, diary of S. Edmund Taylor, 152.

11. Tabernacle Historical Committee, The Taylors of Tabernacle, diary of S. Edmund Taylor, 152.

12. Ibid., 153.

13. Ibid., diary of John A. Taylor, 177.

14. Ibid.

15. Ibid. Although John A. Taylor was a staunch Methodist, his fervent prayers for the Lord to "rule over all for the best" were, without a doubt, for a Confederate victory. Considered a very religious man, John Taylor, nevertheless, like most Southern whites, saw no contradiction between his religious beliefs and his views on slavery.

16. Jesse Burt, *Your Tennessee* (Austin: Steck-Vaughn Company, 1974), 181–83.

17. John Hope Franklin and Alfred A. Moss Jr., *From Slavery to Freedom: A History of African Americans* (New York: McGraw-Hill, 1994), 216.

18. Burt, *Your Tennessee*, 182–83.

19. Ibid., 189.

20. Herbert G. Gutman, *The Black Family in Slavery and Freedom*, 209. Historians Joel T. Williamson and William S. McFeely found a close connection between post-emancipation land use and familial and kin beliefs. Gutman notes that Williamson research left him with "the distinct impression that even as most freedmen left the slave villages they spent their lives on farms carved out of plantations within a few miles of the place of their servitude." But the extended kin networks among the plantation blacks were sufficient reason to remain in a local familial and social setting. Moving a few miles allowed an immediate family to cut loose from the symbol of its servitude and yet remain attached to the kin networks that had developed among them as slaves.

21. In Genovese, *Roll, Jordan, Roll*, 70–71, a plantation manual is quoted: "'Tis but just and humane, when they [slaves] have done their duty, to treat them with kindness, and even sometimes with indulgence." Genovese notes this and other statements on the master and slave: "These ideal statements tell us much more about the actual practice than might be imagined, for although a good master should be 'kind,' circumstances must first allow him to be kind. He must fulfill his duties to his slaves; they will, of course, do their duty to him and respond positively to his demands, so that his kindness and even indulgence may become natural gestures. Kindness does not define this social idea; kindness crowns it."

22. Tabernacle Historical Committee, *Taylors of Tabernacle*, 242. According to John A. Taylor, "this rapid increase among the Negroes was mainly due to the care, and attention which they received from their sympathizing mistress."

23. Gutman, *The Black Family in Slavery and Freedom*, 87, discusses the many young slaves who lived through the Civil War and Reconstruction and probably became the parents of twentieth-century African Americans. Slave children born in the 1840s or the 1850s (like Tamar) grew up in a slave community made up of interrelated but well-defined immediate families. This allowed slave children to

absorb values from parents, grandparents, other adult kin, and adult non-kin. They were not socialized simply by an owner or an overseer; the choices they later made as adults were shaped by socializing experiences rooted within the developing slave community itself.

24. In Brownsville, as in other southern communities, it was common for former slaves and their descendants to address all adult blacks as "aunt" or "uncle," even though the families were not related by blood. Gutman, *The Black Family in Slavery and Freedom*, 217–18, quotes a free black, born in 1848, who said, "the white people did not permit us to say 'Mr.' and 'Mrs.' to each other, so, the children, for 'manners's sake,' were taught to call the older people, 'aunt' and 'uncle.'" According to plantation etiquette, this form of address was considered a mark of respect from the younger slaves to the older slaves. Slaves maintained a rigid enforcement of the law of respect to elders.

25. Gutman, *The Black Family in Slavery and Freedom*, 199. The continuity of social order depends upon the passing on of tradition, knowledge, and skill, and of manners, morals, religion, and taste, from one generation to the next.

26. Ibid., 93, 185–97. Naming practices linked generations and showed an awareness among the slaves of the "sheer importance of kinship."

27. Tabernacle Historical Committee, *Taylors of Tabernacle*, xv.

28. Ibid.

29. Zaidee Taylor Blackwell, "Recollections of Kinfolks Meeting," in Tabernacle Historical Committee, *Taylors of Tabernacle*, 612–13. Zaidee is the daughter of William and Hattie Taylor.

30. Ibid., 612.

31. BHCHS, "Edmond Taylor," in *History of Haywood County*.

3. ON SPRINGFIELD ROAD

1. "Haywood County Roads in Good Condition," *Brownsville States-Graphic*, June 4, 1926.

2. Richard A. Couto, *Lifting the Veil: A Political History of Struggle for Emancipation* (Knoxville: Univ. of Tennessee Press, 1993), 124.

3. Ibid. Couto quotes census figures and states that at this time the number of black landowners in Haywood County was declining rapidly.

4. Franklin and Moss, *From Slavery to Freedom*, 383.

5. James Arnold Baxter, "Charles Allen Rawls: 'A Portrait,' 1907–1977" (master's thesis, Tennessee State Univ., 1982), 14.

6. Franklin and Moss, *From Slavery to Freedom*, 383, describes conditions after World War I, noting that the flight of thousands of African Americans from southern farms after the war did not seem to improve the conditions of those who remained. In many areas, destruction was so extensive that farms were temporarily or permanently abandoned, and both black and white farm laborers were thrown out of work.

7. Lester C. Lamon, *Blacks in Tennessee, 1791–1970* (Knoxville: Univ. of Tennessee Press, 1981), 88.

8. Ibid.

9. Franklin and Moss, *From Slavery to Freedom*, 383.

10. Lamon, *Blacks in Tennessee*, 89.

11. Raymond Wolters, *Negroes and the Great Depression: The Problem of Economic Recovery* (Westport, Conn.: Greenwood Publishing, 1970), 7.

12. John F. Bauman, *In the Eye of the Great Depression: New Deal Reporter and the Agony of the American People* (Dekalb: Northern Illinois Univ. Press, 1988), 22.

13. Ibid.

14. Ibid., 22–27.

15. Lamon, *Blacks in Tennessee*, 88.

16. Wolters, *Negroes and the Great Depression*, 7.

17. See Lamon, *Blacks in Tennessee*.

18. Studs Terkel, *Hard Times: An Oral History of the Great Depression* (New York: Pantheon Books, 1970), 213.

19. "Federal Aid for Drought-Seared Regions Sought," *Jackson Sun*, Aug. 5, 1930.

20. Harvard Sitkoff, *A New Deal for Blacks: The Emergence of Civil Rights as a National Issue*, vol. 1, *The Depression Decade* (New York: Oxford Univ. Press, 1978), 39.

21. Ibid., 35.

22. Ibid., 39.

23. Ibid.

24. Franklin and Moss, *From Slavery to Freedom*, 387. Blacks voted Republican because they did not find it easy to desert the Republican party in 1932. Many remained true to the tradition and voted for the party of Lincoln. Few outside New York were acquainted with Franklin D. Roosevelt, who aroused little enthusiasm as a public figure. They thought a Democratic victory would lead to the ascendancy of southern politicians in Washington and degradation of blacks, as had happened during the Wilson administration.

25. Sitkoff, *A New Deal for Blacks*, 40.

26. Ibid., 26, 40–41.

27. Lamon, *Blacks in Tennessee*, 85.

28. Sitkoff, *A New Deal for Blacks*, 41.

29. Ibid. Ted Morgan, *FDR: A Biography* (New York: Simon and Schuster, 1985), 363.

30. "How the States Voted," *Memphis Press-Scimitar*, Nov. 9, 1932.

4. SWEET GUM TREES

1. Wolters, *Negroes and the Great Depression*, 4.

2. Morgan, *FDR*, 375.

3. Ibid.

4. Wolters, *Negroes and the Great Depression*, 9.

5. Franklin and Moss, *From Slavery to Freedom*, 384.

6. See Wolters, *Negroes and the Great Depression*, and, generally, Morgan, *FDR*, 376–91.

7. Sitkoff, *A New Deal for Blacks*, 52. The great majority of New Dealers accepted discrimination against blacks as an inevitable cost of economic recovery and relief. And the great majority of blacks suffered.

8. Ibid., 50–51.

9. Ibid., 51.

10. Ibid., 53.

11. "Future of Cotton Prices at Stake," *Brownsville States-Graphic*, Feb. 9, 1934.

12. "Gov't. Program Will Aid Cash Basis Farming," *Brownsville States-Graphic*, Feb. 16, 1934.

13. Under the Agriculture Adjustment Administration, farmers received cash benefits for plowing under their cotton, wheat, and tobacco crops and for slaughtering their hogs. Farmers cash benefits rose to billions of dollars under the AAA, but many grants intended for blacks were misappropriated. Many landlords took advantage of illiterate sharecroppers and tenants and kept checks intended for them. Dishonesty led to the organization of the Southern Tenant Farmers Union. Later, payments were provided directly to tenants, but blacks still suffered as white landowners removed them from the land and received the benefits for themselves. Franklin and Moss, *From Slavery to Freedom*, 395; see also, Lamon, *Blacks in Tennessee*, 89.

14. Bauman, *In the Eye of the Great Depression*, 197.

15. By an executive order dated May 6, 1935, certain functions of the Public Works Program (PWA), along with some responsibilities of the Federal Emergency Relief Administration (FERA), were taken over by the Works Progress Administration (WPA) under the direction of Harry Hopkins. While the WPA contracts never included such specific protection for Negro workers as those of the PWA's housing division, Hopkins, after some hesitation, did issue a celebrated administrative order proclaiming that "workers who are qualified by training and experience . . . shall not be discriminated against on any grounds whatever such as race, religion, or political affiliation." Bauman, *In the Eye of the Great Depression*, 203–4.

16. Bauman, *In the Eye of the Great Depression*, 207–9.

17. "County Agents Advise the Planting of Feed Crops Now," *Brownsville States-Graphic*, July 3, 1936.

18. "Triple Slaying on P. H. Bell Farm," *Brownsville States-Graphic*, Jan. 17, 1936.

19. "Public Works Administration Makes Grant for Streets," *Brownsville States-Graphic*, July 31, 1936.

20. "95,000 Checks Due Tennessee Agriculturists," *Brownsville States-Graphic*, Oct. 16, 1936.

21. "Pres. Roosevelt Enters Second Term Wednesday. Pledges to Carry on Fight to Aid Millions in Need in U.S.—Thousands Present," *Brownsville States-Graphic*, Jan. 22, 1937.

22. Ibid.

23. Sitkoff, *A New Deal for Blacks*, 53, writes no clear correlation existed between AAA practices and the black exodus from the cotton counties. More Afro-Americans left the rural South in the period from 1931 to 1933 than in the first two years of the New Deal. More Negroes quit farming toward the end of the thirties, after AAA procedures had been modified to give black tenants a larger share of the benefits, than in the early years of the New Deal, when all the cards were stacked in favor of the white landlord. Regardless of the facts, the claim of Negroes that the AAA drove hundreds of thousands of blacks from the land persisted in the thirties. It gained currency because so much of the first New Deal was in fact discriminatory against blacks.

24. Ibid., 54.

25. With justification the Negro press referred to the NRA with scorn as "Negro Run Around," "Negroes Ruined Again," "Negro Rarely Allowed," "Negro Removal Act," "Negro Robbed Again," and "No Roosevelt Again." No black editor mourned its demise in 1935. Sitkoff, *A New Deal for Blacks*, 55.

26. Bauman, *In the Eye of the Great Depression*, 208.

27. Sitkoff, *A New Deal for Blacks*, 56.

28. Wolters, *Negroes and the Great Depression*, 39.

5. FIGHTING ODDS

1. Sitkoff, *A New Deal for Blacks*, 268.

2. In 1910, the permanent organization was established and announced as its new name the National Association for the Advancement of Colored People. The first president, Moorfield Storg, announced in *The Crisis*, its monthly magazine: "The object of the National Association is to create an organization which will endeavor to smooth the path of the Negro race upward, and create a public opinion which will frown upon discrimination against their property rights, which will endeavor to see that they get in the courts the same justice that is given to their white neighbors, and that they are not discriminated against as they are now all over the country. We want to make race prejudice as unfashionable as it is now fashionable"; Sitkoff, *A New Deal for Blacks*. In Memphis the NAACP was a consistent (and often the only) force in active protest of injustices to blacks through the courts and agencies of the federal government. Kate Born, "Memphis Negro Workingmen and the NAACP," *The West Tennessee Historical Society Papers* (Nashville: West Tennessee Historical Society, 1974, 90.

3. "Application for Charter of Brownsville Branch of the National Association for the Advancement of Colored People," NAACP Administration Files, Group 1, Box G-198, Brownsville Branch, MSLC. The application for the Brownsville charter originally had fifty-four names; two were removed before the application was submitted to the national office.

4. Ibid.

5. Thomas B. Alexander, "Kukluxism in Tennessee, 1865–1869," *THQ* 8 (1949): 203–4.

6. Margaret Edds, *Free at Last: What Really Happened When Civil Rights Came to Southern Politics* (Bethesda, Md.: Adler and Adler, 1987), 161–62.

7. Franklin and Moss, *From Slavery to Freedom*, 357.

8. Sitkoff, *A New Deal for Blacks*, 278.

9. Affidavit of Elisha Davis, NAACP Administration Files, Group 2, Box A-406, Lynching, Brownsville, Tennessee, Elbert Williams, 1941–52, MSLC.

10. Affidavit of Nann Davis, ibid.

11. Affidavit of Elisha Davis, ibid.

12. "Statement of Facts in the Brownsville, Tennessee Case," ibid.

13. Ibid.

14. Elisha Davis to Thurgood Marshall, Special Counsel, Sept. 8, 1942, ibid.

15. Willie Bell Rawls, from her home in Michigan, recalled the events that took place in Brownsville on the night of June 20, 1940. Rawls said she feared the whites had picked up Williams in retaliation for their celebration of Joe Louis's victory over Godoy.

16. Affidavit of Annie Williams, Sept. 11, 1940, NAACP Administration Files, Group 2, Box A-406, Lynching, Brownsville, Tennessee, Elbert Williams, 1941–52, MSLC.

17. Ibid.

18. Ibid.

19. Franklin and Moss, *From Slavery to Freedom*, 341.

20. William "Bill" Rawls, of Rawls Funeral Home, described the finding of Elbert Williams, and the handling and burying of the body by his father, Al Rawls.

21. Affidavit of Annie Williams, Sept. 11, 1940, NAACP Administration Files, Group 2, Box A-406, Lynching, Brownsville, Tennessee, Elbert Williams, 1941–52, MSLC.

22. "Joe Louis Defends Title with Kayo over Godoy," *Memphis Press-Scimitar*, June 21, 1940.

23. "Lynchings Go Down As Cotton's Price Rises, Says Sociologist," *Memphis Press-Scimitar*, Apr. 5, 1940.

24. "Lynched, Elbert Williams," *Chicago Defender*, July 6, 1940.

25. Ibid.

26. "Reign of Terror Follows Tennessee Lynchings, Grand Jury Investigation

Is Promised," *Chicago Defender*, July 6, 1940. The newspaper carried this message in the middle of the article: "Keep Campaigning for Anti-Lynch Law."

27. See Correspondence with Dept. of Justice re Brownsville, Tennessee Case, NAACP Administration Files, Group 2, Box A-406, Lynching, Brownsville, Tennessee, Elbert Williams, 1941–52, MSLC.

28. Ibid.

29. Walter White to O. John Rogge, July 1, 1940, ibid.

30. Walter White to President Franklin Roosevelt, July 1, 1940, ibid.

31. I. L. Newbern to Walter White, July 9, 1940, ibid.

32. The Western Union telegram from Roy Wilkins to President Franklin D. Roosevelt acknowledged that the Justice Department was investigating the specific lynching of Elbert Williams, but they urged that the issue "is much greater than this."

33. O. John Rogge to Roy Wilkins, Aug. 16, 1940, NAACP Administration Files, Group 2, Box A-406, Lynching, Brownsville, Tennessee, Elbert Williams, 1941–52, MSLC. Rogge insisted that the case was "not limited to the alleged lynching Elbert Williams, but is intended to reach all aspects of the case over which the Federal Government has jurisdiction."

34. Walter White to O. John Rogge, telegram, Sept. 3, 1940, ibid.

35. Correspondence with Dept. of Justice re Brownsville, Tennessee Case, ibid.

36. "Grand Jurors End Inquiry into Death, No Evidence of Violence in Haywood Investigation," *Memphis Press-Scimitar*, Aug. 14, 1940. This article reported that more than twenty witnesses had been called before the grand jury and no evidence was revealed that would clear up the mystery.

37. Thurgood Marshall to O. John Rogge, Oct. 29, 1940.

38. "Democratic Standard Bearers Carries 38 of 48 States," *Brownsville States-Graphic*, Nov. 8, 1940.

39. "Jimmie Joe Morris," *Brownsville States-Graphic*, Nov. 8, 1940.

40. Memorandum, Thurgood Marshall to Office, Dec. 9, 1941; Memorandum Dictated by Mr. Thurgood Marshall on December 11, 1941, NAACP Administration Files, Group 2, Box A-406, Lynching, Brownsville, Tennessee, Williams, 1941–52, MSLC.

41. Wendell Berge to Thurgood Marshall, Jan. 23, 1942, ibid.

42. Thurgood Marshall to Wendell Berge, Jan. 30, 1942, ibid.

43. Ibid.

44. Milmon Mitchell to Thurgood Marshall, Feb. 17, 1942, ibid.

45. Thurgood Marshall to Milmon Mitchell, Mar. 17, 1942, ibid.

46. Thurgood Marshall to Victor Rotnem, July 28, 1942, ibid.

47. Davis wrote Marshall from his home in Niles, Michigan, stating his disagreement with the Justice Department dropping his case.

48. Thurgood Marshall to Elisha Davis, Sept. 16, 1942, NAACP Administra-

tion Files, Group 2, Box A-406, Lynching, Brownsville, Tennessee, Williams, 1941–52, MSLC.

49. Memorandum, reinterview with Mrs. Annie Williams Boone, concerning her reference to a "property deal" between Elbert Williams and Elisha Davis, Dec. 12, 1941, NAACP Administration Files, Group 2, Box A-406, Lynching, Brownsville, Tennessee, Williams, 1941–52, MSLC.

50. Faith Berry, *Before and Beyond Harlem: A Biography of Langston Hughes* (New York: Wings Books, 1983), 135.

6. WINFIELD LANE

1. "The War," *Brownsville States-Graphic*, Dec. 12, 1941.
2. Ann Toplovich, "The Tennessean's War: Life on the Home Front," *THQ* 51 (spring 1992): 24. Willie Bell Rawls contributed an article on the African American effort in the war during the segregated 1940s. Rawls recalled the many soldiers and draftees who stayed in her home during the war, and whom she helped entertain. In her interview, Rawls spoke about the apprehension of the young men leaving home to fight for their country.
3. *Brownsville States-Graphic*, Feb. 5, 1943.
4. "U.S. Casualties for Entire War Total 87,304 up to Now," *Brownsville States-Graphic*, June 25, 1943.
5. "Proclamation to the People of the United States," *Brownsville States-Graphic*, Sept. 3, 1943.
6. Point rationing for over two hundred food items and other goods was implemented with an assigned value based on scarcity. Brownsville citizens received ration books that contained stamps for use in purchasing such items as sugar, meats, shoes, and gasoline. Most stamps had an expiration date, requiring them to be redeemed within a limited period of time.
7. "Invasion May Be Near As Bombs Fall," *Brownsville States-Graphic*, Apr. 21, 1944.
8. Circuit Court Minutes, Haywood County, "Indictment for Murder," *State of Tennessee* v. *Mozella Rutherford [and] Lonnie Searcy Alias Bond*, Jan. 22, 1945.
9. Ibid. "Plea of Guilty and Sentence," *State of Tennessee* v. *Mozella Rutherford [and] Lonnie Searcy Alias Bond*, Feb. 1, 1945.
10. "Entire Nation Mourns Death of Franklin D. Roosevelt; Vast Tasks Face Truman," *Brownsville States-Graphic*, Apr. 20, 1945.
11. "Japanese Accept Terms, Local Citizens Join Nation in Celebration," *Brownsville States-Graphic*, Aug. 17, 1945.
12. Ibid.

7. FORCED DANCING

1. See *Brownsville States-Graphic*, Nov. 2, 1948, Jan. 21, 1949.
2. The American golden age lasted only five years, 1945 to 1950, from the end

of World War I to the start of the Korean War. See Gore Vidal, "Making a Mess of the American Empire," *Newsweek,* Jan. 11, 1993, 30.

3. *Brownsville States-Graphic* listed the names of boys from Brownsville and surrounding towns to whom the draft board had mailed orders to report for the armed forces' physical examination, as well as names of those inducted.

4. "Statement of Facts in the Brownsville, Tennessee Case," NAACP Administration Files, Group 2, Box A-406, Lynching, Elbert Williams, 1941–52, MSLC. Despite the efforts of the NAACP and civic-minded individuals, the Department of Justice closed its case files on Brownsville in January 1942. No federal, state, or county investigation resulted in bringing to justice any member of the mob perpetrating intimidation. Still, a full decade later, Elisha Davis held out hope that the Justice Department would prosecute Tip Hunter and other members of the mob who ran some blacks out of town, killed others, and stole their property.

5. Constance Baker Motley to Elisha Davis, ibid. Thurgood Marshall asked Motley to respond, which she did, thanking Davis for "forwarding to us the affidavits of Alene Whitmore Sanders and Jack Adams."

8. THE MOURNING BENCH

1. Andrew Billingsley, *Climbing Jacob's Ladder: The Enduring Legacy of African-American Families* (New York: Simon and Schuster, 1992), 181.
2. Ibid.
3. Ibid., 174.
4. Ibid., 172.

9. WE ARE NOT AFRAID

1. *Brownsville States-Graphic,* July 31, 1959.
2. Charter of Incorporation, Haywood County Civic and Welfare League, May 1959. The quotations from Dr. Boyd in this chapter were obtained by the author from a number of interviews conducted with him in Brownsville and over the telephone.
3. "Delegation of Negroes Protest before State Election Commission," *Brownsville States-Graphic,* July 31, 1959.
4. Lamon, *Blacks in Tennessee,* 102.
5. Ibid., 102–4.
6. "Kennedy Drives for Negro Vote," *Commercial Appeal,* Sept. 2, 1960.
7. "Federal Injunction Sought against 27 White Persons and Two Banks in Haywood County," *Brownsville States-Graphic,* Sept. 16, 1960.
8. Ibid.
9. "Whither Headed?" editorial, *Brownsville States-Graphic,* Sept. 16, 1960.
10. *Brownsville States-Graphic,* Nov. 11, 1960.
11. Ibid.
12. See "Crimes Charged to Race Leader," *Commercial Appeal,* Aug. 4, 1963, and "Core Members Demonstrate," *Brownsville States-Graphic,* Aug. 9, 1963.

13. "Clergy's Pleas Help Quiet Chicago," *Commercial Appeal*, Aug. 4, 1963.

14. "Weinberger 'Cuts Out,'" *Brownsville State-Graphic*, Oct. 11, 1963.

15. "Three Die in Truck-Bus Wreck," *Brownsville States-Graphic*, Nov. 29, 1963.

16. "Two Explosions Cause Damage to House and Garage Monday Night," *Brownsville States-Graphic*, May 20, 1966.

17. "We Are Not Afraid," on display at the Great Blacks in Wax Museum, Baltimore, Maryland.

10. HULLS DINNER

1. "Haywood County Shows Steady Loss in Population Each Year," *Brownsville States Graphic*, May 5, 1967.

2. Between 1940 and 1970, the number of agricultural laborers in Haywood County declined by almost five-sixths; Couto, *Lifting the Veil*, 179.

3. "Economist Sees Further Startling Changes in Tennessee Agriculture," *Brownsville States-Graphic*, Mar. 17, 1967.

4. Ibid.

5. Ibid.

6. "Federal Court Orders Complete School Integration with Choice of Two Plans," *Brownsville States-Graphic*, May 16, 1969.

7. Couto, *Lifting the Veil*, 108.

8. Ibid.

9. "Local School Boards to Answer Justice Department Complaint," *Brownsville States-Graphic*, Feb. 10, 1967.

10. "Notice of School Desegregation Plan under Title VI of the Civil Rights Act of 1964," *Brownsville States-Graphic*, Mar. 17, 1967.

Bibliographical Essay

Noted historian Benjamin Quarles wrote, "Much of the historical information about Negroes must be dug out; it is not readily available in printed form as are the papers of Presidents or other great men or places." Writing *The Legacy of Tamar* required, understandably, the research of people, places, and events where information was not readily available. Therefore, my primary sources were personal interviews and, in many instances, informal conversations. Information gathered from numerous interviews and conversations with Opal Taylor Springfield, my mother, is infused throughout every chapter in this book. Without her sharing memories of the past it would not have been possible to complete this work.

Others who were gracious enough to submit to personal interviews and shed light on the early years in Brownsville, Haywood County, Tennessee, include Ada Averyheart, Brownsville; Dr. Currie P. Boyd, Brownsville; Louise Cook, Decatur, Illinois; William D. "Bill" Rawls, Brownsville; Willie Bell Rawls, Detroit, Michigan; Don Sanders, Washington, D.C.; Charles Springfield, Decatur, Illinois; Clarence Taylor, Romulus, Michigan; Eldred Taylor, New York; Mamie Turner, Brownsville. The formal and informal interviews were invaluable in gathering information concerning family relationships, births, deaths, marriages, migration, early voter registration efforts in the 1940s, the World War II era, the postwar period, and the civil rights struggle of the 1950s and 1960s. These interviews were an important reference source for chapters 4, 5, and 9. The interviews were conducted either in person or via telephone, and in several instances there were follow-up interviews. All notes from these interviews are in the possession of the author.

Sources used to depict the history and early development of Brownsville and Haywood County were Brownsville–Haywood County Historical Society, *History of Haywood County Tennessee* (Walsworth Publishing, Marceline, Mo., 1989); Jesse Burt, *Your Tennessee* (Austin: Steck-Vaughn, 1974); and Weston Goodspeed, *History of Tennessee: From the Earliest Times to the Present* (Nashville: Goodspeed Publishers, 1887). Lester C. Lamon, *Blacks in Tennessee: 1791–1970* (Knoxville: Univ. of Tennessee Press, 1981), is an important reference on the role of blacks in the growth and history of Tennessee. For a political history of Haywood County, Richard A. Couto, *Lifting the Veil: A Political History of Struggles for Emancipation* (Knoxville: Univ. of Tennessee Press, 1993), was valuable not only for its history of Haywood County but also as a guide to other resources on the county.

Tabernacle Historical Committee, *The Taylors of Tabernacle* (Jackson: McCowat-Mercer Press, 1957), was invaluable as a documentation of the early settlers in Haywood County, the life of slaves on the Taylor plantation, and life in Haywood and surrounding counties during the Civil War. It provided the names of Tamar's parents, which heretofore were not known by family members, and important dates of births and deaths. The diaries of John A. Taylor, S. Edmund Taylor, and Robert E. Taylor, and the recollections contained in the book of Kinfolks camp meetings were important sources of reference for chapter 2. For additional information on slave life, I referred to John Hope Franklin and Alfred A. Moss Jr., *From Slavery to Freedom: A History of African Americans* (New York: McGraw-Hill, 1994); Eugene D. Genovese, *Roll, Jordan, Roll: The World the Slaves Made* (New York: Vintage Books, 1974); and Herbert G. Gutman, *The Black Family in Slavery and Freedom, 1750–1925* (New York: Vintage Books, 1976). See also, Andrew Billingsley, *Climbing Jacob's Ladder: The Enduring Legacy of African-American Families* (New York, Simon and Schuster, 1992) for well-documented information, data, and analysis that correct misconceptions and stereotypes about the black family and looks at current issues in the black family.

There are numerous books in print on the Great Depression and on the New Deal and black Americans. I found the following excellent sources: John F. Bauman, *In the Eye of the Great Depression: New Deal Reporter and the Agony of the American People* (Dekalb: Northern Illinois Univ. Press, 1988); Harvard Sitkoff, *A New Deal for Blacks: The Emergence of Civil Rights as a National Issue*, vol. 1, *The Depression Decade* (New York: Oxford Univ. Press, 1978); Studs Terkel, *Hard Times: An Oral History of the Great Depression* (New York: Pantheon Books, 1970); Raymond Wolters, *Negroes and the Great Depression: The Problem of Economic Recovery* (Westport, Conn.: Greenwood Publishing, 1970); and Roger Biles, *Memphis in the Great Depression* (Knoxville: Univ. of Tennessee Press, 1986). An additional source for this historical period and the World War II era is Ted Morgan, *FDR: A Biography* (New York: Simon and Schuster, 1985).

The civil rights movement has likewise been documented at length; however, for my purpose here, only a limited number of these vast sources were used to augment information obtained from newspaper coverage of local and national events, NAACP files, and personal accounts of local citizens and former citizens of Haywood County: Margaret Edds, *Free at Last: What Really Happened When Civil Rights Came to Southern Politics* (Bethesda, Md.: Adler and Adler, 1987); Stephen B. Oats, *Let the Trumpet Sound: The Life of Martin Luther King, Jr.* (New York: Harper and Row, 1982); Paul E. Wilson, *A Time to Lose: Representing Kansas in Brown V. Board of Education* (Lawrence: Univ. Press of Kansas, 1995); and Harvard Sitkoff, *A New Deal for Blacks: The Emergence of Civil Rights as a National Issue* (New York: Oxford Univ. Press, 1978). See also, Mark V. Tushnet, *The NAACP's Legal Strategy against Segregated Education, 1925–1950* (Chapel Hill: Univ. of North Carolina Press,1987).

The Tennessee State Library and Archives, Nashville, is where I began my research on the family. There I found recordings of legal proceedings in circuit court records and county clerk minutes for Haywood County on microfilm. The records on guardians, executors, and administrators of estates were very helpful. Also important in researching my family history were the manuscripts, collections, and death, birth, and marriage records. The U.S. Census records were important in verifying population and farming data and family household information. I relied heavily on the newspapers on microfilm. The Nashville Public Library and the Brownsville Public Library were also utilized in my research. Finally, the Library of Congress, Washington, D.C., yielded the NAACP Branch and Administration files, which contain detailed accounts of the early voter registration efforts and the accompanying mob violence in Brownsville, Haywood County, Tennessee.

Several newspapers were extremely important in providing local coverage of people and events in Haywood County: *Brownsville States-Graphic; Jackson Sun; Commercial Appeal*; and *Memphis Press-Scimitar*. The *Chicago Defender*, while not a local paper, provided news coverage of lynchings across the county in the national campaign for passage of the antilynching bill in Congress. Finally, two other sources valuable for research of local history were *The West Tennessee Historical Society Papers* and *Tennessee Historical Quarterly*.

Suggested as a resource tool for beginning genealogical research is Jesse Carney Smith, *Ethnic Genealogy*. The chapter by Bobby L. Lovett, "Researching Family History," is excellent in that it provides the format, research steps, and other resources for this in-depth approach to researching and writing a family history.

Index

Adams, Jack, 75, 92, 249n5
Alamo, 6
Anderson, Sherwood, 70
Averyheart, Ada Springfield, 38, 41, 44, 147, 232–33
Averyheart, Henry, 44, 60
Averyheart, Jack, 38, 44
Averyheart, Thomas, 209

Ballard, Norma, 171
Baskerville, Cloria Taylor, 38, 43, 59, 67, 73, 77–79, 81, 93–94, 109, 151–53, 226; early years, 2, 8, 10, 25–26, 33
Baskerville, William, 151, 152
Battle of Nashville, 23
Battle of Shiloh, 21
Bells, 6, 102
Berge, Wendell, 92
Berry, Elsie Springfield (Lee), 40, 192, 194, 226
Bilbo, Theodore, 71
black family, 23–24, 138, 241n20
black farmers, 42–43, 46–47, 53–54; exodus from south, 68, 242n6
Booker T. Washington High School, 123
Bond, Dorch, 100
Bond, Irene, 100, 105–6
Bond, John R., 167
Bond, Lawrence, 100, 140
Bond, Mariah, 195
Bond, Nola, 100–101, 139
Bond, Roy, 176

Bond, Suzanna, 100, 141
Bond, Tom, 100, 141, 169
Boyd, Currie Porter (C. P.) 157–60, 163–64, 169, 249n2
Brewer, Joseph, 176
Brownsville, xiii, xv, 63, 68, 70; civil rights, 157–59, 170, 174; Civil War, 21–23; desegregation in, *see* school desegregation; Ku Klux Klan in, 177; location, 6–7, 179–80, 204; and World War II, 102–3

Cannon, Jesse, 214
Carnegie, Andrew, 7
Carver High School, 133, 155, 175–76, 229; last commencement, 199
Chicago Defender, 83–84
Churchill, Winston, 178
civil rights movement, xiv, 71, 173–74; *see also* Haywood County
Civil War, 19–23
Confederate States of America, 19
Congress of Racial Equality (CORE), 159, 170
Cook, Louise Springfield, 40, 55–56, 99, 149, 192–94, 225–26, 233–34
Covington, 6, 214
Crockett County, 2, 179
Crouch, Duarwd, 156

Davidson County, 1
Davis, Cal, 180, 216–17, 220

Davis, Cashier, 74
Davis, Elisha, 73–77, 86–87, 92–94, 134, 246n14, 247n47, 249n4
Davis, Jefferson, 20
Davis, Thomas, 73–74, 77
Decatur County, 157
Delk, George Lewis, 171
Dewey, Thomas E., 108, 127
Doar, John, 163–64
Dotson, Melvin, 158
Drumwright, Strauss, 76
Dupree, Spence, 78, 82, 91
Dyersburg, 102, 139

Eisenhower, Dwight, 163
Estes, James Franklin, 157
Estes, Sleepy John, 131
Evers, Medgar, 173

Fayette County, 2, 15; voter registration drive, 159
Fayette County Civic and Welfare League, 159
Federal Writers Project, xiv
Forked Deer River, 6, 21, 29, 74
Forrest, General Nathan, 13, 23
Fort Donelson, 21
Fort Henry, 21
Fort Pillow, 21; Negro soldiers massacred, 23
Fuller, Charlie, 100, 117–18, 126–27, 129
Fuller, Eva, 100

Grand Ole Opry, 63
Grant, General Uysses S., 21
Graves, George, 158
Great Depression, 42–43, 48–49, 69, 71; *see* migration

Hafford, Dan, 26, 33
Hafford, Tamar Taylor, 2, 8, 10, 25–26, 33, 43
Hardeman County, 2
Harrell, Guy, 89, 131
Harris, Isham G., 20
Hatchie River, 7, 21, 78–79, 81
Haywood County, xiii, 1–2, 24, 40, 111; agriculture, 2, 58, 118, 130, 185–86;

black effort to vote in, 71, 75–76, 81, 86–87, 128, 157, 160, 163–69, 174–75; black landowners in, 41, 46, 242n3; camp meetings in 29; civil rights demonstrations in, 170–74, 177–78; during depression, 51, 63–64; Justice Department investigation in, 86–87, 91–93, 247n36; New Deal in, 53–56; population, xiv, 185, 250n1; settlement of, 15–16; sheriff killed, *see* Hunter, Jack; "Tent City," 159–60; voting in, 49, 90, 128, 166; World War II and, 105, 108, 113, 117; *see also* Ku Klux Klan, lynching, and school desegregation
Haywood County Civic and Welfare League, 157, 167
Haywood County Fair, 123, 161
Haywood County Negro Fair, 123, 161
Haywood Training School, 62, 78, 91
Hess, Beulah Taylor, 27–28
Hoover, Herbert, 46–48, 50–51
Hughes, Langston, 94
Humphrey, Hubert H., 198
Hunter, Sheriff Jack, 156–57
Hunter, Tip, 74, 77; sheriff, 83, 85, 91–93, 111–12, 134, 156–58,165, 249n4

Jackson, 6, 14, 68, 76, 78, 94, 169, 183, 207
Jackson, Ada Springfield, 40, 115, 192, 194, 226, 234
Johnson, Arizona Taylor, 43, 59–60, 78–79, 81, 109, 151–52, 218, 225–26, 228–30, 232; children of, 161; early years, 2, 8–10, 25–26, 33
Johnson, Gilbert, 109, 161, 232
Johnson, Lyndon, 166, 176
Jones, Edna, 171–72
Jones, Willie M., 156

Kennedy, John F., 163, 166, 173–74, 176–77, 249n6
Kinfolks camp meetings, 29–32, 51–52
King, Martin Luther, Jr., 170, 174
Ku Klux Klan, 69–73, 88, 177; *see also* Brownsville

Lanier, Ceily, 162
Lauderdale County, 2

Index

Leigh, Nannie Bell, 102
Lincoln, Abraham, 18, 21–22; assassinated, 23
Lyle, George, 111, 132–33
lynching, 71, 77–88, 92–94; Anti-Lynching Bill, 71, 85, 246–47n26; sociologist's theory on, *see* Raper, Arthur; *see also* Williams, Elbert

Madison County, 2
Malone, Joe C., 176
Mann, Aggie, 100, 108, 110–11, 139
Mann, Albert, 74
Mann, Aleck, 100, 110–11, 117, 126, 139
Mann, Pat, 168
Marks, Julius (Bubber), 81, 106–7
Marshall, Thurgood, 87, 91–93, 134, 247n37, 247n40–48, 249n5
May, Neal, 176
McClanahan, William, 85–86
Mecklenburg County, Va., 15
Memphis, 6, 14, 33, 42, 46, 68, 70, 83, 85, 114, 123, 144, 157, 192
migration, 68; of African Americans, *see* black farmers; Roosevelt's policies on, 68, 245n23
Mississippi River, 7, 18, 58
Mitchell, Milmon, 78, 91–93
Morris, Jimmy Joe, 89–91
Motley, Constance Baker, 134, 249n5

National Association for the Advancement of Colored People(NAACP), xiv, 48, 69, 72, 74–78, 134; charter of Brownsville Branch, 70, 246n3, on lynching, 85–87, 247n32, 247n33; purpose of, 71, 245n2
Nelson, Ford, 144
New Deal programs, 52–53, 62; discrimination in, 68–69, 244n7, 244n13; effect on black migration, *see* black farmers; *see also* Tennessee Valley Authority (TVA)
Newbern, Irma, 85–86, 247n31
Nixon, Richard, 166

Oakview Church, 100, 167
Oakview Elementary School, 100–101, 120, 139, 206

Oswald, Lee Harvey, 177
Outlaw, John, 91

Parks, Rosa, 173
Pearce, Mary Alice, 171
Perry, Lee Andrew, 45, 160
plantation, 17, 23; etiquette, 24, 242n24; familial and kin belief, 16, 241n2, 242n5; master and slave relationship, 24, 241n21; slave naming practice, 25, 242n26
Price, Lettie, 171

Raper, Arthur, 82
Rawls, Al (Charles Allen), 26, 77–78, 111, 133, 224; finding Elbert Williams, 80, 246n20
Rawls, Dan "Boy," 77, 80–81, 94
Rawls, Maude, 77
Rawls, Willie Bell, 77, 93, 102, 246n15, 248n2
Reed, Charles, 74, 77
Reed, George, 72, 76
Rice, Harvey, 73
Ripley, 6, 102
Rogge, O. John, 85–87
Roosevelt, Franklin Delano, 49–52, 62, 85–86, 90–91, 107–8; and black voters, 48, 243n24; death of, 113, 248n10
Rothschild, M., 7, 47, 81
Rotnem, Victor, 93
Ruby, Jack, 177
Rutherford, Ike, 100, 104, 109–12, 116
Rutherford, Mozella, 100, 109–12, 116, 248n8, 248n9

Sanders, Margie (Sis), 168–69
Sanders, Odell, 157–58, 163, 168–69, 177, 191
school desegregation, 186–88, 199–200, 250n10
Searcy, Lonnie (Shorty), 111–12, 248n8, 248n9
Shaw, Dan, 74
slavery, 16–23; marriages, 16, 240n5; naming practices, *see* plantation
Somerville, 2, 6, 102
Sorrelle, Alfred, 3, 11, 14

Sorrelle, Bessie, 3
Springfield, Aaron, 45, 88, 95–96, 98, 101–2, 106–7, 108, 117, 121, 123, 125, 134, 197, 224, 237; joins service, 128–29
Springfield, A. D., 35–36, 41, 68, 76, 149, 206, 218–19
Springfield, Ada Shaw, 41, 48, 67, 114–15, 194–95, 203, 224, 226
Springfield, Asalean, 56, 137, 223, 236
Springfield, Avery, 40, 194, 225
Springfield, Betty, 119, 139–41, 143, 148, 176, 221, 236
Springfield, Brown, 36, 38, 40, 48, 129, 147, 149, 169, 189, 192–95, 213, 224
Springfield, Charles, 40, 194, 225, 234
Springfield, Clarence, 95, 98, 101, 108, 136, 139, 142, 155, 169, 205, 224
Springfield, Cloria, 60, 96, 137, 194, 205, 224, 236
Springfield, Crettie Mae, 48, 51, 147, 149, 189, 192–93, 195
Springfield, Dan, 40, 45, 48, 147, 149, 184, 191, 194, 225
Springfield, Dave, 41, 232
Springfield, Dorothy, 129, 139–41, 143–44, 148, 188–89, 202, 236
Springfield, James Edward, 48, 129, 213–14
Springfield, Jim, 43–45, 48–49, 64–65, 67, 73, 76, 98, 110, 114–15, 204, 224–27, 232, 237; automobile accident, 189–93; death of, 194–96; farming, 53–55, 57, 61–62; as landowner, 41–42; and reign of terror, 88–90
Springfield, Jim Howell, 44–45, 88, 95–96, 101–2, 106–7, 117, 120–23, 125, 128, 130, 200, 204, 223–24, 237
Springfield, Lawrence, 48, 67
Springfield, Lee, 55, 96, 98, 108, 117, 125, 127, 130, 132, 198, 204, 214, 216–17, 221, 223–24, 228, 236
Springfield, Lois, 95, 101, 136, 139, 142, 154–55, 169, 197, 224, 236
Springfield, Lucille, 48, 149, 184
Springfield, Norman, 135
Springfield, Opal Ree, 114, 139, 141, 143, 148, 169, 189, 194, 236
Springfield, Opal Taylor, 51–52, 123–24, 128–29, 133–35, 226, 231–34; civil rights era, 157–60, 164, 166–68, 172–74, 176–77; during World War II, 95–96, 102–8, 113–14; early years, 2, 8–10, 25–27, 29, 31–33; family reunion, 197, 200, 204, 207; farm life, 65, 119–22, 127, 136, 141–42; and Grandpa Jim's accident, 189–96; her faith, 215–16; joins Springfield family, 34–37, 38–40, 43–48; Key Corner Street, 154–56, 161; later years, 210–14, 217–22; life after farming, 179–84, 201–3; move to Winfield Lane, 97–100, 101, 109–12, 206; and post WW II changes, 116–18, 138–39, 143; raising young family, 56–63, 67; reign of terror, 73–76, 78–80, 82–83, 91; on school and education, 137–38, 185, 187–88, 199, 236–37; sisters' death, 152–53, 228–30; Tonnie's death, 223–25; tradition of church, 144–47, 149–51, 209; voting, 198
Springfield, Salathiel, 48, 96, 98, 117, 121, 125, 127, 129–32, 197, 224, 237
Springfield, Shirley, 108, 139, 155, 169, 224, 236
Springfield, Tonnie, 35–40, 43–49, 51, 61–63, 124, 128–129, 133–34, 199–200, 205, 226; civil rights era, 157–58, 160, 164, 167–70, 177; during World War II, 95–96, 103–4, 106–8; family reunion, 197–200, 204, 207; farm life, 101, 119–22, 125–27, 136, 141; his father's accident, 190–93, 194–96; Key Corner Street, 153–56, 161; as landowner, 54–58, 64–68; last days, 221–23; later years, 210–20; life after farming, 179–80, 182–89, 201–3; move to Winfield Lane, 97–100, 109–12, 114–15; post WW II changes, 116–18; reign of terror, 73–76, 78, 80, 87–90; and tradition of church, 144–47, 149–51, 209; voting, 198
Springfield, Tony, 48, 56, 96, 98, 106, 117, 121, 124–25, 128, 198, 204, 223, 236
Springfield, Wallis, 67, 101, 136, 139, 221, 228, 236
Springfield School, 55, 124, 161, 233

Index

Stanton, 2, 102, 175–76
State of Tennessee v. Mozella Rutherford and Lonnie Searcy Alias Bond, 111, 248n8, 248n9
States Graphic, xiv, 61, 90, 102, 107, 118, 165, 217
Sternberger, Joseph, 7, 47
Sugarmon, R. B., Jr., 175
Sullivan, George W. (Buddy), 164–65, 171–72

Tabernacle Church, 5, 15; as New Hope Church, 29, 231; *see also* Kinfolks camp meetings
Tamm, Emil, 7, 47
Tamm, Nathan, 88
Taylor, Benjamin Franklin, 6, 8–10, 14
Taylor, Betty, 10, 28, 32, 38, 119, 128
Taylor, Clarence, xvii, 28, 72, 75, 82, 84, 95, 234–35
Taylor, Dempsy, 5, 8, 10–11, 13, 28–29, 32–33, 35–38, 43, 68, 84, 119, 128
Taylor, Eldred, 28, 84
Taylor, Emma, 32, 231
Taylor, Edmund, 15–16, 18, 240n1, 241n11
Taylor, Harrison, 35, 73
Taylor, Hattie, 30–31, 33, 52, 242n29
Taylor, Howell (Reverend), 15–16, 25–26, 29–30
Taylor, Howell Y., 2–6, 9–10, 13, 44, 99, 226, 227, 229; estate of, 7–8, 25, 240n7
Taylor, Isabel, 16, 18–19, 21–22, 24, 60, 227, 240n1; children of, 17
Taylor, James (Meedie), 28, 79, 234
Taylor, John A., 18–23, 24, 30
Taylor, Lizzie Hess, 27, 34–35, 38, 73, 234
Taylor, Mary Springfield (Meg), 40, 115, 149, 192, 194, 226, 134
Taylor, Ora, 2–3, 6–9, 13, 25, 27, 226–27
Taylor, Polk, 2–3, 5–6, 8–14, 226–29, 237
Taylor, Richard, 15–16, 18
Taylor, Sam, 16, 19–22, 24, 227, 240n1; children of, 17
Taylor, Tamar, 2–3, 5–6, 8–15, 25–26, 28–33, 39, 43, 59–60, 226–28, 237; death of, 51–52; on plantation, 18, 22–24, 240n1, 241–42n23

Taylor, Thomas Lewis, 5–8, 13, 27–29, 33, 79, 84, 227
Taylor, Walter Howell, 2–6, 8–9, 25
Taylor, William, 15, 30–31, 242n29
Taylor's Chapel Church, 5, 9, 15, 24, 35–37, 47, 60, 231; as school, 27; location, 29
Tennessee River, 1
Tennessee State University (A&I) 137, 202, 236
Tennessee Valley Authority (TVA), 53, 117
Thornton, Harbert, 57–58, 67, 72–73, 97–99, 187
Thornton, John, Jr., 187, 221
Thornton, John, Sr., 59, 95, 99, 108, 114, 191–92
Tipton, County, 2
Transou, Cherry Springfield, 40, 43, 129, 226
Truman. Harry S., 108, 127; begins Korean War, 129, 248–49n2
Tullahoma, 102
Turner, James, 171
Turner, Jeanette, 171
Turner, Lee Wilson, 171
Turner, Mamie, 171
Turner, Norvell, 158, 167
Turner, Wilbia, 171
Turner, Willie Lewis, 171
Tyus, Emma, 124, 153

Vietnam War, 177

Waddell, Vernise Springfield, 40, 115, 149,
Walker, Buster, 75–77, 85, 87, 91
Wallace, George, 173
Weinberger, Eric, 170–72, 175, 249n12, 250n14
White, Lily, 120, 155
White, Walter, 70, 85, 247n29
Whiteville, 2
Whitten, Billy, 131
Wiley, Robert Lewis, 171
Wilkie, Wendell, 90
Wilkins, Roy, 86
Williams, Annie, 77–80, 87, 246n16, 248n49

Williams, Elbert (Dick), 27; abduction and lynching, 77–81, 134, 160, 234, 249n4; federal investigation of lynching, 85–87, 91–93, 248n49; national media attention, 83–84, 246n24; speculation about killing, 81–82, 88, 93–94, 246n15

Williams, Nat D., 144

Willow Grove Baptist Church, 47, 69, 74, 160, 192, 194–95, 224

Wills, Mann, 10, 14, 25, 60, 229

Wilson, Woodrow, 1

World War II, 91, 95–97, 102; the end of, 113, 248n11; rations during, 103–8, 248n6

Wright, Louis, 70

www.ingramcontent.com/pod-product-compliance
Lightning Source LLC
Chambersburg PA
CBHW030306080526
44584CB00012B/463